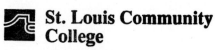

Who Gets the
Good Jobs?

Who Gets the Good Jobs?

Combating Race and Gender Disparities

ROBERT CHERRY

RUTGERS UNIVERSITY PRESS
New Brunswick, New Jersey, and London

Library of Congress Cataloging-in-Publication Data

Cherry, Robert D., 1944–
    Who gets the good jobs?: combating race and gender disparities / Robert Cherry
        p. cm
    Includes bibliographical references and index
    ISBN 0–8135–2920–4 (cloth: alk.paper)—ISBN 0–8135–2921–2 (pbk. : alk. paper)
    1. Discrimination in employment—United States. 2. Sex discrimination in
    employment—United States. I. Title.

HD4903.5.U58 C46 2001
331.13'3—dc21   00–045684

British Cataloging-in-Publication data for this book is available from the British Library.

Manufactured in the United States of America

For Shelley

Contents

Figures and Tables

Preface

This book is the product of two overlapping concerns. The first is my frustration that recent debates over anti-discrimination policies are between two hopelessly flawed positions—maintaining all current policies or dismantling them completely. The intensity of the struggle between these two polar positions leaves little room for a more reasoned, and necessary, "third" way. The second is more personal: a desire to reestablish unity between my emotional and intellectual attitudes concerning race and gender disparities in capitalist societies.

Since the 1960s, race and gender disparities have been a major focus of academic and political disputes both across the political spectrum and within each section of that spectrum. I have spent most of my adult life involved in this political discourse from within the left. The unifying theme within the left was an agreement that capitalism required race and gender divisions for its very existence. However, there were sustained conflicts between those who believed that all workers were harmed by these divisions and those who believed that white males benefited from these divisions, gaining a privileged position both at the job and in the home. My strong inclination, reflecting both political and intellectual activities, was to side with the former position and reject the "identity" politics that flowed from the latter.

My anger toward capitalism was also fueled by the utter indifference the corporate elite seemed to have toward the plight of an underclass that grew during the post–Vietnam war era. Most glaring was the decision in 1980 to plunge the economy into a severe recession in order to protect financial wealth being eroded by inflation. This recession was really a depression for inner-city urban communities as the official adult black unemployment rate soared over 20 percent. I was angered by society's response to use drug laws to warehouse the black unemployed in prisons just as the vagrancy laws of Elizabethan England were used to control a displaced peasantry. Both liberal and conservative academics chipped in by promoting "blaming the victim" ideologies, sometimes reminiscent of the debate at the beginning of the twentieth century between conservatives who believed that the new immigrants from southern and eastern Europe were genetically inferior and liberals who believed that they were culturally inferior. In this context, I saw all suggestions that dysfunctional behavior of inner-city residents contributed to the persistence of poverty as reactionary and a defense of the status quo.

Over time, however, it became harder and harder to sustain intellectually some of my long-held positions. As I read more labor history, it became clear that capitalists rarely initiated race and gender divisions but simply accommodated to the demands of white men. It was difficult to see how capitalists could have promoted Jim Crow laws that restricted their access to cheap black labor. At the same time, evidence began to accumulate that at least some of the adaptations of black men and women to the depression-like conditions they were enduring were worsening their situation and could not be ignored. In addition, the continued entry of blacks and women into professional occupations and corporate management could no longer be considered mere tokenism. These new intellectual assessments created tensions with the emotional truths I had nurtured for decades.

These tensions were most apparent at the time of the publication of Andrew Hacker's *Two Nations: Black and White, Separate, Hostile, Unequal.* Hacker's theme that blacks are hopeless victims of a racist society that is responsible for the persistence of unyielding inequality seemed to go against my intellect even though it fed my emotional truths. Three years later, the publication of the conservative response to Hacker's book by Stephan and Abigail Thernstrom, *America in Black and White: One Nation Indivisible,* reopened the same tensions. While the book's claims were clearly excessive, parts did appeal to some of my newfound intellectual sensibilities: black improvement was undeniable, certain government programs were difficult to defend, and some aspect of dysfunctional behavior had to be confronted. However, it totally conflicted with my emotional truths.

As I struggled to find compatibility between my head and my heart, it became clear that both analyses were deeply flawed. It was not simply because one was too pessimistic and the other too optimistic about black progress. It was not simply because one saw dominant American society as exclusionary while the other saw it as completely open. It was because neither fully understood both the strengths and weaknesses of capitalist societies. The profit motive has both the ability to ameliorate and to exacerbate race and gender disparities. Therefore, both theoretical insights and historical contexts are crucial to determining whether capitalism will be an ally or an enemy in the fight for race and gender equality.

Who Gets the Good Jobs? is the product of this intellectual and emotional journey. It begins with some theoretical insights that I believe are crucial to the logic of capitalism. The book then holds these theories up to the historical record in order to understand how race, gender, and nativism shaped labor market outcomes prior to the 1960s civil rights legislation. The knowledge gained from these chapters provides a foundation for understanding (1) why the advances made as a result of civil rights legislation have been both substantial and limited, and (2) which public policies are helpful and which are not in the struggle against remaining race and gender earnings and employment inequities. I hope this journey has produced a document that can be helpful in determining how we can proceed to building a more humane and equitable society.

Acknowledgments

This book and my understanding of the social and labor market dynamics has benefited immensely from the effort and counsel of many friends and colleagues. Most important, Steve Fraser and Carey Harrison helped shape the way I approached the stories this book tells and encouraged me to abandon the passive voice I had become accustomed to. Not only did this force me to make choices I was avoiding, enhancing my own understanding, it also gave the material more clarity that was critical to its readability and, ultimately, its ability to be published.

Individual chapters also were aided by efforts of others. Suggestions by James Cronin, Gregory DeFreitas, Susan Greenbaum, Alice Hughey, and Donna Wilson were especially helpful. Comments at seminars presented at University of California-Riverside, University of South Florida, and Boston University improved the presentation of a number of chapters.

Rutgers University Press also nurtured this project. In particular, Marlie Wasserman made me think clearly about the way I presented material to a readership of noneconomists and about the book's organization. Cecilia Cancellero and Debbie Self did superb jobs at various stages of editing, and Alison Hack and Marilyn Campbell shepherded the manuscript through the production process in an efficient and supportive manner.

Who Gets the
Good Jobs?

1 | Deciding Who Gets the Good Jobs

An Overview

As the new millennium dawns, racial and gender earnings and employment inequalities are alive and well. In March 2000, the U.S. Government offered $508 million in an attempt to settle more than one thousand individual lawsuits brought against the federally funded Voice of America by female workers. These women documented how managers routinely hired and promoted men, ignoring more qualified female applicants. The government made this settlement offer only after losing forty-six of the first forty-eight individual suits brought to trial. Beyond blatant examples of discrimination, occupations dominated by women continue to have lower wages than occupations that are dominated by men. In order to counter these inequities, President Bill Clinton proposed that Congress allocate $27 million to the Equal Employment Opportunity Commission (EEOC) and urged passage of Senator Thomas Daschle's Paycheck Fairness Act, which requires the federal government to set wage guidelines for various occupations. Supporters of this legislation hope that these guidelines will prod employers to create more gender equity in the labor market.

A similar lawsuit filed by disgruntled black employees of Coca-Cola threatened to disrupt their annual shareholders meeting. One plaintiff, Kimberly Orton, spent years at the company and was paid less than white employees she supervised. "You have a low-trust environment," said another black employee, citing large numbers of blacks

1

in the lowest-paying jobs, with just a handful at the top levels. Even Federal Reserve chair Alan Greenspan, not known for criticisms of market capitalism, felt it necessary to chide U.S. businesses for the persistence of discriminatory employment practices. In a speech to the National Community Reinvestment Coalition, Greenspan urged firms to eliminate the "distortions that arise as a result of discrimination."[1]

While these realities have led some, like President Clinton, to articulate ways to strengthen anti-discrimination policies, the 1990s witnessed concerted and largely successful efforts to eliminate them. These efforts have been particularly effective in mobilizing opposition to special admissions programs at top universities. In Michigan, Texas, and California legal challenges to these programs, in the courts and at the ballot box, have already substantially constrained the ability of public colleges to use race as a factor in their admissions process. These battles against anti-discrimination policies raise fundamental issues of equity and diversity. The ideological positions of the combatants are so deeply held that these conflicts can accurately be characterized as "religious" wars.

Supporters of government anti-discrimination policies claim that, if not for the force of government, even the modest gains made by women and African American men in the last few decades would not exist. They predict a return to the patriarchal past for women and Jim Crow–like conditions for blacks if these policies are eliminated. They point to the precipitous decline in black freshmen enrollment at the University of California's Law School—from thirty-six to five—after Proposition 209 outlawed special admissions policies. From this perspective, any suggestion that there are even modest problems with current anti-discrimination policies is dangerous, creating a fault line that will be seized by opponents who want nothing less than their total dismantlement. Similarly, opponents reject any compromise. They dismiss the barriers to equality that might remain if the government completely abandoned these policies as minor impediments.

A broad attack on all aspects of anti-discrimination policies is found in Stephan and Abigail Thernstrom's highly acclaimed book, *America in Black and White*, which documents a dramatic improvement in the economic, political, and social position of blacks since World War II. Noting the gains made before 1970, the Thernstroms reject any notion that government anti-discrimination policies have been responsible for postwar improvements. Around the same time, *Fortune* magazine published a special issue on black senior executives in corporate America. Rather than viewing these individuals as mere tokens, the magazine argued that they represented the final step to a new era where blacks are judged by merit and not by the color of their skin. More recently, in response to President Clinton's call for government-determined wage guidelines, American Enterprise Institute economists claimed that the gender "pay gap is phony." As evidence, these economists pointed to thirty-year-old women, without children, who have virtually the same earnings as thirty-year-old men with comparable skills. Citing the striking rate at which women have entered well-paying professions, including law and medicine, they dismissed evidence of workplace inequality.[2]

In today's America, similar perceptions of labor market equality are broadly disseminated by the media and politicians. Conservatives argue that improvements in the quality of education have been most responsible for the substantial decline in race and gender earnings gaps over the last half century. According to them, perceptions of labor market discrimination persist only because many blacks and feminists have become comfortable with victim status. It is this dysfunctional attitude, conservatives maintain, which explains any remaining income disparities. More broadly, conservatives contend that affirmative action and feminism, not discrimination or patriarchy, are the root causes of many of society's contemporary societal ills.

Simultaneously, those at the other end of the political spectrum claim that there has been virtually no change in discrimination from the pre–civil rights era. According to the left-leaning Economic Policy Institute, racial income disparities have grown since 1980 as black wages have not kept pace with inflation. They also discount the recent reduction in the female-to-male earnings ratio since it is primarily the result of a decline in male wages (after adjusting for inflation) rather than a rise in female earnings.[3]

Some left-wing commentators go even further. They suggest that the exclusionary barriers, supposedly outlawed by 1964 civil rights legislation, remain as strong as ever. These barriers persist because "people with power have an interest in discrimination and firms adapt to oppressive relations elsewhere in society." Work teams may become integrated on the shop floor, "but a new division of labor may emerge that maintains the subordination of women and minorities."[4]

Those who argue that substantial discrimination persists cite evidence from the medical profession. *New York Times* reporter Natalie Angier claimed that "female physicians still suffer from what might be called stipendicitis; an acute failure of the wallet to perform as expected."[5] She found that in virtually all medical specialties female physicians make less than 85 percent as much as male physicians. Female cardiologists earn only 63 percent as much as their male counterparts.

The most negative assessment of the post–civil rights era is presented by economists William Darity and Samuel Myers. They believe that corporate leadership increasingly finds large sections of the black population expendable, leading to anti-natalist policies. They single out Planned Parenthood's focus on birth control and abortions as the primary method of alleviating poverty among blacks. Instead of allowing blacks to enter the mainstream of the economy, Darity and Myers maintain that corporate leaders have chosen to use prisons to house them. As a result, since 1970, the prison population has quadrupled. Though only 12 percent of the population, by 1990 the number of blacks equaled the number of whites admitted to state and federal prisons. By the early 1990s, over 50 percent of urban black men, aged eighteen to thirty years old, had some relationship to the criminal justice system: either jailed, on probation, or awaiting trial.[6]

This book attempts to bridge the gap between these two polar positions. I am troubled by the attempt by the Thernstroms and other conservatives to shape data to suggest that income disparities no longer reflect discrimination. Government intervention was necessary thirty years ago to undermine discriminatory labor practices, and it continues to be necessary today. However, the Thernstroms were correct to reject leftist notions that the capitalist profit motive has been responsible for race and gender inequities. In professional labor markets, government policies complement the profit motive in promoting merit-based hiring practices.

In particular, I part with leftists who suggest that capitalists benefited from labor practices which excluded black and female workers. Capitalists profit from policies that expand labor supplies since they put downward pressure on wages. Indeed, this is the reason for unqualified corporate support of open immigration policies and the elimination of government welfare programs. In contrast, policies that restrict labor supplies are generally costly. As a result, except in isolated cases, capitalists did not promote policies that limited the ability of firms to hire female or black workers.

In the 1960s, civil rights legislation outlawed exclusionary hiring practices. This legislation encouraged a hiring system that focused on

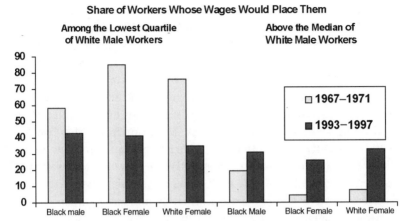

Figure 1.1 Changes in Relative Earnings, 1967–1997. *Source: Finis Welch, "Economic Well-Being in the United States,"* American Economics Review *89 (May 1999): 1–16.*

the profit-enhancing ability of the workers employed. In this system, workers would be judged by the skills they possessed rather than their race or gender. Since they did not financially benefit from excluding particular groups, profit-seeking firms had little reason to resist merit-based hiring procedures. Thus, there has been a fundamental change in the hiring process so that women and black men in high-paying jobs can no longer be considered the beneficiaries of mere tokenism.

The shift toward greater labor market equality has been substantial. There was a dramatic improvement of the earnings of women and black men relative to white men over a thirty-year period, 1967 to 1997.[7] During the 1967–1971 period, for example, 85.1 percent of black women had earnings which would have placed them in the lowest quartile of the white male earnings distribution; only 4.7 percent had earnings above the median white male earnings. In contrast, during the 1993–1997 period, 41.2 percent of black women had earnings that would have placed them in the lowest quartile of the white male earnings distribution while 25.9 percent had earnings above the median white male earnings (see Figure 1.1). Similar improvements occurred for black men and white women. While clearly equality has not been reached, one cannot trivialize the extent to which a large share of white female and black workers has escaped low-wage labor markets and now earns more than the median white male worker.

These improvements require us to take the theories of discrimination developed by the conservative economist Gary Becker more seriously. He pioneered the notion that exclusionary barriers were unprofitable, and this book builds on his work in an attempt to understand the origins of and the eventual undermining of discriminatory hiring practices. It parts company with conservatives, however, by rejecting their belief that these potential financial losses *alone* compel capitalists to actively oppose exclusionary barriers. Most important, this book rejects conservative claims that wage discrimination is unlikely to persist in unregulated capitalist societies. While there is now substantial upward mobility for blacks, white women, and immigrant workers, data clearly show that wage discrimination and employment barriers continue to persist throughout our society.

Interestingly, a number of left-wing writers have begun to suggest that capitalism has the ability to overcome race and gender employment barriers. Ellen Meiksin Wood, former editor of the preeminent U.S. leftist journal, *Monthly Review*, wrote: "I do believe that capitalism can tolerate a degree of formal equality between races and genders that no previous system was able to do."[8] Indeed, Karl Marx and Friedrich Engels suggested this very point when discussing the impact of capitalist production on women and children. Engels thought that the incorporation of working-class women into the production process would cause "the last remnants of male domination in the proletarian home [to lose] all its foundation."[9] Marx echoed this view: "However terrible and disgusting the dissolution, under the capitalist system of the old family ties may appear, nevertheless modern industry, by assigning as it does an important part in the process of production, outside the domestic sphere, to women, to young persons, and to children of both sexes, creates a new economic foundation for a higher form of family and of relations between the sexes."[10]

Marx believed that in the long run, the capitalist labor process would be antagonistic to any restrictions that limited labor supplies. However, he was well aware that capitalism might, for a time, accommodate whatever forms of oppression it inherited. Accommodation is most likely when it facilitates divide-and-conquer strategies to weaken working-class militancy.[11] Maintaining racist, nativist, and patriarchal divisions in the workplace has often allowed capitalists to undermine unionization and weaken the ability of all workers to fight successfully for material, social, and political objectives. When explaining the origins and maintenance of the Jim Crow system, the Marxist sociologist Oliver Cox stated, "Every segregationist barrier is a barrier put up between white and black people by their exploiters."[12]

Some leftists have emphasized that cultural factors, rather than direct economic considerations, may be the root cause of the persistence of discriminatory behavior. The political activist Harold Baron argued that profits are too meager to explain why capitalists have maintained a social system that has so much potential for social disruption. He claimed that once a whole set of discriminatory institutions is developed and ideological rationales embraced, they are sustained even when they no longer serve financial interests. The sociologist Allan Johnson also rejects the view that patriarchy persists because it serves corporate financial interests. He believes that patriarchal values are so deeply rooted and so important in preserving male privilege that they will persist even when corporations implement anti-discrimination policies.[13]

Historically, the resilience of discriminatory institutions and ideologies, and the usefulness of divide-and-conquer strategies, may explain why firms maintained discriminatory labor practices for so long. However, these policies can only forestall the long-run tendency of capitalism to undermine exclusionary barriers, especially in professional occupations. Eventually, the cost of these exclusionary policies and the benefits from merit-based hirings are too great. Most important, once government undermines the legality of discriminatory practices, firms will be willing to change their employment policies. This is especially the case if labor militancy is so weakened that divide-and-conquer strategies no longer have value.

This hopeful vision of merit-based hiring is consistent with some recent data gathered by former college presidents William Bowen and Derek Bok.[14] They surveyed black and white men and women who matriculated at a group of elite colleges in 1976 (see Figure 1.2). When considering the average earnings of those graduates who were working full-time in 1995, grouped by their class rank, the data clearly suggest that gender inequality remained. Female graduates who ranked in the top third of their college class were able to earn only as much as male graduates who ranked in the bottom third. However, it does appear that racial equality had been achieved. In virtually all groups, black graduates had at least the average earnings of white graduates with the same class rank. The only exception was among men who ranked in the lower third of their graduating class, a group that disproportionately comprised children of wealthy white alumni.

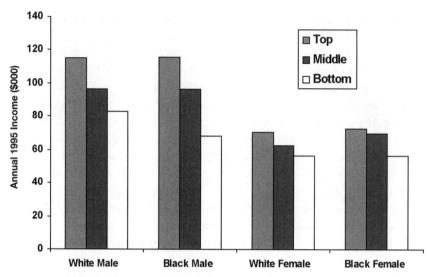

Figure 1.2 Mean 1995 Income by Class Rank, Gender, and Race for 1976 Cohorts. *Source: William Bowen and Derek Bok,* The Shape of the River *(Princeton, N.J.: Princeton University Press, 1998).*

Importance of Social Class Distinctions

During the pre–civil rights era, women, blacks, and immigrants were uniformly subjected to oppressive conditions so that class differences within each of these groups were of minor importance. Civil rights legislation aided white women and black college graduates to gain entry to managerial and professional occupations. This legislation, however, has not been as helpful for white women and blacks with anything less than a college degree. As a result, there has been growing income inequality among workers in these two groups. In contrast, during the most recent economic expansion, income inequality among white men has declined.

The efforts of white men themselves contribute to the fact that discrimination has been most persistent in blue-collar occupations. In the better-paying jobs, including the construction and the building trades, white men have been active initiators of discriminatory policies rather than pawns manipulated by capitalists. A wide spectrum of leftists, including Paul Baran and Paul Sweezy and Ray Franklin and Solomon Resnik, have argued, even when capitalists have no personal animus toward women or nonwhites, racist and sexist labor market policies persist because of their inability to change the behavior of supervi-

sory personnel.[15] These lower levels of management are often populated by white men imbued with racist and patriarchal values that dis-
tort their judgments on the capabilities of individual workers. However,
even when these managers are able to focus on corporate profitability, they must take into account the potential hostility of white male
line workers to female and nonwhite workers. Often these managers
conclude that the disruption to the production process that integrat-
ing their work force might cause would be more costly than any benefits from hiring qualified black or female workers. The privileged
position of white male workers in the job queue is further enhanced
by the widespread hiring procedure of relying on the recommendations from current employees when job openings occur.

Discriminatory hiring practices often put blacks at the end of the
hiring queue. When the number of job seekers is greater than the number of jobs available, black workers will be disproportionately unemployed. In some parts of the country, where employment trends have
created a surplus of noncollege graduates, racial queuing has created
a large racial employment gap. This is most apparent in the Midwest
where a substantial amount of blue-collar jobs were lost, particularly
in the automobile and steel industries. Typical of the region is Illinois where, in 1995, 75.2 percent of all white men over sixteen years
old were employed while the black male employment rate was only
56.6 percent.[16]

Despite these disparities, the severe employment difficulties experienced by adult black men can be substantially overcome if the
economy runs tight labor markets. When national unemployment rates
fell below 5 percent, employers could no longer indulge their own racist
and sexist attitudes or those of their white male workers. Due to labor shortages, firms were forced to hire welfare recipients and less-
educated black men from poor neighborhoods. As a result, the black
unemployment rate fell from 10.2 to 7.2 percent between 1997 and
March 2000. Tight labor markets have also enabled low-wage workers to experience real earnings growth for the first time in over two
decades. Between 1986 and 1996, the typical low-wage worker saw
the purchasing power of hourly earnings drop more than 6 percent—
from $7.11 to $6.66 when measured in 1998 dollars. By the spring of
1999, however, wage growth raised hourly wages to $7.19.

Tight labor markets alone, however, will not eliminate black employment problems. A substantial reason for the decline in the unemployment rate of black men has been their decision to abandon active

job searches, leaving them uncounted as part of the active labor force, and hence not included in official unemployment statistics. As will be documented more fully later, the 1997 unemployment rate of adult black men, aged twenty to sixty-four years old, would have been as high as 18 percent if adjustments were made for these labor force withdrawals. This indicates that discriminatory practices are widespread and that vigorous enforcement and expansion of affirmative action in blue-collar occupations is quite necessary.[17]

Unfortunately, there has been little effort to correct race and gender inequality outside of professional labor markets. According to conservatives, a culture of poverty has created dysfunctional behavioral traits among a large share of black youths, making them unemployable. Additionally, conservatives contend that women are often more motivated by familial goals of marriage and motherhood than by their careers. As a result, many choose occupations which complement their personal lives even though these choices have limited earnings potential. While not embracing these stereotypes, liberals also ignore race and gender inequities within blue-collar occupations. While admitting that these inequities exist, for the liberal wing of the Democratic Party, any focus on the plight of the working poor and lower middle class would be difficult to accept. "It would constitute an implicit confession that Democrats are paying less attention to the nonworking poor."[18]

This unwillingness of liberals to confront discrimination in working-class occupations was most evident in the 1980s, when feminists were focusing on pay-equity issues. They found that invariably those job categories that were male dominated were assigned a higher pay scale within corporations than those that were female dominated. Feminists documented that these pay-scale patterns persisted even when companies determined that the skill requirements and job responsibilities in the male-dominated job categories were the same as in the female-dominated job categories. In response, feminists mobilized and united around demands for the government to institute comparable work regulations that would force corporations to pay female and male workers equally if they were found to have comparable skills and responsibilities. Similar policies had been successfully implemented in Australia and Canada, but, unfortunately, after some initial success, the U.S. comparable-worth movement died because liberals where unwilling to support it.[19]

Even among some left-leaning critics of unregulated capitalism, there has been a reluctance to focus on the plight of blue-collar black and female workers who have stable employment but, due to discriminatory practices, earn less than their male counterparts. Instead of highlighting the general injustices these workers face, these critics have emphasized the maltreatment of a subsection of this labor force: immigrant workers who are employed in the most unstable and unsafe jobs. In August 1997, newspapers reported an example of the inhumanity experienced by workers on the periphery of the labor market when the government freed thirty deaf Mexican women who had been working in virtual slavery in New York City. This story complemented a growing literature on the abuse of illegal workers.

These examples provide a strong moral indictment of capitalism: the ability of the powerful to exploit the powerless. Critics often use them as a springboard to make generalizations concerning the indifference of capitalist societies to basic human needs. How can a capitalist society call itself humane, they argue, when it allows millions of children to grow up in poverty with deficient housing, medical care, and/or sustenance? These critics claim that capitalism may work in a nondiscriminatory manner for those who can fully participate in the system, but those who cannot are treated horribly.

Capitalism is culpable for much inhumanity visited on the defenseless. However, this is an overly pessimistic viewpoint that understates the willingness and capacity of the capitalist system to absorb those who are on the margins. Since the middle of 1997, the national unemployment rate has remained below 5 percent, the best the economy has done in a generation. In many regions the unemployment rate became so low that employers had to recruit individuals from outside their local labor markets to meet demands. After an initial reluctance to hire welfare recipients, firms realized that many of their stereotypical fears were unfounded. Some companies are even focusing on employment possibilities for prisoners.

Social critics often fail to fully analyze the impact of capitalism on those who are initially on the periphery of the economy. It may be that capitalism is liberating them from even worse alternatives. Moreover, it is possible that many workers are employed temporarily by firms which offer unfair wages and unsafe working conditions. Once they've gained experience, workers may be able to find better jobs. In addition the most exploitative companies, because of their small size and outdated technology, may be driven out of business by the forces of competition, enabling capitalism to cleanse itself of these reprehensible employment situations. Finally, benefits often accrue to consumers not corporate shareholders. For these reasons, the plight of exploited workers is complicated and an unqualified condemnation of their employers and/or the capitalist system may be misguided. Most important, focusing on workers on the periphery can deflect much-needed attention away from the continued discrimination experienced by the vast majority of black and female workers without a college degree, especially when political and legislative battles must be prioritized.

Another example of how critics of unregulated markets have placed working-class disparities on the back burner is their decision to make the defense of special admissions programs a priority. These programs have increased the access of blacks and white women to elite U.S. universities, postgraduate professional schools, and corporate boardrooms. Nationally, there has been significant mobilization against the ending of race-based affirmative action at the University of California's elite Berkeley campus but silence about the many years of reduced funding of the state's university system that educates the majority of blacks and other students. Downplaying K–12 education and the inadequacies of working-class colleges, the focus remains on giving a select few a break at elite institutions.[20]

In defense of these efforts, Robin Kelley rejects any notion that middle-class blacks no longer are victimized by racism:

> While corporate boardrooms and the halls of government might appear more integrated, racism continues to cut across class lines. From Texaco to Denny's, from the New Jersey Turnpike to the groves of academe, middle-class blacks face discrimination every day. We constantly hear stories of so-called minorities and women experiencing glass ceilings in the world of business, of talented black professionals second-guessed because of affirmative action, of black executives having to endure racial slurs at work or harassment from those who police the exclusive clubs of the bourgeoisie.[21]

Kelley has contempt for those who oppose continuing emphasis on the remaining discrimination faced by the black elite. He believes that they ignore the continued power of white-skin privilege and wrongly presume that race and class are in competition.[22] Kelley's arguments would support set-aside programs that allocate a specified percentage of government contracts to businesses owned by underrepresented groups. Interestingly, set-aside policies originated with

President Richard Nixon, who wished to promote black capitalism as a solution to inner-city problems. These policies are quite problematic, however, not only because they are subject to abuse and institutionalize racial preferences, but also because they have had little impact on the growth of black business ownership.

Similarly, the continued defense of special admissions policies must be questioned. In pursuit of diversity goals, many top universities admit black and Latino applicants with much weaker test scores and high school records than white applicants. To cite one representative example, in 1995 the University of Michigan Law School had dramatically divergent entrance for their white and black applicant pool. Whereas almost 80 percent of white applicants admitted had at least a 3.50 undergraduate grade point average (GPA), almost one-half of black applicants accepted had less than a 3.25. Whereas 95 percent of white admittants had an undergraduate GPA of at least 3.25 *and* a Law School Aptitude Test (LSAT) score of at least 164, only 8 percent of black applicants admitted met these standards.[23] Whatever the benefits to those individual black and Latino students who are accepted, these policies undermine notions of fairness and generate resentment.

Kelley's vision would also support a trickle-down theory of progress: promoting a black elite—an updated version of W.E.B. Du Bois's Talented Tenth—that may eventually aid their working-class brothers and sisters. However, without direct government action to benefit the other 90 percent, special admissions policies trade popular progress for representation in elite education institutions and corporations.

Conservatives like the Thernstroms seize on the inadequacies of set-aside and special admissions programs to attack all aspects of affirmative action, including employment policies that have been quite effective in countering the biases inherent in a hiring process dominated by white men who are quite comfortable hiring through "old boys" networks. Indeed, this was exactly the outcome in California where Proposition 209 eliminated affirmative action completely. To avoid further setbacks, it would be wise to defend vigorously the employment components of affirmative action.

The choice, however, should not be between maintaining the status quo or completely eliminating government policies to promote diversity in colleges and in the business community. At universities, class-based policies can be tailored to aid black, Latino, Asian American, and white working-class applicants. Under these alternative policies, colleges would make significant use of an applicant's socioeconomic background in the admissions process. Strivers who have overcome hardships can be identified and offered support services so that they can succeed in a competitive college environment. These alternative polices would broaden class diversity at universities without necessarily limiting racial diversity.

In addition, developmental policies can provide skill preparation and enhanced intellectual opportunities to disadvantaged youngsters through government-funded after-school and summer programs. These programs would enable students to meet the same skill requirements as other college applicants. In the business world, the government could provide the capital and managerial training that would enable entrepreneurs from underrepresented groups to compete on an equal footing with other firms, rather than setting aside a portion of contracts for minority-owned businesses. In the short run, these changes would somewhat reduce black and Latino representation in elite universities and the number of government contracts those businesses secure. However, developmental policies are the most effective way to ensure race and gender equity in the long run and to promote fairness that is crucial to the long-term success of any progressive movement.

Chapter Coverage

Central to the conservative view that government intervention is unnecessary is the belief that competitive markets will self-correct for any unfair outcomes. The next two chapters detail the origins of this pro-market model and explain why it dominates the discourse within economics. This model shapes the thoughts of individuals as diverse as Booker T. Washington and George Soros. It also underpins the policy recommendations of a leading liberal economist, Paul Krugman, who believes that workers on the global assembly line benefit from the employment opportunities offered by transnational corporations.

In the hands of conservatives, the pro-market theory becomes a weapon against government anti-discrimination legislation. Since markets are highly competitive, firms work on small profit margins. In this environment, employers cannot afford to sacrifice economic efficiency by refusing to hire qualified applicants from groups they dislike. As a result, skills and behavioral traits—not gender, race, or ethnicity—determine labor market outcomes. Thus, conservatives maintain, government intervention is unnecessary and risks being counterproductive.

Chapters 2 and 3 also identify the reasons why the conservative application of the pro-market model is faulty. Though most markets are competitive, there are many firms in uncompetitive markets that may not suffer significant profit losses if they refuse to hire qualified workers from groups they dislike. They may be able to pass the higher costs along to their consumers. In addition, firms in competitive markets may find it profitable to discriminate if they are following the preferences of their customers. Nor does the pursuit of efficiency necessarily lead firms to seek the most productive workers available. If it is costly to thoroughly evaluate individual applicants, owners might find it cost-effective to rely on group profiling in their initial screening. Unfortunately, the use of group profiling often excludes qualified applicants from underrepresented groups. For these reasons labor legislation is required to counter discriminatory practices, especially when firms employ blue-collar workers.

The next three chapters focus on the history of U.S. exclusionary barriers: Jim Crow legislation which restricted black employment; male breadwinner policies which discriminated against women; and immigration laws which excluded foreign workers. In each case, we find that capitalists rarely profited from these exclusionary barriers. Instead, these barriers were promoted by other groups: Jim Crow by plantation owners, male breadwinner policies by social reformers, and immigration restriction by unions. Since generally these barriers did not entail significant financial costs, capitalists chose to accommodate rather than actively oppose them. Only when free market options became politically viable or too profitable to ignore, did capitalists begin to consider the elimination of exclusionary barriers. As a result, it was only after World War II that capitalists began to oppose Jim Crow policies and legislation that barred the employment of married women. Their willingness to accommodate for so long suggests that capitalists eliminate discriminatory practices only when the cultural and political environment changes, as it did during the last half of the twentieth century.

The next two chapters assess to what extent civil rights legislation closed racial and gender employment and earnings gaps, allowing us to judge the success of blacks and women in entering the mainstream of the U.S. economy. Statistical studies suggest that the closing of these earnings gaps has been substantial, especially in professional occupations. The divergence between professional and nonprofessional labor markets, however, has resulted in growing inequality among blacks and among women. While the impact of the very tight labor markets during the 1990s is encouraging, evidence indicates that more attention to the enforcement of anti-discrimination legislation within nonprofessional labor markets is necessary to address remaining racial and gender disparities.

The final three chapters assess various policies that might reduce the remaining race and gender disparities. Although equal employment and pay-equity legislation should be strengthened, I am not as sanguine with respect to the two nonlabor market components of affirmative action: government set-aside programs and special admissions programs. While these two policies may have been justified in the past, contemporary evidence calls them into question. These chapters document more fully the wide disparities in admissions standards when race-based procedures are used and elaborate on the positive effects of alternative class-based and developmental policies when they have been implemented.

Besides race and gender specific policies, black and female workers in nonprofessional labor markets can be aided by a number of government policies that lift the bottom of the wage distribution. They include policies to aid union organizing, increase the minimum wages and extend living wage ordinances, sustain full employment, and enhance the earned income credit. Each of these proposals can complement the direct anti-discrimination policies identified in the previous chapters. In addition, these proposals provide benefits to a broad working-class constituency, increasing the likelihood that they can be enacted.

These eleven chapters provide a comprehensive overview of the labor market experience of various groups of workers. The historical sections demonstrate the complex political and economic forces that influenced labor market practices. These factors limit the value of simple economic models of labor market discrimination. They can provide some useful insights and direction but must never be allowed to trivialize concrete analyses of real world events. In particular, we must reject generalizations that place all or none of the blame on the capitalist system or that minimize economic class when determining which policies to prioritize. Only by becoming less ideological and more pragmatic can we hope to overcome the remaining race and gender labor market inequities that have victimized too many people for too long.

2 | The Profit Motive

How It Can Benefit the Powerless

When Adam Smith was awarded a university position in Scotland in the 1750s, he had just witnessed the final suppression of the Scottish clans, enabling the British feudal aristocracy to gain unconstrained hegemony over the entire British Isles. Smith was no ally of the British feudal order and, instead, considered capitalism a more humane alternative. While he never witnessed full-blown capitalism, Smith was able to observe its beginnings through the workings of a few industrial enterprises. In *Wealth of Nations*, Smith used these observations to develop his view that unregulated capitalism would transform societies by promoting economic growth and individual freedom. No longer would material standards of living remain stagnant and no longer would individuals be constrained by institutional and feudal restrictions.

Smith envisioned unregulated capitalism as having the ability to correct for any unethical outcome, thereby maximizing the social good. This notion of self-correcting mechanisms, often labeled as the invisible hand, undermined any need for the heavy-handed institutions Smith associated with feudalism. Indeed, a diverse group of individuals, including Booker T. Washington, George Soros, and the liberal economist Paul Krugman, have judged that unfettered markets offer the best chance for societies to improve the general welfare of their average citizens.

Pro-market advocates contend that one of the advantages of the invisible hand is the role it plays in eliminating discriminatory labor market practices. Looking back at the integration of baseball in 1947, the conservative journalist Steve Sailer suggests that competition among owners was responsible for giving black players a place in the major leagues and, as such, illustrates how self-interest can promote racial fairness.[1] While Sailer recommends reliance on market mechanisms, he fears that in government monopolies, including police and fire departments, or in labor markets dominated by unions, legislation is necessary to prevent discriminatory practices.

It is true that employers are generally harmed financially by exclusionary employment practices, especially when they sell in highly competitive markets. It is also true that self-regulating mechanisms will eliminate the worst labor market abuses that victimize the most defenseless groups within the population. However, this should not lead to a glorification of unfettered capitalism and an attack on all forms of government intervention to protect the well-being of workers. On the contrary, government and institutional intervention must accompany market mechanisms to ensure that all workers are treated fairly.

The Invisible Hand Thesis

To have unregulated or laissez-faire capitalism means that government does not engage in any policies that constrain the production and employment decisions of individual firms. The sole role of government is to provide an institutional environment that enables market activities to function as efficiently as possible. This environment includes legal protection of private property, the enforcement of legal contracts, and policies that promote competition and facilitate informed decision making. Among liberals, this institutional environment should also include full employment and maybe some restrictions on international capital movements. In both liberal and conservative variants of laissez-faire capitalism, however, once the necessary environment has been created, there is no room for government policies which infringe on the ability of individuals to choose the products they desire and the jobs that they want.

The distinction between government policies that create the necessary environment and those that are intrusive is most obvious when we consider issues of product and job safety. Legislation that requires full disclosure of product and worker safety information would allow both consumers and workers to make informed decisions. Full disclosure regulations are consistent with laissez-faire capitalism because they do not infringe on the decision making of firms, consumers, or workers. In contrast, product or industrial safety regulations constrain individual choices. The government is telling individual consumers and individual workers that they cannot make certain informed choices; persons can neither buy products nor work in factories the government considers unsafe.

Early critics voiced concern that in unregulated capitalist economies, owners would be guided only by their self-interest rather than the social good. In this environment, the powerless would be exploited by the powerful. These critics pointed to the squalid living condition of workers during the early stages of capitalism and its vicious treatment of children. Indeed, southern slaveholders argued that these abuses demonstrated the *moral* superiority of the feudal plantation economy, where the paternalistic obligations of the elite protected the weak. As one defender of slavery, George Fitzhugh noted that retailers take advantage of ignorant customers and those who need credit. He pointed to the struggle among desperate men and women, underbidding one another to get employment. Fitzhugh lamented, "This process of underbidding never ceases so long as employers want profits or laborers want employment. It ends when wages are reduced too low to afford subsistence, in filling poor-houses, and jails, and graves."[2]

Self-Regulating Mechanisms

Pro-market advocates agree that, at times, capitalism can exploit the weak. In some industries, firms sometimes obtain excessive profits by overcharging their customers. However, high profits encourage other firms to enter this industry. Industry supply increases, forcing all firms to lower their prices and their profits. Thus, the competitive process undermines the ability of owners to exploit consumers in the long run.

Pro-market advocates also suggest that self-regulating mechanisms operate in labor markets. If one group of workers is underpaid relative to their productive worth, other employers have an incentive to offer them higher wages and better working conditions. This creates a bidding process among competing firms, especially if labor markets are fully employed. This competition eventually enables all workers to earn a wage consistent with their productive worth. Once more, a competitive process eliminates unfair market outcomes.

These pro-market views completely undermine any notion that capitalists are more powerful than the consumers they sell to or the workers they hire. According to them, in markets for goods and services, consumers are sovereign. If capitalists produce goods and services not desired, households would shift their purchases to other more responsive firms. In the labor market, it is workers who are sovereign. If some firms are unwilling or unable to compensate them fairly, workers will gain employment from other more responsive firms.

Smith did not believe that competition would *completely* eliminate the power capitalists had over workers. He understood that owners had the advantage of controlling the number of jobs available and the greater ability to outwait workers in a strike. However, Smith remained optimistic for a number of reasons. A central feature of capitalist economies was their ability to sustain permanent economic growth. In a growing economy, even if benefits were unequally distributed, Smith believed that workers would experience a rising material standard of living. As a result, he had faith that the natural workings of supply and demand in labor markets would result in a rising wage, not only enabling (male) workers to support their families, but also providing funds to purchase "luxuries" such as tobacco, sugar, rum, and beer.[3]

Smith also believed that, despite market pressures, most capitalists would not be motivated by self-interest alone. He believed that they were moral men who would also be motivated by sympathy for others and propriety. Moreover, Smith was convinced that this goodwill would be matched by the increased work effort of their grateful employees. Additionally, providing a liberal subsistence to workers would increase their productivity by increasing their health and giving them the vitality to sustain effort more continuously. In this regard, Smith's views were consistent with the contemporary efficiency wage theory, which will be discussed in the next chapter. However, the opinions of Smith were in conflict with the later writings of the social critic Thomas Malthus, who believed that higher wages for the working classes would lead them to become lazy.[4]

Booker T. Washington and George Soros

Booker T. Washington and George Soros can both be considered pro-market advocates even though one represented the interests of the poorest participants in the economy and the other, its wealthiest. Both believed that the social good is best served when individuals are motivated by self-interest and unencumbered by government regulations.

In Booker T. Washington's time, more than 90 percent of blacks lived in the South. For the vast majority of southern whites, the social good included notions of white superiority and domination. Reflecting these attitudes, laws were being passed to limit blacks politically and financially. In this environment, Washington was asked to speak on behalf of blacks at the 1895 Atlanta World's Fair.

Washington decided to discuss his views on the appropriate strategy for improving the economic well-being of blacks. He emphasized the economic advantages the planters and industrialists derived from their employment of blacks:

> As we have proved our loyalty to you in the past in nursing your children, watching by the sick-bed of your mothers and fathers, and often following them tear-dimmed to their graves, so in the future, in our humble way, we shall stand by you with a devotion that no foreigner can approach, ready to lay down our lives, if need be, in defense of yours, interlacing our industrial, commercial, civil and religious life with yours in a way that shall serve the interest of both races.[5]

Washington placed his faith in the market system, for he believed that "no race that has anything to contribute to the markets of the world is long in any degree ostracized." Washington considered "agitation [for] social equality the extremest folly; . . . progress will come to us [as a] result of severe and constant struggle rather than [by] artificial forcing." While recognizing the importance of legal rights, he claimed that "it is vastly more important that we be prepared for the exercise of these privileges."[6]

Given the prevailing racist attitudes among whites, Washington believed that black workers would benefit only if planters and industrialists made hiring decisions on a purely profit-motivated basis. Qualified black workers could gain employment only if white employers separated their economic interests from their social values. Raising his hand, Washington proclaimed, "In all things that are purely social we can be as separate as the fingers, yet one as the hand in all things essential to mutual progress."[7]

A century later, George Soros made his pronouncements on the social and economic efficacy of unregulated market capitalism. On the one hand, Soros became one of the richest men in the world through financial speculation on world markets, and during the 1990s, his maneuvers led to dramatic changes in country currencies, causing havoc to some national economies. On the other, Soros annually donates hundreds of millions of dollars to support economies making the transition to a market system.

Soros readily accepts the observation that, in capitalistic endeavors, he acts amorally, making decisions based solely on their profitability. He agrees that some of the time the short-term consequences can be harsh. However, he believes that it would be counterproductive to create barriers that stifle market dynamics. If an activity is unprofitable, government subsidy would only waste valuable resources that could be more profitably used elsewhere. Soros could cite the British government's support of the coal industry during the 1960s and 1970s, and support for domestic steel in Belgium and agricultural industries in France during the 1980s and 1990s as ways in which government resources and policies simply delayed inevitable economic transformations. Thus, for Soros, market efficiency is always consistent with following market signals as quickly as possible—the hallmark of profit-seeking capitalists.

Soros is concerned, however, that many societies will reject this capitalist ethos. He has been particularly involved with countries created by the breakup of the former Soviet Union, now making their transition from command to market economies. Soros rejects the need to intervene in domestic markets in these countries but instead focuses on the development of the required infrastructure. In order to strengthen support for the market, Soros has invested heavily in the creation of cultural institutions that he hopes will generate the necessary market values.[8]

After the 1997–1998 Asian economic crisis, Soros somewhat readjusted his commitment to unregulated capitalism. He began to worry about the instability created by international capital flows. This led him to support some international financial controls to reduce the very currency speculation on which he made much of his fortune. Soros now also believes that governmental stimulative policies should be used to maintain production and incomes in developing countries already harmed by capital flight. However, both of these proposals are best considered an expansion of the necessary infrastructure in which individual markets must operate, rather than a repudiation of the pro-market model.

Predatory Capitalism

Critics of unfettered capitalism point to its predatory nature and its potential to abuse the most powerless, most de-

fenseless groups in society. Dickensian England and contemporary
sweatshops in Southeast Asia present images of brutal treatment of
children and young women and seem to shatter the pro-market vision
that competition undermines the power of corporations to take advantage of individual workers.

It is easy to see why most caring people sympathize with these
critics. However, in opposition Paul Krugman contends that outcries
over the abuses experienced by Asian workers employed by
transnational corporations are misplaced. He questions these indict-
ments because he believes that while "fat-cat capitalists might benefit from globalization, the biggest beneficiaries are, yes, Third World
workers." He highlights improvements in diet and the drop in mal-
nutrition. Krugman notes that though "a shocking one-third of young
Indonesian children are still malnourished . . . in 1975, the fraction was
more than one-half."[9]

For Krugman these benefits are the result of the workings of the
invisible hand:

> These improvements have not taken place . . . [as] the result
> of the benign policies of national governments, which are as
> callous and corrupt as ever. It is the indirect and unintended
> result of the actions of soulless multinationals and rapacious
> local entrepreneurs, whose only concern was to take advan-
> tage of the profit opportunities offered by cheap labor. It is
> not an edifying spectacle; but no matter how base the motives
> of those involved, the result has been to move hundreds of
> millions of people from abject poverty to something still aw-
> ful but nonetheless significantly better.

Krugman infers that the rise in real wages is experienced by large
groups of rural and urban workers since the growth of manufacturing
has a ripple effect throughout the economy. He contends that "pressure on the land becomes less intense so that rural wages rise; the pool
of unemployed urban dwellers always anxious for work shrinks, so
that factories begin to compete with each other, and urban wages also
begin to rise."

Questioning the sincerity of his critics, Krugman wonders why the
image of Indonesians sewing sneakers for sixty cents an hour evokes
so much more sympathy than the image of other Indonesians earning
half that trying to feed their families on tiny plots of land. He maintains that critics are motivated by feelings of guilt from benefiting from

the cheap consumer goods produced on the global assembly line: "Unlike the starving subsistence farmer, the women and children in the sneaker factory are working at slave wages for our benefit—and this makes us feel unclean."

Krugman focuses on the weak points in the arguments of critics: that global markets harm workers in emerging economies and promote complacency—consumers should admit that they benefit and shut up. However, just because workers may be somewhat better off, does not mean that we should not be concerned with the "awful conditions" that persist. Krugman overstates the positive effects of industrialization on workers. With high unemployment, desperate peasants are bountiful, enabling transnationals to continue to expand without pressures to raise wages or to improve working conditions substantially.

Krugman also ignores the harmful spillover effects of unregulated market growth: the abuse of women *outside* the factory system. In Thailand, to foster industrialization, government policies encourage the migration of girls from rural areas to urban manufacturing centers. Excess supplies not only kept wages down but also forced into prostitution many young women who had responsibilities to send money back to their rural families. In Malaysia, when manufacturing plants closed down during recessions, many young women could not afford to return to rural areas and had no alternative but to become prostitutes in order to maintain themselves and their families. If prostitution were not bad enough, many of these young girls contracted AIDS and other diseases. Similar abuses have followed the development of factories in the *maquiladores* zones in Mexico. Young women who are drawn into prostitution are subject to violence; hundreds have been found murdered over the last few years.[10]

Finally, Krugman's suggestion that consumers should passively accept the benefits they receive from the global assembly line is inappropriate. In response to labor abuses in the carpet-making industry in India, workers' rights groups have devised a logo that identifies rugs not made by child labor.[11] Many manufacturers have decided that this logo more than compensates for the higher labor costs associated with adult employment. Negative publicity, including threatened boycotts, has also caused Nike to improve the wages and working conditions of its Indonesian and Vietnamese labor force.

The most successful attempt to use consumer power to improve labor conditions has been on college campuses. Currently, $2.5 billion worth of college-name merchandise is sold nationwide each year.

Student protests have pressured administrators at dozens of major universities, including the University of Wisconsin, Cornell, and Duke to agree that all companies that produce college-name apparel will meet certain wage and working-condition requirements. In addition, firms will be required to disclose the names and locations of their factories, making independent monitoring easier.[12] By 2000, the majority of college-name merchandise met these requirements.

Evolving Competition

When capitalism enters new markets, the initial impact is often devastating. For example, the feminist sociologist Dorothy Smith contends that the emergence of capitalist relationships intensifies patriarchal oppression. The early North American homestead is a case in point. Pre-capitalism, it was characterized by relative equality of the sexes. This changed once capitalism became more developed, forcing farmers to emphasize cash crops sold in highly competitive markets. Owing to their small scale and undercapitalization, these farmers were always on the brink of bankruptcy. Increasingly, women's labor was substituted for hired labor; "her time and energy, indeed her life, were treated as inexhaustible."[13] Women were virtually imported into Canada in this period to serve these functions.

John Kenneth Galbraith addressed the problems that owners of small-scale firms face in fiercely competitive markets. He argued that these owners try to offset the higher technical productivity of their large-scale competitors by working longer and harder. Since reducing labor costs is paramount, these owners aggressively oppose unions, minimum wage legislation, or whatever might increase wage costs.[14] As a result, Galbraith considered those who labor in the competitive sector doubly harmed: harmed because for small-scale firms, the use of technological innovations that could raise productivity and wages is limited and because competitive pressures force wages and working conditions down to the lowest levels the labor market can bear.

The belief that competitive pressures lower wages is also found in the writings of Karl Marx. In nineteenth-century England, uneven development characterized the garment industry, as large-scale manufacturers competed against small-scale rural domestic producers. These small-scale producers could not utilize the newest technologies because they had neither the capital nor scale of operation necessary. Instead, they sought out women, children, and others made destitute by unemployment. These "cottage industry" laborers were among the most exploited workers of the day. Like Galbraith, Marx blamed competitive pressures for leading to the most extreme abuses since competitive pressures force owners to rob "the workman of the conditions most essential to his labor, of space, light, and ventilation."[15]

However, Marx believed that there were limits to the abuses workers could bear: "The cheapening of labor-power, by the sheer abuse of the labor of women and children, by the sheer robbery of every normal condition requisite for working and living, and by the sheer brutality of overwork and nightwork, meets at last with natural obstacles that cannot be overstepped."[16] Once these limits are reached, most small-scale firms would still have cost disadvantages and they would be driven out of the industry. Thus, Marx believed that self-regulating mechanisms would eliminate the most extreme abuses workers endured after a period of time.

The Pro-Market Model and Labor Market Discrimination

If labor markets treat workers equitably, earnings disparities among workers must reflect productivity differences. This idea has led pro-market economists to infer that if African Americans, women, or immigrant men are paid less than white native-born men, it must be due to their inferior skills and/or weaker work ethics. This view was widespread at the beginning of the twentieth century when economics, like most of the academic professions, contained racist assumptions.

Virtually all of the leading economists at the time believed that blacks were *genetically* inferior while there were disagreements as to the reasons for the inferiority of the recent white immigrants. The "liberal" wing of the profession believed that cultural factors explained their inferiority while the "conservative" wing pointed to genetics. These conservatives feared that continued unrestricted immigration would undermine the United States and characterized the pending doom as "race suicide." Articles presenting these viewpoints could be found in all the leading economics journals up through the early 1920s. When legislation eliminated further immigration from eastern and southern Europe, economics journals finally became silent on "racial" issues.[17]

During the 1930s, the fight against racism was embraced by radical movements, particularly the U.S. Communist Party. In 1931, seven blacks were convicted of raping two white women in Scottsboro, Mississippi. There seemed to be strong evidence that they were convicted without any proof of guilt. The Scottsboro Case was used to exemplify the situation facing blacks in the South, and anti-racist sentiment developed throughout the nation.[18] As the radical-led movements grew, many anti-racists left the NAACP, an organization committed to legislative reform rather than grass-roots struggles for radical change. While grass-roots movements were unable to exert sufficient political pressure to force the passage of national anti-lynching legislation, their threat did move President Franklin Roosevelt to agree to anti-discrimination regulations in all defense-related production facilities in 1941 and to reduce the sentences of the Scottsboro men. Most important, growing sensitivity to racial oppression provided the background for the successful integration of the armed forces and baseball in 1947 and support for educational desegregation after the *Brown v. Board of Education of Topeka* decision in 1954.

This radical anti-racist movement took for granted that government intervention was necessary because capitalists benefited from racism. In response, the Carnegie Commission funded studies, coordinated by the Swedish economist Gunnar Myrdal, which reached alternative conclusions. In *The American Dilemma*, Myrdal and his associates totally rejected the radical position that the capitalist profit motive promotes racism. They urged readers to reject radical politics and instead return to supporting the legislative reform strategy of the NAACP.[19]

Myrdal posited a "cumulative process" in which he adopted the nascent culture-of-poverty arguments then developing in the social sciences—ideas that had been applied by the "liberal" wing of the economics profession to buttress their claims that the new immigrants were culturally inferior.[20] According to Myrdal, restrictive policies increased the dysfunctional behavior of blacks: laziness, reliance on criminal activities, and lax sexual mores. The growing dysfunctional behavior blacks exhibited, in turn, reinforced negative black stereotypes held by whites that only strengthened their support of racist policies. Moreover, these stereotypes persisted, not because white racists benefited financially, but because of the dysfunctional behavior blacks exhibited.[21]

Despite Myrdal's protestations and further corporate funding to promote an alternative viewpoint, radical views continued to enjoy broad support.[22] It was not until Gary Becker's work, and the elimination of radical elements within the academy during the McCarthy period, that the pro-market model of discrimination gained preeminence within the economics profession. In his 1957 work, *The Economics of Discrimination*, Becker generally ignored key aspects of the radical view: the effects of divide-and-conquer strategies on corporate profits and on the wages of preferred (white) workers. Instead, he focused on the way corporate profits are impacted when firms refuse to hire nonpreferred (black) workers. His work suggested that there was no need for government intervention. Exclusionary barriers, he maintained, are unprofitable and will be eliminated by the self-regulation of markets.[23]

The Simple Pro-Market Model

Looking more closely at the hiring decisions of firms in highly competitive industries, it is clear that they must offer their workers the going wage and working conditions generally accepted in the marketplace. Their only real decision is how many workers to hire.

Now suppose that a firm decides to hire six workers, where the productivity of the twelve best applicants, comprised of six white and six black workers, is known (see Figure 2.1). If the firm hires solely on the basis of merit, it would hire the six most productive workers— three black and three white workers. However, suppose that the owner has a preference for white workers. The fourth-best white applicant produces forty units per hour, which is only slightly less than the forty-five units per hour produced by the third-best black applicant. Given his racial preferences, the owner might very well choose to hire the less-productive white applicant.

What about hiring the fifth-best white worker? This worker is capable of producing only thirty units per hour. To hire this white worker requires that the firm must forgo hiring the second-best black applicant who would have produced fifty-five units per hour. Here the productivity losses are more substantial and might be too much for the owner to accept.

This exercise suggests that when productivity differences between applicants are small, owners may exclude qualified workers from the group they dislike in favor of the slightly less-qualified workers from the groups they prefer. These same owners, with the same set of biased preferences, will react differently if the productivity differentials among applicants are substantial. In this case, hiring less-qualified workers from preferred groups causes substantial productivity losses—

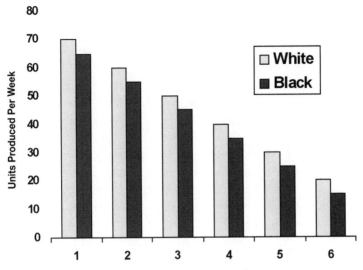

Figure 2.1 Productivity of the Twelve Best Applicants

losses that are likely to encourage owners to reject exclusionary hiring practices.

Hiring practices will also be influenced by market structure. If firms
face fierce competition, they may not be able to pass along the productivity losses from exclusionary practices to their customers. As a
result, these labor practices will have an adverse impact on profits.
Since firms in highly competitive environments often have low profit
margins, they might even be unwilling to exclude qualified black workers from employment when the productivity differentials are small.
In contrast, firms in less competitive industries are more able to pass
along productivity losses to customers as either price increases or lower
quality goods. Since these firms will suffer limited profit losses even
when productivity losses are substantial, they are more likely to maintain unfair hiring practices.

Applications of the Pro-Market Model

As indicated earlier, pro-market advocates point to
the integration of baseball as evidence of the powerful effect of market forces.[24] Professional baseball was organized during the 1870s. A
decade later, Cap Anson, a future Hall of Famer, refused to allow his
team to play against black baseball players. In response, the major

leagues became all white. During the 1920s, with the popularity of Babe Ruth, baseball became the national pastime and attendance and incomes grew. As the pro-market model predicts, entrepreneurs like Bill Veeck wished to purchase weak teams at bargain prices and improve them by hiring better-skilled and lower-paid black ballplayers. Steve Sailer writes, "Like all direct challenges, though, this was rebuffed by the autocratic Commissioner of Baseball, Judge Kenesaw Mountain Landis. After the Chicago Black Sox threw the 1919 World Series, the owners had restored faith in the game by appointing Landis, who was famed for his strict moral standards—one of which was Segregation Forever."[25] After Landis's death in 1944, the new commissioner, "Happy" Chandler, refused to enforce any ban on black ballplayers, opening the way for profit-seeking owners. In 1947, the owner of the Brooklyn Dodgers, Branch Rickey, broke the color line in the National League by employing Jackie Robinson. When Veeck was finally able to purchase the Cleveland Indians in 1948, the color line was broken in the American League.

To determine the impact of integration on team performance, the average number of victories for each team during the years 1946 to 1949 is taken as a benchmark, since during this period integration had little effect on the competitiveness of teams. There are two measures of integration used: (1) the first year each team had a *starting* black player; and (2) the total number of starting positions each team filled with black players over the thirteen-year period from 1947 to 1959 (see Table 2.1). Using either of these criteria, eleven of the sixteen teams fell into two groups: five which rapidly and strongly integrated, and six which had not really begun integration by 1959. For example, the Cleveland Indians belonged to the first group, with its first starting black player in 1948 and with black players filling an average of about two starting positions per year during this time period. In contrast, the Philadelphia Phillies had only one starting position in one year (1957) filled by a black ballplayer.

Integration should have improved team performance since some black players available were better than some white players. Teams that remained segregated would be less productive and not perform as well. Teams that integrated rapidly averaged 7.2 *more* wins per year during the 1950s than during the benchmark years. In contrast, teams that were not meaningfully integrated by 1959 averaged 6.6 *fewer* wins yearly during the 1950s than during the benchmark years.

One might ask why the pace of integration was relatively slow.

TABLE 2.1 Impact of Integration of Baseball on Team Performance, 1947–1959

TEAMS	BLACK STARTERS First year	BLACK STARTERS Number 1947–59	AVERAGE NUMBER OF WINS 1946–49	AVERAGE NUMBER OF WINS 1950–59	DIFF.
Milwaukee	1950	18	83.2	85.7	2.5
Los Angeles	1947	27	92.0	91.6	−0.4
San Francisco	1950	22	75.8	81.8	6.0
Chicago (WS)	1950	24	64.4	87.4	23.0
Cleveland	1948	25	85.2	90.2	5.0
Average					7.2
St. Louis	1958	2	88.0	77.7	−11.1
Philadelphia	1957	1	73.8	75.1	1.3
Washington	–	0	62.6	63.7	1.1
Detroit	–	0	87.4	71.4	−16.0
Boston	–	0	94.6	80.0	−14.6
New York	1959	2	94.6	94.1	−0.5
Average					−6.6

Why were there still six teams that had not integrated more than a decade after Jackie Robinson broke the color line? Pro-market theory suggests that it was because the profit motive was weak. Since team revenues and costs were quite low, winning or losing resulted in only small profit differences. Unlike Rickey and Veeck, most owners had made their fortunes elsewhere and considered baseball a hobby. They could easily afford to accept small financial losses so that they could hire according to their personal preferences.

In the 1960s, television revenues increased players' salaries and potential revenues to team owners. This dramatically increased the gains from having a winning team and the losses from having a losing one. No longer could owners afford to treat their teams as personal hobbies. They could maintain discriminatory preferences in their purely social activities, but they could not afford to use them when employing ballplayers. By the mid-1960s all baseball teams were strongly integrated. Thus, at least within the mainstream of the economics profession, empirical evidence and the rigor of the analysis seemed to convincingly demonstrate that when corporate profits are significantly harmed, exclusionary employment barriers become too costly to maintain in highly competitive industries.

Pro-market advocates argue that the government, correspondingly, is likely to be the most discriminating employer. Since the government has no profit motive, it has little concern for productivity and can hire solely on the basis of personal preferences. In support of their viewpoint, pro-market advocates point to the period prior to World War II when virtually no blacks were hired in a wide range of government occupations.[26]

Since the civil rights acts of the 1960s, the government has hired a disproportionate number of black workers. Between 1965 and 1982, 65 percent of all black professionals were hired by government and other nonprofit institutions.[27] For supporters of civil rights legislation, the large gap between the hiring practices in the public and private sectors was evidence that the private sector had been slow to change its discriminatory policies. However, conservative pro-market advocates have an entirely different explanation: reverse discrimination. The conservative economist Thomas Sowell claimed that, after the 1960s, government agencies continued to determine hiring decisions on the basis of public sentiment rather than merit. Since the new public sentiment favored the previous victims of discrimination, blacks now became *over*represented in the federal government.[28]

Implications for Theories of Discrimination

Competitive market mechanisms are not responsible for the deplorable conditions workers on the periphery of market economies endure. Generally, the spread of the market system has improved the conditions of workers compared to their situation in pre-capitalist economies. Moreover, even when there is an initial deterioration, market mechanisms eliminate the most severe abuses that occur in small, technologically backward firms. In agriculture, the emergence of agribusinesses has undermined the worst abuses experienced by farm workers employed on small-scale "family" farms. Today, the emergence of superstores, like Wal-Mart and Costco, have benefited those retail workers who no longer must seek employment in "family" grocery stores.

Despite the optimistic views of pro-market advocates, market mechanisms alone are not capable of eliminating completely the unfair conditions faced by powerless workers. Living in societies with large excess labor supplies, workers, especially those who have limited skills, still must adapt to the needs and desires of their employers. Only direct government intervention can rapidly counter the unfair conditions these workers face. In addition, the demise of small-scale enterprises, in which the most extreme abuses occur, would be accelerated by industrywide government regulations. Minimum wage and industrial safety regulations today, as child labor laws did in the past, undermine the ability of small-scale enterprises to compensate for their technological backwardness by reducing wages and working conditions.

Finally, unfettered capitalism has been particularly damaging to the interests of women. In Dickensian England, five-year-old girls toiled spinning silk while teen-age women contracted tuberculosis in textile factories and cottage industries that struggled for survival. Today, it is primarily women who populate the global assembly line, laboring for inadequate wages under unsafe conditions. In addition, this environment promotes prostitution, murder, and disease for many women who can take little consolation from the fact that most may be slightly better off than those who remain locked in patriarchal pre-capitalist communities. Rather than being complacent, consumers can speed up the process of adjustment by supporting activities, like those on college campuses, which force transnationals to raise living standards and working conditions of their employees worldwide.

Within the domestic economy, there are situations in which government intervention to protect workers is unnecessary. In highly competitive industries, where profit margins are already low, exclusionary policies place firms at a severe disadvantage and can even lead to bankruptcy. In this instance, unfair hiring practices have very little to offer profit-seeking owners.

The integration of baseball became a textbook example of the potential power of market forces to undermine discriminatory practices. Before any national legislation would have required it, baseball owners ended exclusionary practices, enabling employment of ballplayers to be determined by skills rather than the color of their skin. While owners could maintain discriminatory behavior in their personal lives—belonging to segregated country clubs, living in segregated neighborhoods, and sending their children to segregated schools—they could not maintain exclusionary hiring practices if they were to be financially successful.

There are logical political implications of the pro-market model. Pro-market proponents contend that it was necessary to eliminate legislation, like Jim Crow, which placed employment restrictions on firms. Once these restrictions were eliminated, the profit motive would guide firms to hire the most productive applicant. Not only did they believe that further civil rights legislation was unnecessary, pro-market proponents feared that this legislation would create new forms of discriminatory behavior. Reflecting this viewpoint, the conservative economist Milton Friedman wrote that while he deplored bigotry, he deplored government legislation that restricted the actions of those he considered bigots even more. "In a society based on free discussion," Friedman maintained, "the appropriate recourse is for me to seek to change their views and their behavior, not to use coercive power to enforce my tastes and my attitudes on others."[29]

Friedman was so fearful of the coercive power of government that he considered the civil rights laws passed in the United States during the 1960s the equivalent, philosophically, to the Nuremberg laws passed in Nazi Germany during the 1930s. Both sets of laws tried to legislate attitudes; one made it illegal to hire nonpreferred workers, while the other made it illegal not to hire them.

The pro-market model demonstrates that there are incentives for firms to hire in a nondiscriminatory manner. However, most pro-market advocates ignore other factors which might result in economic benefits to discriminating firms. Especially when the efficiency benefits from hiring the most productive job applicants are meager, these other factors may dominate employment decisions. In that case, exclusionary employment barriers can persist in the absence of government intervention. The next chapter will detail ways in which profit-seeking capitalists can benefit from exclusionary employment policies.

3 | It's Not Personal
When Hiring the Best Worker Isn't Profitable

The pro-market model is seductively simple: The profit motive will discipline owners to hire the most productive workers or suffer unacceptable losses. No government, no moral suasion is necessary; self-interest and competitive forces will do the job. Unequal incomes by race and gender may persist, but they will be the result of skill or behavioral differences, not discriminatory labor practices.

Critics do sometimes allow emotions to cloud their thoughts and overstate the case against market capitalism. However, this chapter will detail the reasons why the profit motive alone is not enough to end discriminatory practices. Some of the underlying assumptions of the pro-market model will be examined to demonstrate that the efficiency incentives to hire in a nondiscriminatory manner are not nearly as robust as pro-market advocates suggest. Benefits to owners from discriminatory behavior, which may dominate hiring decisions, will be identified also.

Discrimination by Competitive Firms

In the pro-market model, firms suffer productivity losses when they hire less-productive job applicants. These productivity losses can be substantial in an industry such as professional sports. In baseball, there are starting center fielders who have a .250 batting average and hit only three home runs while others have a .300

batting average and hit thirty home runs. With such measurable productivity differentials, it would be quite costly to hire on the basis of
personal preferences. In these situations, it is definitely cost-effective
to invest extensively in screening applicants. In baseball, substantial
scouting resources are expended, as well as substantial funds to pay
for minor league teams. Thus, it is not surprising that once television
revenues transformed baseball from a hobby to a business, owners felt
the need to separate their personal preferences from their business
decisions when hiring players.

Can we, however, generalize from this experience to other industries and other occupations? Are there situations in which the productivity differences among applicants are so meager that even
competitive firms will not be discouraged from engaging in discriminatory hiring practices? While owners might want to hire the most productive workers, they may not initiate a comprehensive search if it is
costly to obtain productivity information on job applicants. Owners
may end up using arbitrary hiring procedures because the additional
screening costs are unlikely to yield substantially better employees.
Moreover, when firms adopt exclusionary practices, though they may
suffer some efficiency losses by not hiring the most productive job
applicants, there are sometimes other ways in which they benefit
indirectly.

Limited Productivity Differentials among Applicants

While there are quite large differences in produc-
tivity levels among ballplayers, this might not be sufficient to force
owners to always hire *all* of their employees in a nondiscriminatory
manner. Within baseball, we can distinguish between the employment
of athletes and nonathletes—managers, coaches, and office personnel.
In 1989, the economist Gerald Scully noted that although blacks were
paid very well and, in many ways, had come to dominate professional
sports, their role has been restricted to the playing field. In his own
words, "Baseball has taken on the appearance of a white man's game
which employs well-paid African American gladiators."[1]

After highly publicized racist remarks by a baseball executive in
1987, Commissioner of Baseball Peter Ueberroth prodded team owners to double the number of blacks and Latinos hired in nonplayer
positions within the next year. However, virtually all of these hirings
were low level; few were to decision-making positions. Even after these

affirmative action hirings, of the 130 coaching positions, minorities held only a total of sixteen. There were no black trainers, no black umpires in the American League, and only six in the minors. Despite the urging by Peter Ueberroth, when clubs appointed thirteen new managers, general managers, and presidents, none was black.[2] Though there has been modest improvement in the last decade, blacks and Latinos are still underrepresented in nonplayer positions.

Moreover, even the modestly positive experience in baseball cannot necessarily be transposed to other professional sports. In particular, television contracts in professional football reduce the financial benefits gained by having an improved team. Unlike baseball, there is only one national television contract, negotiated collectively by the National Football League. As a result, each team receives the same television revenues regardless of its performance.

For many years, this had the effect of deemphasizing performance so that there were many incidents when teams would release superior athletes because of alleged "attitude" problems. Scouting was not as thorough-going and black players from smaller colleges were not as likely to gain employment as white players from football college powerhouses. Only during the last decade, with the emergence of luxury box seats and the sale of merchandise by individual teams, have the financial incentives to have a winning team become as decisive in football as in baseball.

Since some owners deemphasized winning, the Oakland Raiders' Al Davis was able to field championship NFL teams during the period 1970–1985. Much of his success reflected a willingness to employ players with "attitude" problems who were cast off from other franchises. One possible explanation for this was that Davis, unlike most of the other football owners, had no outside sources of income. He was not a millionaire who had bought a football team as a "hobby." For him, the modest financial incentives of having a winning team were sufficient. In this regard, Davis paralleled Branch Rickey and Bill Veeck. Once financial incentives increased for other football owners, Davis lost his edge. As a result, since the mid-1980s, his teams have not been able to maintain their excellence.

Outside of sports, it is likely that productivity differentials would be too small to influence employers to hire fairly. For example, there are many talented musicians who could be hired as third or fourth chairs in concert orchestras throughout the United States. In virtually all these orchestras, the hiring decisions are made by men who, not surprisingly, favor other men. This was demonstrated when some orchestras shifted to using a screen during auditions so that the gender (and race) of the musician was hidden. Under this "blind" audition procedure, twice as many women were selected as under the traditional method of selection.[3]

Productivity differences are the smallest when young workers are hired for less-skilled positions. Between 1989 and 1992 there were a series of employment audits to test hiring biases in these types of jobs. For each advertised job opening, a white and a black individual were sent, matched for qualifications and demeanor. Audits found that white applicants were more likely to reach higher stages in the hiring process than their matched black applicants. In an Urban League study, in 73 percent of the cases, paired white and black applicants had the same outcome. However, in 20 percent of the audits, the white applicant received more favorable treatment: either going to a higher stage in the application process or being hired when the black applicant was not. In only 7 percent of the audits did the black applicant receive more favorable treatment. This study strongly suggested that in these labor markets, hiring decisions are significantly influenced by personal preferences.[4]

Consumer Preferences

When firms are providing services, their customers may be sensitive to the personal characteristics of workers. In sports, some owners once claimed that they were reluctant to hire black ballplayers because their customers would attend games only if it was an all-white team. During the 1950s, this was the rationale given by August Busch for his reluctance to integrate the St. Louis Cardinals baseball team. During the 1970s, the owner of the basketball team in Cleveland made a similar claim: now the issue was, would fans attend if the *entire* starting lineup was black? Evidence seems to indicate that when teams are winning, fans are able to put their racial preferences aside.

Consumer preference may make a difference, however, when productivity gains are modest. This may very well explain why the largest accounting firms—the old Big Eight—resisted hiring Jewish (and black) accountants for more than a decade after civil rights legislation. These firms reasoned that many of their clients were reluctant to have Jews and blacks visit their premises. The black or Jewish accountants, who could have been hired, may have been only slightly superior technically—at best, they might have been able to do firm audits slightly faster than their present accounting employees. In this situation, the accounting firms could have only slightly lowered their fees by hiring black and Jewish accountants. Without major differences in productivity levels that would have resulted in large fee differentials, there was no financial incentive for clients to separate their personal preferences from their business decisions. As a result, the Big Eight firms felt they must accommodate their clients' preferences and not hire black or Jewish accountants to do outside audits.

Concern for consumer preferences has been the rationale given by elite New York City restaurants for their unwillingness to hire women to wait on customers. Restauranteurs excluded women because they felt their corporate image was enhanced when their cuisine was served by men. They also desired to convey the elegant ambience found in elite European restaurants. In 1999, New York state attorney general Eliot Spitzer filed suit against the Cipriani restaurant family in an effort "to overturn longstanding practices that prevent women from obtaining lucrative jobs in many of the city's most expensive steak-houses and French and Italian restaurants." Mr. Spitzer claimed, "This type of insidious behavior creates a glass ceiling within the restaurant industry. Women are being denied lucrative jobs and a stepping stone to more prestigious positions."[5]

Group Profiling

The pro-market model ignores the cost to firms of obtaining information on the skills of job applicants. Critics contend that firms will use group profiling to reduce their initial screening costs, especially when productivity differentials are small. Group profiling can be based on personal hostility to particular groups. Owners can decide to save the hiring expenses of screening applicants by immediately excluding those from groups they dislike. If the savings in screening costs are substantial, they may offset the productivity losses incurred from not hiring the most productive job applicants, which increases the likelihood that firms will engage in exclusionary practices.

Group profiling is even more likely if there is evidence that one group has more undesirable qualities than others. For example, suppose there is evidence that on city streets after 11 P.M., 2 percent of young black men but only 1 percent of young white men are carrying illegal goods. Let us assume that the police department has the capability of stopping two hundred young men nightly. Since black youths are twice as likely to possess illegal goods, police can maximize the illegal goods obtained by focusing *solely* on black youths. Note that this group profiling can be effective even though 98 percent of black youths stopped will not be in possession of illegal goods.

The likelihood that group profiling would dominate hiring practices is especially high for desirable jobs where there are many qualified applicants. Since comprehensively evaluating each individual applicant can be quite time-consuming, a quick profiling of applicants is often cost-effective. Suppose that employers perceive that there is a higher likelihood of inferior skills among a particular group of applicants. Group profiling would eliminate *all* applicants from this group since there are more than enough qualified applicants from other groups to choose from.

Group profiling can be based on factors other than race. At the author's own college, there was an opening to hire one entry-level economist. When we advertised in a national publication, 180 recent graduate students applied. We had to decide how much time to spend screening these applications in anticipation of interviewing twenty-five candidates at an upcoming national convention. There were five members on the screening committee. If just ten minutes were spent evaluating each application, this would be thirty hours per committee member. We decided to complete the screening process quickly by focusing on the school each graduate had attended. Since we had many applicants from first-tier graduate programs, we immediately eliminated virtually all applicants from second-tier schools. After completing this initial screening, we gathered extensive information on the candidates we chose to interview. Subsequently, the department brought three candidates to campus. Each candidate made a presentation and was interviewed by a group of economics majors and the entire economics faculty.

Once candidates made it to the interview stage, they were judged on their individual merit. During the initial screening process, however, group profiling was used to limit the allocation of scarce personnel resources. Since this is a procedure used by most economics departments, it undoubtedly afforded weaker candidates from first-tier graduate schools many more opportunities to be interviewed than it did stronger candidates from second-tier graduate programs.

Group profiling precluded the certainty that the best applicant for our position was interviewed. The additional screening costs necessary to guarantee that this applicant would be interviewed were too large when compared to the expected benefits. Even if the best applicants were from weaker schools, they would have been only slightly better than the applicant we eventually hired using our arbitrary screening process. Thus, when productivity differentials among applicants are small, group profiling is likely to exclude virtually *all* qualified individuals from groups that are perceived to have, *on average*, lower performance.

In the 1970s, group profiling was most prominently identified with the inability of women to obtain managerial positions. Firms expected that many women would voluntarily quit after a few years to get married or take care of children. Rather than doing extensive screening to identify which female applicants were more strongly career-oriented, firms simply eliminated all women from the applicant pool. As a result of these perceptions, female college graduates were excluded from many high-paying professional occupations and instead crowded into less-prestigious and lower-paying female-dominated ones.[6]

Even within low-paid occupations, group profiling can substantially damage the employment prospects of qualified workers. Suppose that employers believe that, on average, black workers have higher rates of absenteeism and lateness than white workers. If they had a sufficient number of white applicants, employers might screen out *all* black applicants. Employers realize that among their black applicants, some are rarely late or absent. However, since the productivity differences are not perceived to be substantial, it would not be worth the increased screening costs to find these efficient black applicants. This kind of group profiling might help to explain the high black unemployment rate.

Group profiling substantially undercuts two tenets of the pro-market model: that (1) exclusionary policies reflect purely personal preferences and (2) exclusionary policies will be costly to firms. Exclusionary policies can occur even when decision makers do not have a personal preference and simply make screening decisions based on group statistics. Moreover, discriminatory behavior persists because the reduction in screening costs substantially offsets meager productivity losses resulting from exclusionary practices.

Since group profiling has historically been one of the major sources of discrimination, affirmative action guidelines focus on the demographic composition of the applicant pool at each stage in the hiring process. As a result, when my department did its initial screening, affirmative action candidates from second-tier graduate schools remained in the pool. They were interviewed at the national convention and judged on their individual merit.

Critique of Group Profiling

We can certainly question the decision of police departments to use racial profiling, in view of the undue burden it places on the vast majority of blacks who are law abiding. We can certainly point to the shortcomings of group profiling in hiring practices. However, if group profiling is based upon accurate information on group differences rather than on personal animus, there will have to be a trade-off between efficient law enforcement and civil liberties and between the efficient use of hiring resources and the fair evaluation of all qualified applicants.

While group profiling sometimes raises conflicts between equity and efficiency, it is also often based on statistical misinterpretations. Let me give an example from my own experience. At Brooklyn College, I teach a large introductory course. Whenever I give an examination, a number of students are late. At some point, it seemed to me that these were disproportionately nonwhite students. First, my perception might have been based on preconceived notions. That is, if I began with the belief that black students lack punctuality, I might notice black students who are late and subconsciously minimize the extent to which white students are also late. As a result, I may treat black lateness as a general principle but white lateness as exceptions to the rule.

Second, let us suppose I found that black students were indeed disproportionately late for exams. How should this be interpreted? Presumably, I should see if factors *other than race* could explain this phenomenon. For one thing, students who come late may be disproportionately weaker students, as measured by their scores on previous examinations. If black students make up a disproportionate share of weaker students, they will make up a disproportionate share of students coming late to exams. In this case, lateness may not be due to race but instead, due to skill level.

The ability to separate race from other factors is an inherent problem with interpretation of *aggregate* statistics. For example, there is some statistical evidence that black workers have higher rates of absenteeism than white workers. If this is a manifestation of *racially distinct* behavioral differences, firms could justify their adoption of group profiling procedures whenever there are a sufficient number of white

Table 3.1 Absenteeism by Race and by Occupation

	ABSENTEEISM (%)			EMPLOYMENT (%)	
RACE	*Good jobs*	*Bad jobs*	*Average**	*Good jobs*	*Bad jobs*
Black	2.0	6.0	5.2	20	80
White	2.0	6.0	4.0	50	50

* For African Americans, 2.0(0.2)+6.0(0.8)=5.2; for whites, 2.0(0.5)+6.0(0.5)=4.0

applicants. The problem is that these aggregate statistics do not indicate how black and white absenteeism relate to *specific* jobs.

Let us assume that the labor market can be divided into two subgroups: "good jobs" and "bad jobs" (see Table 3.1). Good jobs are those jobs where there are substantial nonwage benefits, expectations of upward mobility, and decent working conditions. Bad jobs are dead-end jobs with few benefits and generally unpleasant working conditions. The absenteeism rate equals the percentage of workers who are absent on any given day. Table 3.1 was constructed with the following assumptions:

1. Black workers have the *same* absenteeism rates as white workers in each job grouping.
2. Absenteeism rates are *higher* for bad jobs (6 percent) than for good jobs (2 percent).
3. A larger share of black (80 percent) than white workers (50 percent) are employed in bad jobs.

Since white workers are equally distributed between the two subgroups, the overall white rate is a simple average of the absenteeism rates of each group, (6+2)/2 = 4.0 percent. For black workers, since 80 percent are employed in bad jobs, the overall absenteeism rate is a weighted average, 0.8(6)+0.2(2) = 5.2 percent.

Just as the illustrative data suggest, studies have found that job characteristics "play a decisive role in predicting employee behavior."[7] When black and white youths were employed at jobs with the same characteristics, there was no difference between their rates of absenteeism. These studies suggested that black youths are not very different than white youths. If given decent jobs, they will behave just as responsibly. These studies demonstrated that the use of group profiling may not even be efficient, let alone equitable.

Offsetting Benefits

Whether group profiling is due to the use of group averages or to personal animus, qualified black and female workers are excluded from better-paying positions. As we have seen, the resulting increase in productivity is somewhat offset by a reduction in hiring costs. Firms may benefit in other ways as well. In particular, excluded workers adapt by shifting to less-desirable occupations. This increases the number and skills of workers in these occupations. As a result, firms are able to hire highly qualified workers at lower wages in other less-sought-after employment categories. A simple example will illustrate this relationship.

Law firms do not hire only lawyers. They also hire paralegals and legal secretaries. For many years, major law firms used group profiling and excluded female lawyers. A noted case is the experience of Supreme Court justice Ruth Bader Ginsburg. When she graduated second in her law class at Columbia University, she was unable to secure a position at any of the major corporate law firms in New York City. This exclusionary barrier caused many women who wished to enter law to adapt their career aspirations. Many of them reluctantly shifted to becoming paralegals and legal secretaries. Thus, law firms benefited indirectly by having somewhat better-qualified (and somewhat lower-paid) support service workers.

The ability of capitalists to place qualified black workers in secondary tracks within their companies was illustrated by the hiring practices of Henry Ford. During the 1930s, black workers were generally excluded from all well-paying jobs. Henry Ford was the only automobile manufacturer who hired black workers. In his River Rouge plant, the largest automobile assembly plant in the world, black workers comprised 12 percent of the work force. Within the automobile plants, however, some jobs were much less desirable, such as foundry work. It was to these positions that black workers were assigned. Despite the harshness of their working conditions, the black workers were quite thankful for the jobs and were hard-working and loyal to the company. Thus, the efforts of black workers in the foundry more than compensated Ford for the modest productivity losses that resulted from their exclusion from more preferred employment positions.

The experience of these black workers is also a concrete example of the misinterpretation of group averages. Beginning in the 1920s, black workers became a significant presence in northern labor markets. At that time, many northern employers believed that black workers were inferior to whites and interpreted their movement from job to job as a weak commitment to industrial work. On the surface, Ford company data seemed to support these views: Black workers had higher turnover rates than white workers. However, economists Warren Whatley and Stan Seto found that this high turnover rate was the result of black workers being disproportionately assigned to occupations, like those in the foundry, which had the highest turnover rate for all workers. Within each individual occupation, black workers had a lower turnover rate than their fellow white workers.[8]

Even when firms do not employ those who adapt to exclusionary policies, they still can benefit indirectly. For example, suppose that a company has fluctuating, volatile demand. If it relied on its own internal production, there would be periods in which workers would earn substantial overtime and other times when the company would have high labor costs when it maintains employment despite low demand. As an alternative, the company may outsource the volatile portion of its demand to other suppliers, enabling it to maintain stable employment and production in its own plants. The contractors who supply the volatile portion of demand are less desirable companies that generally hire excluded workers. Thus, these excluded workers bear the brunt of volatile production, enabling the discriminatory firm and its workers to have stable employment and production.

Discrimination by Firms in Noncompetitive Industries

When firms face fierce competition, profit margins are low, and they cannot afford to sacrifice economic efficiency for personal reasons. However, what if producers are not in a competitive environment? For example, many firms are in industries that are difficult to enter so that competition is limited. In this environment, existing firms obtain excess profits and can afford to indulge their personal preferences. In addition, government agencies do not have a profit motive so they have no economic incentive to hire the most productive worker. Indeed, pro-market economists suggest that because they lacked any profit motive, government agencies have historically had the most discriminatory hiring practices. These economists cite evidence that prior to the civil rights era, government agencies hired fewer women and blacks than the for-profit sector. Since the civil rights era, they maintain, government agencies have begun to favor these groups so that the growth in black and female employment has been higher in the nonprofit than the for-profit sector. Using the examples of the FBI and Texaco, however, this section indicates that in most instances hiring decisions continue to discriminate against blacks and other underrepresented groups of workers.

The pro-market model implies that firms in less competitive industries will be nondiscriminatory as long as they attempt to maximize their profits. In contrast, critics contend that there are a number of ways in which discriminatory hiring practices profit these corporations. There are situations, highlighted in the following pages, in which providing additional benefits to workers can actually lower production costs and how this can have an impact on the race or gender distribution of the work force. In these cases, capitalists may also profit by preserving, within their work force, racial divisions that are maintained through discriminatory hiring practices.

Discriminatory Personal Preferences—
Texaco and the FBI

Civil rights advocates generally reject any notion that the fast growth of black employment in many government agencies during the 1970s reflected unfair preferences. Indeed, these advocates note that some government agencies continued to have limited nonwhite employment, particularly those agencies, like the FBI and the Corps of Engineers, which are relatively insulated from public purview. In 1989, while 9 percent of FBI employees were black, only one of its field offices (Puerto Rico) was headed by a black, and less than 2 percent of senior officers were black. In 1990, the FBI had to settle a class-action lawsuit with three hundred veteran black agents who were judged by a federal court to have been systematically denied promotions.

The most glaring example of abuse was the experience of Donald Rochon. A veteran of the Los Angeles police force, Rochon took a pay cut to join the FBI in 1983. At the Omaha office, he was subject to numerous racist actions. For example, fellow agents defaced a family photograph on his desk by taping a picture of an ape's head over his son's. His supervisor told investigators that these pranks were "healthy" and a sign of an "esprit de corps." After Rochon transferred to the Chicago office, the harassment intensified. For example, another agent forged Mr. Rochon's signature and handwriting on forms for two insurance polices in 1985, one for death and dismemberment coverage, the other for burial costs. When the FBI was forced to act after finding out the identity of the harassing officer, it decided that a fourteen-day suspension without pay was sufficient punishment. In response, white agents in the Chicago office chipped in to pay the penalized officer's salary for the two weeks. Recalling a three-year campaign of harassment by fellow agents, Mr. Rochon stated, "I couldn't believe this was happening. It was like I was in a time machine, and someone had turned the clock back from the 1980's to the 1950's."[9]

In 1990, Latino employees won a similar lawsuit against the FBI. Texas federal district judge Lucius Bunton found that "Hispanic agents tended to receive assignments that demanded Spanish language skills and offered no opportunity for career advancement." Rather than contesting the ruling, the FBI director William Sessions said, "Each of the 11 agents will be promoted to a position which best serves their needs and the needs of the FBI." Only fifteen of the nearly one hundred veteran Latino agents eligible to file did so, because of feared retaliation by non-Latino supervisors. "Listen, I might have gotten a promotion out of it, but they might have promoted me to Timbuktu as a form of punishment," said a Latino agent. "I wasn't going to risk that."[10]

The same pattern seems to be prevalent within the Corps of Engineers. In Pennsylvania, black workers were systematically subject to racist harassment. *New York Times* columnist Bob Herbert reported,

> Two black employees . . . were draped in chains and had shackles placed on them by their white co-workers. This was considered hilarious. Photographs were taken and . . . widely circulated. . . . [Another worker, Stanton Greenwood,] walked into a locker room and saw a life-sized poster of four armed men in Ku Klux Klan robes surrounding a black man with a noose around his neck . . . Mr. Greenwood told an Army equal employment opportunity counselor about the harassment, and he noted that blacks were almost always relegated to the lowest-paying menial jobs. When word got out that Greenwood complained, a co-worker threatened to shoot him. One day Mr. Greenwood arrived at work to find that someone had gone into his locker and stuffed human feces into his work boots.[11]

A similar situation existed in Mississippi. *New York Times* columnist Ken Sack reported that black workers had "for years endured racial slurs and discriminatory personnel practices by white authorities." He found that "sleeping quarters, bathrooms and mess halls were segregated by race. While white workers were assigned semi-private quarters in the front of boats, blacks slept 10 to 12 to a room in the aft." He noted that the chief administrator condoned racist behavior where "white workers regularly used racial epithets to refer to black counterparts in their presence" and promoted a white supervisor who was particularly abusive to black workers even though he had exhibited consistent alcohol problems while piloting the boat.[12]

Civil rights advocates reject the claim that industries are generally competitive enough to be relied upon to eliminate discrimination in hiring. They note the oil industry as an example. In 1996, Texaco was forced to settle a class-action lawsuit, agreeing to pay $176 million to its fourteen hundred black employees. The lawsuit noted that, due to the hostile environment, the percentage of black employees at Texaco fell from 9.8 to 8.3 percent between 1984 and 1995, and that blacks never represented more than 3.75 percent of its management staff. It was also noted that not one of the five hundred most senior oil industry executives was either black or Latino.[13]

These recent Texaco policies mirror its previous policies toward Jews. While there has been some improvement since the mid-1980s, in a survey of the six major oil companies done in 1978, only five of the three hundred top executives were Jewish. The study by Ira Gissen concluded that this resulted from "recruitment avoidance, promotion levels beyond which Jews cannot go, non-assignment to certain job areas, and stereotyped employment (i.e., in such departments as legal, accounting, and research)."[14]

Gissen's findings were consistent with employment practices in many other industries, including commercial banking, which is dominated by a few large firms. For example, a 1973 American Jewish Committee study did not find a single Jew among the 176 senior executives of the fifteen largest U.S. commercial banks, eight of which were headquartered in New York City. Even at middle-level management, there were only 14 Jews out of 1,757 executives. A decade later, Simon Rifkin, a longtime Jewish leader and corporate director, still contended: "Jews have traditionally been successful bankers and yet if you look at most of the commercial banks you will not find a Jewish name at all. . . . The same is true of insurance companies. I would say the same is true of the bigger corporations."[15]

Economists Steve Slavin and Mary Pradt surveyed 1972–1973 recruitment patterns of major corporations. They documented the same kind of recruitment avoidance mentioned in the Gissen study. A wide disparity between corporate interviewing at colleges with low Jewish enrollment and similar colleges with high Jewish enrollment was found. While corporations in the Fortune 500 made a total of more than forty visits a year to colleges with a Jewish enrollment of less than 20 percent, they averaged less than twenty visits to comparable colleges with Jewish enrollment of more than 30 percent.[16]

Divide-and-Conquer Strategies

Radical economists suggest that racism creates and/ or solidifies divisions within the working class. These divisions can weaken the ability of workers to unite to form effective unions. At the end of the nineteenth century, divisions between native workers and immigrants undermined unionizing efforts in northern manufacturing. Just after World War I, northern capitalists used blacks as strikebreakers to undermine union struggles. And after World War II, racism in the South created a pool of cheap labor, enabling corporations to shift production away from more costly unionized labor in the Northeast and Midwest.

Michael Reich tested the hypothesis that racial unity would adversely affect the income of capitalists, using 1960 and 1970 data from the largest forty-eight metropolitan areas. Reich had to select measures for each of his variables. For income going to capitalists, he used the share of local income going to the richest 5 percent of households. For a measure of racial unity, he used the ratio of black-to-white family income in each area. Reich reasoned that the smaller the income gap, the more likely black and white families would find common ground on which to unite.[17]

Reich found that metropolitan areas with less racial inequality had a smaller share of total income going to capitalists than metropolitan areas with greater racial income inequality. His results held, even after including other factors that might explain variations in the amount of money capitalists were making. Moreover, just as the divide-and-conquer model would predict, Reich found unionization efforts were influenced by the degree of racial unity. In metropolitan areas where there was less racial income inequality, there was also a higher percentage of workers in unions.

Reich argued that a racially divided working class was less able to defend social spending programs against political attacks. As racial income inequality increased, per capita expenditures on social services declined. Since local governments must have balanced budgets, lower per capita expenditures translate into lower taxes. Thus,

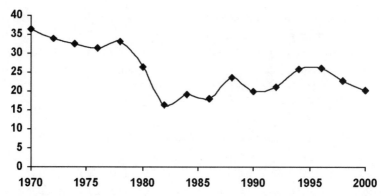

Figure 3.1 Corporate to Personal Federal Tax Ratio, 1970–2000. *Source:* Economic Report of the President *(Washington, D.C.: Government Printing Office, 2000), Table B78.*

Reich claimed that declining racial unity aided the wealthy by lowering the local taxes they paid.

While Reich studied urban areas, the same pattern should also hold at the federal level. Many radicals contend that racial divisiveness increased during the 1970s. According to Reich's model, this would have made it easier to cut back social spending in order to finance tax cuts beneficial to wealthy households. Consistent with this thesis, the tax rate for households with income over $250,000 fell from 90 percent in 1980 to 36 percent by 1986. It fell even further in 1997, when legislation reduced the tax on capital gains from 32 to 18 percent.

In addition, corporations have been able to avoid high rates of federal taxation. For most of the 1970s, corporate taxes were about one-third the level of personal taxes (see Figure 3.1). At the end of the 1970s, however, tax changes lowered corporate taxes dramatically so that, by 1990, they were only one-fifth as much as federal personal taxes.

Finally, and maybe most important, radicals argue that racial divisions enable capitalists to scapegoat blacks as the cause of social ills, deflecting the anger felt by white workers and their families away from the wealth-owning class. During the 1980s, there was a dramatic decline in the overall earnings and employment of adult men. For example, between 1979 and 1989, after adjusting for inflation, the usual weekly wage of the median male worker fell by 4 percent. For the male worker who was at the twenty-fifth percentile, his real wage fell by 11 percent. In addition, employment became more uncertain. The share of adult men who worked full-time for at least eight years fell from

79 percent for the period 1970–1979 to 70 percent for the period 1980–1989. The decline was even more dramatic for those with less education. Among male high school graduates, the decline was from 84 to 72 percent; among high school dropouts, from 52 to 30 percent.[18]

One might have expected that the resulting anger among male workers would have led to a united working-class movement to confront corporate greed. Unfortunately, that white male anger appeared to be deflected toward various scapegoats: foreigners, women, and blacks. In the 1988 presidential campaign, ideology was harnessed to shift concerns to black criminality, typified by the "Willie Horton ad," which focused on the perceived lenient treatment of convicted felons. During the 1992 presidential campaign, there was an attempt to shift blame to feminists for the alleged undermining of family values, typified by Dan Quayle's attack on the TV series *Murphy Brown,* for glorifying unwed mothers. During the 1996 campaign, the scapegoats became affirmative action beneficiaries and immigrants, as was shown by support for California's initiatives to end affirmative action programs and to withhold government benefits from immigrants. Meanwhile, corporate taxes continued to decline, working-class wages continued to stagnate, and capital gains tax reforms aimed at benefiting the richest households were promoted.

The radical divide-and-conquer theory serves to explain why capitalists have been major funders of anti-tax movements—movements which have used race as an unspoken argument against government social spending programs. The divide-and-conquer theory, however, tells us very little about how individual capitalists make employment decisions. For example, it is certainly possible that individual capitalists, whose personal contributions help fund racist political campaigns, may not discriminate in hiring decisions. Indeed, as discussed in chapter 2, this is exactly the separation that Booker T. Washington anticipated when he counseled blacks to ally themselves with white capitalists rather than white workers.

The divide-and-conquer strategy can also be effective when firms employ an all-white work force. In the early part of the twentieth century, owners had the ability to use black strikebreakers to undermine unionization efforts of their white workers. During the 1930s, the Ku Klux Klan promoted the idea that even though unions might marginally raise white wages, it was not worth a few cents to be forced to work in racially integrated workplaces.[19] As a result, racist white southern workers supported anti-union legislation, particularly the so-called

right-to-work laws, which made it illegal for unions to require workers to pay dues, even when they had voted for union representation.

Capitalists have also benefited when they've employed an integrated but segmented work force. This was the situation at the end of
the nineteenth century when northern capitalists employed native-born
craft workers and unskilled immigrant workers. Racist theories promoted the notion that immigrants were inferior, undermining any ability of native and immigrant workers to unite. Similarly, when Henry
Ford hired black workers in the 1930s, he created disunity among his
work force. Even though these black workers had the worst jobs in
his automobile plants, they were grateful for the employment. As a
result, they and the black community initially allied themselves with
Henry Ford rather than the United Automobile Workers (UAW), fore-
stalling union organizing efforts at his Ford Motor Company.

The Efficiency Wage Theory

In most labor markets, worker productivity im-
proves with length of employment making labor turnover costly. For
these reasons, firms might find it cost-effective to offer their current
workers a wage premium. Since workers realize that they are being
paid above their productive worth, there would be lower quit rates,
reducing training costs. Also, the loyalty this policy engenders might
raise worker productivity and reduce monitoring costs. If the increased
productivity and reduced monitoring and training costs are greater than
the wage premium, these firms would have lower production costs.

Mainstream economists believe that this *efficiency wage theory*—
where firms can lower their production costs by paying workers premiums above the going market wage—is most prevalent in larger firms
which undertake long-term planning. A historical example most often cited is the case of Ford Motor Company. When Henry Ford instituted his assembly-line production technique, Ford Motors experienced
very high turnover and absenteeism rates. Owing to the competitive
wages Ford paid, the company had no trouble finding replacement
workers. However, in an attempt to reduce turnover rates and increase
worker productivity, Ford changed his wage policies. In January 1914,
Ford doubled wages to five dollars per day for all workers who were
employed for at least six months. Almost immediately, worker behavior
changed. The quit rate fell by 87 percent, the discharge rate by 90 percent, and the absenteeism rate by 75 percent. Morale and productivity increased, enabling Ford to improve profitability.[20]

A variant of efficiency wage theory is provided by left economists associated with the Social Structure of Accumulation (SSA) school.[21] They believe that during the early post–World War II period, firms in the noncompetitive sector valued labor stability and their workers received wage premiums as a result. While many production workers benefited somewhat from this arrangement, David Gordon believed that the lion's share of the wage premiums went to managers and other supervisory personnel: "Executives could enhance their power and prestige by, as it were, expanding their retinues. Feudal baronies prospered and grew in the European countryside in the eleventh–thirteenth centuries. And the equivalent of feudal baronies prospered and grew in U.S. corporations in the postwar period."[22] With the growth of global competition, firms sought to reduce the wage premiums paid to workers. Gordon lamented that, in order to protect their continued wage growth, corporate managers reverted to a "big stick" approach to force down wages of production workers.

Just like Adam Smith and efficiency wage theorists, Gordon thought that this was shortsighted, since paying wage premiums could have maintained loyalty and productivity. He pointed to statistics that indicated that countries with the most cooperative labor-capital relationships tended to have the highest rates of productivity growth. Thus, in Gordon's view, the big-stick approach reflects the interests of middle managers but not of long-term corporate profitability.

Most relevant to our discussion, the efficiency wage theory has been used to explain why, for some profit-seeking firms, hiring an all-white and/or all-male work force is rational behavior. According to the pro-market model, this should cause production costs to rise. However, what if white male workers perceive noneconomic benefits from working in an all-white, all-male environment? In this case, firms can substitute exclusionary hiring practices for wage premiums.

In addition, in the absence of exclusionary practices, white male workers might threaten to disrupt the production process. Historically, this disruption often took the form of strike activities. Today, Randy Albelda, Dick Drago, and Steve Shulman contend, "White males exert pressure in a more covert fashion. Women coworkers may be sexually harassed. Black coworkers may be ostracized, ignored, or subtly informed that they got their new job through quotas rather than qualifications."[23] Facing declining worker morale and a disruptive workplace, management might choose to adopt exclusionary employment practices.

Table 3.2 Black and White Male Employment Rates at the Peak and Trough of Business Cycles, 1973–1999

YEAR	BLACK MEN		WHITE MEN	
	Emp. rate (%)	*Change*	*Emp. rate (%)*	*Change*
1973	67.5		76.5	
1975	60.6	-6.9	73.0	-3.5
1979	63.4	2.8	75.1	2.1
1982–83	56.2	-7.2	70.5	-4.6
1989	62.8	6.6	73.7	3.2
1992	59.1	-3.7	71.1	-2.6
1999	63.1	4.0	72.8	1.7

Not only might an all-white, all-male workplace reduce the probability of a disrupted production process, it might allow management to "maintain a positive relationship with its white male workers by encouraging them to feel that they have exclusive rights to certain jobs."[24] As the efficiency wage theory contends, this develops worker loyalty, increasing productivity and reducing training and monitoring costs.

There are also indirect ways in which benefits provided to workers result in limiting the share of black workers. If individual merit is the only consideration, firms would want the widest discretion in their choice of hirings and layoffs. By contrast, when layoffs occur, workers would prefer that seniority determine who is terminated, eliminating uncertainty for most workers. When firms hire, workers would rather that applicants be chosen through personal recommendations, allowing them to provide employment opportunities to their friends and family members.

The use of networking to provide job applicants and seniority to determine layoffs is not the most efficient method of making personnel decisions. The firm is not necessarily laying off the least productive workers nor hiring the most productive workers available. However, the compensating gains in worker loyalty makes these accommodations cost-effective. Unfortunately, black workers are adversely affected in these situations since they tend to have less seniority and fewer informal networks than white workers.

Evidence exists to demonstrate the harm to black workers when networking and seniority practices are utilized (see Table 3.2). The data show national employment for black and white men at the peak and the trough of the most recent business cycles. Note that in each year, the black employment rate is substantially below the white rate. This lower rate of black employment is consistent with the view that using informal networking to determine new hires adversely affects the employment of black workers.

The data in Table 3.2 also indicate that black male employment is more volatile than white male employment. In each contraction, the decline in black employment rates was substantially larger than the decline in white employment rates. In each expansion, black employment grows more rapidly than white employment. This is consistent with the pattern we would anticipate when firms use seniority to determine layoffs. Since black workers have less seniority, they would be the first to be laid off during economic contractions and the first to be hired on during expansions.

Concluding Remarks

Key assumptions underpinning the pro-market model may be inconsistent with the situation in many hiring situations. When employers have personal animus toward particular groups, discriminatory practices can persist as long as they do not face fierce competition and/or as long as skill differentials among job applicants are meager. Indeed, these possibilities may explain why despite integration on the playing field, baseball owners still tend to exclude nonwhite job applicants from nonplaying positions. They also explain hiring practices in the oil industry and commercial banking where firms are insulated from competitive pressures.

Exclusionary practices can persist in occupations where obtaining productivity information is costly. In these situations, firms may exclude all individuals from groups which are perceived to have productivity levels, on average, below other applicant groups. Interestingly, owners are engaging in these practices even when they have no personal aversion to members of the excluded group. Employers simply judge it is not worth the added screening costs to identify the small number of applicants from the lower-productivity group since they would be only marginally more qualified than those who would otherwise have been hired. In addition, discriminatory firms may obtain substantial benefits indirectly. Their exclusionary practices may enable them to hire more-qualified employees at lower wages in less-desirable job categories or to obtain supplies at lower costs from other firms which hire the excluded workers.

Discriminatory hiring practices may persist also because they create divisions among workers that lower their bargaining power, enabling capitalists to lower wages. These divisions may enable corporations to lower the taxes that they pay and to scapegoat excluded groups for the problems the majority of workers face. The efficiency wage theory suggests that capitalists may find that gains from having a loyal and grateful all-white, all-male work force outweigh the productivity losses from the exclusion of qualified black and female job applicants. Finally, the adoption of informal hiring procedures and seniority procedures when determining layoffs, while beneficial to the firm, indirectly limits black and female employment.

4 | Race before Class
Jim Crow Employment Practices

The Civil War had the potential for revolutioniz-
ing social relationships in the South. The conflict
reduced the wealth and power of large landowners, reduced the gap
between black and white farmers, and opened up opportunities to a
free black populace. The political, social, and economic gains made
by southern blacks were, however, severely constrained, first, by the
ending of Reconstruction in 1877 and then, by the Jim Crow laws which
developed. Beginning in the 1890s, the "separate but equal" doctrine
accelerated the trend in southern states to segregate blacks and whites.
Blacks went to separate schools and medical facilities, and employers
were eventually required to segregate their work force. Not surprisingly, black schools and medical facilities were inferior and increasingly higher-waged jobs were reserved for white workers. Only after
the passage of civil rights legislation in 1964 was this pattern halted.

The following assessment of the economic aspects of the Jim Crow
era details the role of capitalism in its origin, maintenance, and elimination. In particular, I evaluate first the pro-market model which suggests that capitalists should have rejected the racially exclusionary
components of Jim Crow and, instead, should have been active supporters of the movement against them. Secondly, the impact of Jim
Crow on the earnings of southern black and white workers and farmers and the expectation that whites benefited from Jim Crow while

blacks were harmed are examined. Thirdly, the reasons why blacks remained in the South for so long after the institution of Jim Crow, only decisively leaving in large numbers after World War II when the mechanization of cotton undermined southern agricultural employment, are explored. Factors affecting the benefits and costs of migration out of the South and factors constraining that choice are discussed. In particular, attention is paid to the reasons why industrial expansion in the North relied upon immigrant rather than black labor and how this impacted the southern wages of both black and white workers.

My intentions are to provide important insights into understanding the economic dimensions of Jim Crow, particularly, that southern blacks experienced substantial progress during the latter part of the nineteenth century, which discouraged northern migration. In addition, it documents the disastrous impact that 1930s federal economic policies had on southern black employment. However, what follows should not be considered a comprehensive history of the Jim Crow era. For southern blacks, the Jim Crow era represented more than simply severe income inequality. This era continued the slave tradition of considering blacks as a people who were less than human and who could be terrorized at the whim of the white populace. The terror was most symbolized by the wide acceptance and participation of southern whites in lynching activities. In some black communities, the simple ability to survive could be considered a heroic act.[1] Nonetheless, Jim Crow's arbitrariness and violence have had a lasting imprint on the consciousness of the African American community.

A limitation of this section is its emphasis on the situation of black men. Black women were employed outside the home to a much greater extent than white women. During the period 1890 to 1930, black and white female labor force participation rates were approximately 40 percent and 15 percent, respectively.[2] However, black women had a narrow range of paid occupations. Except for positions as teachers in black schools, black southern working women were employed almost entirely as either domestic servants or as agricultural laborers. For example, these two occupations comprised 88 percent of all employed black women nationally in 1900 and still 78 percent in 1930. Black women were also subjected to physical terror and abuse. However, since the focus here is on capitalist labor markets, and competition between white and black labor, the story of the struggle of black women under Jim Crow is generally excluded.

The Origins and Impact of Jim Crow

For virtually all slaveholders in the antebellum South, the majority of their wealth was not in land or buildings but in slaves. Rather than focusing on land improvements or investments in fixed capital stock, slaveholders were primarily interested in maximizing the market value of the human beings they owned. This lack of attachment to local community was reflected in the lack of canal building, town development, use of fertilizer, or mineral exploration. Their preoccupation with the value of slaves led slaveholders to make decisions that impeded economic development. When the cotton market improved in the 1850s, they pulled slaves out of commercial textile production despite the higher rates of return available there. As a result, whereas in New England, textile production grew at 2.5 percent annually during both the 1840s and 1850s, in the South it grew at 5 percent annually during the 1840s but *declined* during the next decade.[3]

The Civil War revolutionized the southern economy, not simply because emancipation expropriated the planters of their most valuable assets, but because now they had to make decisions based on the *immovable* capital they owned. It was only when land was their most valuable asset that the planters began to undertake conservation measures, to use fertilizer, and to focus on improvements in the local economy, including town and inland railroad links.

With easier access to midwestern agricultural markets, plantations began to increasingly specialize in cotton. Between 1860 and 1880, southern production per capita of both corn and hogs fell by more than 40 percent while cotton production expanded. In addition, the growing use of fertilizer revitalized the older eastern cotton areas. By 1880 a plantation belt, where cotton was produced exclusively, dominated the economies of six southern states: Arkansas, Alabama, Georgia, Louisiana, Mississippi, and Texas.

This resurgence of cotton production did not, however, reestablish the older relationships between former slaves and planters. Since blacks were free, they could no longer be coerced into becoming wage laborers who would be supervised in the same gang labor system used during slavery. Instead, the dominant relationship had free blacks working on plantation land as independent farmers. The planter would rent the land under a variety of conditions. For some families, it would be a fixed rent, while in the majority of cases, it was for a fixed share of the output; hence the term *sharecroppers*. Moreover, planters made these arrangements with white families who also became sharecroppers and tenant farmers.

The high fertility rate among both white and black women—20 to 25 percent higher than in the Midwest even after adjusting for rural-urban differences—meant that the supply of labor increased substantially. Initially, this was not a problem. Cotton is a much more labor-intensive crop than hogs or corn, so that the shift to cotton specialization substantially increased the demand for southern farm labor. In addition, free blacks were unwilling to work the long hours associated with slavery so that their individual labor supply declined. These factors, together with the growth of cotton demand, initially offset the adverse consequence of high fertility on the economic status of southern farm workers and sharecroppers.

The shift to cotton specialization was completed by 1880. At that point, continued high birth rates began to create a growing imbalance between agricultural labor demand and labor supplies. This imbalance had two predictable consequences. First, the amount of land per sharecropper and independent farmer fell substantially. Between 1880 and 1900, average farm size in the plantation states decreased from 155 to 96 acres, whereas in the Midwest average farm size increased from 122 to 145 acres. Secondly, the gap between farm wages in the Midwest and the South grew. Whereas the wage for a farm laborer in the South remained constant after adjusting for inflation, it grew by almost 50 percent in the North. Thus, the North-South wage differential rose from 20 percent in 1880 to 80 percent by 1900.

After 1880, world cotton prices fell dramatically. In the South, this worsened the situation for both black and white sharecroppers, leading them to make common cause. A multiracial populist movement arose which attacked the power of plantation owners. Small independent producers formed alliances to lower the cost of credit and to improve the marketing of their output. Together with sharecroppers, they attempted to wrest political control of state governments away from the plantation owners.[4]

At first, the planters used election fraud to maintain political power. They also tried to use conservative blacks to dissuade others from joining the multiracial populist movement. For example, the planters selected Booker T. Washington to make a speech at the 1895 Atlanta World's Fair. As mentioned earlier, Washington counseled blacks to accept a second-class status in return for steady work. As expected, he urged them to maintain an alliance with planters and emerging capitalists rather than rely on political reforms through an alliance with poor whites.

Ultimately, however, the planters relied on the political system that they controlled. Seizing on a number of Supreme Court decisions, they instituted poll taxes and literacy voting requirements that virtually disenfranchised all blacks and a modest number of whites. Together with legislation that implemented the separate-but-equal doctrine, they eliminated the foundation of the multiracial populist movement. Over the next half-century, these racial exclusionary policies were expanded and the inferior social, political, and economic status of blacks in the South was institutionalized in a system that came to be known as Jim Crow.

Jim Crow and Capitalists

The objective of the planters was to undermine the unity of black and white farmers; they had no interest in expanding racial exclusionary policies to employment. Throughout the Jim Crow era, planters continued to hire farm workers without regard to race, and about one-half of their sharecroppers were white. There was, however, a secondary objective of planters that did have adverse economic consequences for black workers: the impact of disenfranchisement on educational expenditures.

As an outgrowth of the Reconstruction era, public education in the South was primarily funded by state legislatures. In most southern states, this led to a substantial underfunding of education. The economic historian Robert Margo estimated that, in 1890, expenditures per pupil were 43 percent lower and the school year was two months shorter in the South than outside the South. Since some state legislatures allocate these funds evenly, underfunding had an equally adverse effect on both black and white children in much of the South.[5]

With disenfranchisement, however, there was a shift of funds away from black schools. In plantation areas, where there were substantial numbers of black students, by separating the funding of black and white schools, Jim Crow made it easier to increase educational funding for white students. In non-plantation areas, local counties found it easier to supplement state aid since the additional funds were overwhelmingly used to serve only white students. As a result, among the three plantation states for which comparable data are available, from 1890 to 1910, real per white pupil instructional expenditures increased by 250 percent while they were virtually unchanged for black pupils.

By 1910, Margo estimates that per pupil instructional expenditures on black students averaged only 26 percent as high as it did for white pupils in the six plantation states. While this lower expenditure was partly due to the higher salaries paid to white teachers, it primarily reflected overcrowding and the shorter school year in black schools. The gap was most severe in counties in the six plantation states which had majority black populations, counties that contained 37 percent of all blacks living in the South. In those areas, the average instructional expenditures on black pupils were only 14 percent as much as on white students. In addition, black public high schools were virtually eliminated. By 1910, only sixty-four existed in the entire South. Not surprisingly, the gap in literacy between blacks and whites remained large. In 1910, 40.4 percent of southern black men but only 9.4 percent of southern white men were illiterate.

Planters consistently opposed improving education because they feared that rising literacy rates would reduce the supply of labor willing to become farm workers or sharecroppers. Southern industrialists were not as opposed to educational expenditures since factory work often required some literacy. Indeed, in Birmingham, Alabama, industrialists, desiring stable family-based workers, funded both white and black education substantially more than in rural areas.

Whereas the planters hired without regard to racial preferences, this was not the case in industry. As southern manufacturing expanded, industrial production was generally divided along racial lines; some industries hired virtually only whites, while others hired primarily black workers. By 1910, the textile industry dwarfed all other traditional manufacturing areas (see Table 4.1). Throughout the entire period, 1880–1930, no more than 2 percent of textile operatives were black. In contrast, in 1910, blacks comprised 60 percent of the operatives in tobacco and 45 percent of the semi-skilled workers in the iron and steel industry.

There were a number of reasons why racial segregation in manufacturing followed racial rather than regional lines. In agriculture, there was an abundance of individuals with the necessary skills; when farm workers or sharecroppers left, they could be replaced easily by comparably skilled unemployed workers. This was not the case in manufacturing since individual workers gained industry-specific skills over time. If they left, replacing them with new employees who had no previous industrial experience was costly. Moreover, in an ever-expanding industry, it was crucial to retain a core of experienced workers.

Table 4.1 Manufacturing Employment, 1880–1930

INDUSTRY	EMPLOYMENT (000)		
	1880	*1910*	*1930*
Textiles	16.4	145.6	270.0
Tobacco	23.1	31.6	37.0
Iron and Steel	8.1	11.0	18.2
Printing	3.2	19.8	25.1
Foundry/Machines	5.3	23.3	22.0

Source: Gavin Wright, *Old South New South* (New York: Basic Books, 1986).

The economic historian Gavin Wright suggests that this was the main reason why textile production became virtually all white. With the withdrawal of slave labor from textile production during the 1850s, those workers with industrial experience after the Civil War were virtually all white. Since experienced workers were white, it followed that in the 1870s and 1880s, *before* the institution of legal exclusionary practices, the new workers hired would also be white.

One might think that white workers recruited to mill towns would have higher wages than black workers who had no option other than working in agriculture. In this case, mill owners would be paying a wage premium for accepting racial exclusionary rules. The dynamics of labor markets, however, undercut this tendency. If initially mill owners were paying a substantial wage premium, more white farm workers would seek employment in textile mills. Given the large labor pool of agricultural workers, there would continue to be an excess supply of white workers seeking employment in mills as long as there was a significant pay differential. As a result, mill owners could eliminate the wage premium and still obtain all the white workers they desired. Thus, white millworkers earned essentially the same as white and black farm workers.[6]

In the beginning, families were recruited to mill towns because, without the ability to recruit women independently, it was the only alternative. Reflecting this pattern, in 1880 the majority of workers in southern mills were women and there were numerous accounts of the maladjustment of adult men who could not acclimate easily to industrial life. Eventually, however, men became more comfortable and efficient in this world. Children would begin in the mills at twelve years of age. While many teen-age men would leave the mill town for agricultural employment, those that remained developed skills that made them valuable employees. By 1900, adult men began to dominate operative positions.

Many mill owners experimented with black workers. Some were forced to close because of the objections, often violent, of the white communities in which they located. However, even when there was no conflict, owners were unable to sustain black mills. The reason was quite simple: Since blacks had been excluded from mill towns, mill owners were unable to hire a large enough core of experienced black workers. Since they could not have an integrated work force, they were at a productivity disadvantage compared to white mills.

Two related actions of southern industrialists strengthen the belief that a shortage of workers with industrial experience, not racial animus, was the reason for the failure of these black mills. First, the need for skilled workers to provide a core work force seemed to shape the location of new textile mills. According to Wright, "Mills tended to locate in established textile centers or adjacent to them, and the industry became more concentrated geographically over time."[7]

Secondly, Wright points to labor recruitment of tobacco workers. During the antebellum period, tobacco manufacturing was done by slaves so that, after the Civil War, it was an industry in which black workers domi∞ ted. Just as in textile production, this initial advantage was sustained because of the value of experienced workers to employers. As a result, when tobacco manufacturers initiated production in new areas, they would often pay the transportation costs to attract experienced black workers from distant locations rather than hire inexperienced local white workers.

Experience of Southern Black Workers
Under slavery, black field hands worked long hours in a gang labor system. The harshness of this system was so uninviting that planters were unable to reintroduce this system after the war. As a result, black labor supplies decreased substantially, especially for women and children. Roger Ransom and Richard Sutch estimate that, on average, blacks were willing to supply only about 68 percent as much labor as they had supplied as slaves (see Table 4.2).[8]

Despite the substantial labor supply reductions, despite informal employment restrictions, and despite physical violence, southern blacks experienced continued progress during the first thirty years after the Civil War. In 1880, the per capita income of black sharecroppers and

Table 4.2 Estimates of Labor Supply of Enslaved Blacks (1850s) and Free Black Workers (1870s)

	HOURS WORKED PER YEAR			
	Men	*Women*	*Children*	*Average*
Enslaved Blacks	3,510	3,045	2,231	2,674
Free Black Workers	2,870	1,625	1,222	1,818
Percent Decline	19.2	46.6	45.2	32.0

SOURCE: Roger Ransom and Richard Sutch, *One Kind of Freedom* (New York: Cambridge University Press, 1997).

their family members was 29 percent higher than the per capita income of comparable slave families. Ransom and Sutch note, "[Even] assuming all food was purchased at credit prices rather than cash prices . . . sharecroppers would have experienced an improvement of 11.5 percent in material income."[9] When leisure gains are included, the welfare of individual blacks nearly doubled between 1860 and 1880.

The historian Robert Higgs presents further evidence of the robust growth of black incomes. He estimates that per capita black incomes during the last third of the nineteenth century rose by about 2.7 percent annually after adjusting for inflation. This improvement was experienced not only by black farm workers, but also in a wide range of occupations available to southern blacks. Black progress can also be inferred from the substantial growth of black property ownership. In Georgia, which has the most detailed records, the value of property owned by blacks grew at an annual rate of 9 percent between 1875 and 1892.[10]

Experience of Southern White Workers

The last two decades of the nineteenth century were difficult times for most southern whites. Population growth continued to reduce the size of the average family farm while credit requirements pushed independent farmers away from self-sufficiency into cotton production. When the cotton price continuously declined between 1880 and 1895, it had substantial adverse consequences for independent white farmers, leading many to forge an unsuccessful multiracial populist movement.

After the defeat of this multiracial movement, white workers increasingly embraced overtly racist policies. The dramatic shift is reflected in the political activities of Tom Watson, a leader of the multi-racial Georgia populist movement. In 1893, he led two thousand white farmers on an all-night ride to save black farmers from being lynched. After Negro disenfranchisement, Watson shifted away from multiracial unity and by 1906 became "the outstanding exploiter of endemic Negrophobia."[11]

During the next two decades, cotton prices rebounded. This did not, however, benefit all cotton farmers since the price rebound was due to reduced supplies—the spread of the boll weevil infestation—rather than increased demand. Beginning in Texas at the turn of the century, the infestation spread eastward, reaching Louisiana in 1902, Mississippi in 1907, Alabama in 1909, Georgia in 1914, and South Carolina in 1917. On average, in these five states, the number of acres on which cotton was planted fell by 27.4 percent once infestation was complete. With fewer acres planted, there was a dramatic decline in the number of workers who could earn a living by farming.

The reduction in the demand for farm labor not only stimulated migration but also intensified the racist movement among southern whites. In 1915, South Carolina passed legislation eliminating the ability of black and white workers to be employed in the same facilities. In four representative southern states, the percentage of apprentices who were black fell from 24.8 percent in 1890 to 11.1 percent in 1920.[12]

These racially exclusionary practices eventually benefited white nonfarm workers. Whereas in 1907, the most typical wage of black and white nonfarm workers was virtually the same, in 1926 the typical white wage was 40 percent higher than the typical black wage. Whereas in 1907, 35 percent of white workers earned less than the black median and only 15 percent earned more than double the black median, by 1926 only 15 percent of white workers earned less than the black median while 35 percent earned more than double the black median. Summarizing this shift, Wright states:

> In Virginia during the 1920s, an explicitly racial wage differential had emerged, in clear contrast to the prewar relationship. . . . The widest gap was in the building trades, which were heavily unionized by the 1920s by unions that had become more, rather than less, racially exclusive. Increasingly, "black jobs" and "white jobs" were coming to be associated with "low-wage" and "high-wage" employment. . . . Even in tobacco, traditionally the industrial employer of blacks, a noticeable

spread could now be seen between wages for "white" and "black" jobs.[13]

These benefits went to only a modest proportion of the white work force. The vast majority of white workers were still engaged in agricultural work where the decline in cotton acreage created a glut of labor. As a result, agricultural wages declined dramatically compared to textile wages. Whereas between 1909 and 1918, both wages were virtually the same, over the next decade agricultural wages declined to about 75 percent of textile wages. Indeed, this excess white labor supply enabled owners to undermine the working conditions of textile workers. The proportion of textile factories that had night shifts rose from only about 20 to 30 percent in the period 1909–1918 to 52 percent by 1926. Thus, white workers still continued to be impoverished, with many migrating out of the South.

The debilitating situation of southern agricultural workers—both black and white—was reflected in the statistics on pellegra, a condition that caused severe gastric disturbances, skin eruptions, and nervous disorders. Joseph Goldberger demonstrated conclusively in 1915 that pellegra was due to poor diets, especially when there was reliance on corn products. However, the Pellegra Commission relied on a paper by the Harvard biologist C. B. Davenport and reported in 1917 that pellegra was an infectious disease which affected individuals who had a genetic predisposition. Davenport was an enthusiastic supporter of eugenics, whose biology textbook was used in German universities, and his research was funded by the Kellogg Foundation, a major producer of corn products. The commission report provided an excuse to do nothing about the growing pellegra problem. As a result, it remained widespread in the South, killing an average of 1,763 white people and 1,775 black people annually between 1923 and 1941.[14]

The Timing of Northern Migration

The first major wave of black northern migration occurred during the decade after the beginning of World War I. There is a substantial split among researchers as to the reason why black workers did not flee the South earlier, especially when industrialization in the North could have provided a growing number of entry-level positions. Traditionalists, including economist Jay Mandle and historian Jacqueline Jones, focus on the inhibiting role of discrimination in both the North and the South.[15] In contrast, revisionists like Gavin

Wright focus on factors other than discrimination, including the relatively low productivity of black workers which limited their value to northern employers, black preferences which limited their desire to migrate out of the South, and the expanding employment opportunities in southern urban areas.

The Traditional Viewpoint

The traditional viewpoint contends that racism limited the ability of blacks to migrate. In the South blacks feared violence if they moved, especially if they owed money to white planters. In the North, racist exclusionary employment practices limited economic benefits to black migrants. The main source of northern discriminatory employment practices was the trade unions. Between 1882 and 1900, northern white workers engaged in at least fifty strikes when employers attempted to integrate the workplace.[16] These actions were largely successful so that in many cities, including Detroit and Philadelphia, there were virtually no black workers employed by manufacturing companies until the 1930s. In describing the situation in Detroit, Warren Whatley and Gavin Wright note: "Resistance to hiring blacks in factories was so great that it took more than six months of combined effort by the Society of Prevention of Cruelty to Children, the Poor Commission, and the YMCA to secure a manufacturing job for a 15 year old black boy of unusual mechanical ability who wanted to secure a trade to support his mother and six younger brothers and sisters."[17] Even when strikebreaking activities enabled some black workers to gain an industrial foothold, they suffered employment disadvantages. In northern and midwestern regions, black unemployment rates were fifty to one hundred times higher than white rates.[18] In trying to explain the success of trade union actions, W.E.B. Du Bois stated:

> The object of the trades union is purely business-like; it aims to restrict the labor market. . . . Here is a chance to keep out of the market a vast number of workmen, and the unions seize the chance. . . . The chief agency that brings about this state of affairs is public opinion. . . . Where a large section of the public more or less openly applauds the stamina of a man who refuses to work with a "Nigger," the results are inevitable. . . . If they could keep out the foreign workmen in the same way they would; but here public opinion within and without their ranks forbids hostile action.[19]

These racist attitudes seemed to be endemic among white unionists, even in those unions like the United Mine Workers (UMW) that
had a significant black membership. In its official publication, the UMW
argued that "labor unions upheld the 'Caucasian ideals of civilization'
[and] were the white man's best hope in the contest for 'domination,'
and [urged] its members to purchase products 'made by white men.'"[20]

Racial wage disparities were quite widespread in the absence of
organized labor. These disparities encouraged even the most racist
southern capitalists to hire black workers. At the same time, they intensified white antagonism to black workers. Unions fought back whenever firms attempted to hire lower-waged blacks, especially when they
were used to replace white workers. The two famous examples of this
kind of protest were the 1909 strike of white railroad brakemen in Georgia and the 1897 strike of white textile workers in South Carolina.

Sometimes unions would be willing to allow black workers to be
employed as long as they earned the same pay as white workers. However, the 1922 Chicago commission found many examples of owners
who would "only use the Negro when he would want to maintain a
lower standard of wages, but when compelled by force of circumstances
to pay a living rate of wages, immediately a request would be made
on the organization that the Negro be removed and a white man fur-
nished."[21] Thus, even when unions fought for equal pay for equal work,
they often inadvertently undermined the employment of black workers.

Northern anti-black practices also had an adverse impact on white
southern workers. Black migration to northern jobs would have substantially reduced the southern supply of agricultural workers. This
supply reduction would probably have increased the wages planters
had to pay agricultural laborers and the benefits offered to sharecroppers and tenant farmers. In turn, this would have caused mill owners
to raise the wages which they paid their workers or at least have given
white workers more job security. Northern exclusionary practices discouraged black migration. As a result, southern wages did not rise,
and white workers continued to feel that black workers threatened their
employment.

Black migration also would have lessened the regional wage differentials which existed. While black migration would have raised
southern wages, it would have somewhat lowered northern wages.
Thus, the persistence of the regional wage gap reflected economist Barbara Bergmann's crowding hypothesis: When black workers are excluded from northern manufacturing jobs, they crowd southern labor

markets, depressing the wages of both white and black southern unskilled workers.

Between 1914 and 1920, there was a dramatic increase in the migration of both black and white southerners to the North. Whereas between 1900 and 1910, 263,000 individuals left the South, 1.2 million left during the next decade. As expected, this labor supply shift caused a substantial decline in the interregional wage gap. Between 1914 and 1920, the gap between wages in the North and in the six plantation states fell by an average of 15.7 percent.

Traditionalists also contend that many southern states placed substantial restrictions on the ability of northern companies to recruit that raised the cost of migration. They argue that many southern blacks were unable to migrate because of their need to borrow money from planters during the planting season. By charging exorbitant rates of interest for the consumer goods purchased before harvest, many black sharecroppers were heavily indebted to planters. Since many black sharecroppers were unable to pay off the debt, traditionalists contend that this made it impossible to migrate. Focusing on the power of the planters, Jacqueline Jones states: "Black and white croppers throughout the South continued to believe that they risked bodily harm to themselves if they left a place over the objections of its owner; and they were right."[22]

There is no doubting the physical dangers southern blacks faced. State records indicate that during the first three decades of the twentieth century there was an average of eighty lynchings yearly. These lynchings were not secret actions done by isolated individuals. They were often public spectacles, where blacks were literally burned at the stake, in order to send a "message" to all blacks. In general, these abuses were ignored by the federal government. Despite extended efforts during the first two decades of the twentieth century, W.E.B. Du Bois could not convince the U.S. Census to collect data on lynchings. Most telling was the indifference of President Franklin Delano Roosevelt, who was unwilling to support anti-lynching legislation during the 1930s, even after his landslide victory in 1936.[23]

Revisionists Explanations

The traditionalist viewpoint is seriously flawed. It suggests that the ebbs and flows of migration were dictated by the interests of planters. In contrast, revisionists believe that migration was primarily determined by the preferences of southern blacks. Certainly, these two issues meshed when the boll weevil spread, dramatically reducing the amount of land that could be planted. A 1918 Department of Labor report stated: "It seems quite clear that the exodus had its main start and recruited its largest numbers in those sections which suffered most from the boll weevil and the floods. . . . Many of the employers turned the Negroes out with nothing to live on."[24]

However, this report goes on to emphasize how it was primarily the preferences of blacks that dictated migration. Where rural Negroes felt secure or had educational opportunity for their children, none migrated:

> Dougherty County, Ga., furnishes an interesting example of the effect of consideration and kindly treatment of the Negroes on the part of the whites. This county has lost few Negroes in comparison with the counties all about it. . . . [Few Negroes] if any, usually leave the neighborhood of a good school in such a locality. Around the Calhoun Colored School, in Lowndes County, Ala., there are perhaps a hundred Negro farmers, who, through the instrumentality of the school, have been able to buy and pay for their lands. Not one of these men has been attracted away by the opportunities in the North; and other Negroes in this neighborhood, though living under hard conditions on great plantations, declare that they remain on account of the good school for their children.[25]

Second, revisionists reject claims that restrictions on mobility explain why blacks did not migrate north before World War I. Revisionists point to a large body of evidence that shows a high degree of turnover of sharecroppers. Their mobility was not northward, however, but westward from Georgia and the Carolinas to southwestern cotton-producing states. Black movement to Kansas, Arkansas, Oklahoma, and Texas between 1878 and 1910 dwarfed the migration of blacks to the North.[26]

Third, revisionists reject the picture of black southern life painted by traditionalists like Jones, who assert that "compared with other American workers, Southern sharecroppers and tenants experienced remarkably little improvement" between 1870 and 1930.[27] While the post–Civil War South was no paradise, this bleak picture ignores the improving economic situation of southern blacks during the first three decades after the Civil War. As previously discussed, during the last third of the nineteenth century, despite all the impediments faced, the standard of living of southern blacks grew substantially. These rising living standards may have played a part in their decision to remain in the South.

Fourth, it is clear that southern blacks were concerned with non-material factors, as evidenced by their unwillingness to work under antebellum conditions even though it would have been financially rewarding. Consistent with this value system, there is some indirect evidence from more recent surveys that southern blacks who may have been tempted by material rewards were resistant to migration for familial and cultural reasons. Eva Mueller and William Ladd conclude,

> Negroes on the whole seem to have stronger emotional and family ties to their current place of residence than the white population. . . . The survey shows that only 6 percent of Negro families, in contrast to 21 percent of white families, have no relatives in the community where they are now residing. It should be added that 48 percent of Negro families but only 37 percent of white families, reported that all their close friends are living in their current place of residence. These contrasts are important since . . . moving plans are particularly low among families who have all or most of their relatives living near them.[28]

Fifth, urban areas in the South offered a favorable alternative to risky and more alienating northern migration. In southern urban areas, there was a more favorable climate to the hiring of black workers in craft trades than in the North. It was not because southern owners were less racist than their northern counterparts. It was primarily because, in the absence of unions, black workers could underbid white workers. For example, in Georgia, in virtually all trades, urban black workers were paid 10 to 20 percent lower than white workers.[29]

Since southern unions were generally weak or nonexistent, blacks gained a foothold in many crafts. Indeed, throughout the South, blacks had a "fair chance only in those localities where white labor unions do not dominate." Referring to Mississippi, Du Bois noted: "As there are no trade unions in the state to interfere, colored mechanics find work without difficulty." Whereas in southern cities blacks were almost equally as likely to obtain manufacturing and craft employment as whites, in northern cities they were only one-half as likely. Thus, there is wide support for the summary statement: "Compared to the

North, blacks found a cornucopia of skilled occupations open to them in the South."[30]

Southern cities often offered blacks improved educational opportunities. Many southern whites agreed with the position voiced in the *American Federationist* that with five-cent cotton, there were "hordes of negroes ready to drop their plow-shares for work at almost any price in town for the sake of the education which the state gratuitously offers their children."[31]

While by the beginning of the twentieth century black employment opportunities in the North were limited, the latter part of the nineteenth century was actually a time for optimism, especially in the Midwest. During the Civil War, Irish immigrants rioted against black workers because "it was degrading to see blacks working as equals . . . and more so while our brothers were out of employment." However, over the next twenty years, black codes in Illinois and segregated schools in Chicago were eliminated so that "the community of the free was accepted as a normal part of city life. The tradition became set that Negroes could compete for power and prestige in the economic and political sphere."[32]

These changing conditions enabled early black migrants to northern cities to develop niches in a number of lines of work: as waiters, coachmen, barbers, janitors, and domestic servants. Reflecting these advances, the editor of the first black Chicago newspaper wrote in 1878, "Conflict between the races was not very great . . . [and] successful Negroes of the era, many of them former slaves, interpreted their own careers as proof that someday black men would be accepted as individuals and Americans."[33]

The employment situation of black workers began to deteriorate in the 1890s as new immigrants competed for jobs. A 1905 study of Chicago concluded, "It is quite safe to say that in the last fifteen years the colored people have lost about every occupation that was regarded as particularly their own. In barbering, bootblacking, cooking, hotel and restaurant waiting, and janitors in office buildings, now less than twenty percent are black."[34] Its author contended that this shift was the result of fair competition not racist hiring practices. Similarly, a Boston study suggested that the loss of barbering was at least partially the result of the inability of black owners to upgrade their establishments. New York City studies also claimed that black servants, whitewashers, and waiters were replaced by better educated, more sophisticated, and harder working immigrants.[35]

Even those sensitive to the discrimination black workers faced in the North during this period agreed that at least part of the reason for the loss of employment was fair competition. A Tuskegee instructor stated, "The exclusion of young colored men from the machine shops of the North and South is not due so much to prejudice as to their inability to do the best work."[36] In explaining the disadvantage black craftsmen had when brought into fierce competition with the new immigrants, Du Bois said: "Now the Negro mechanic could not . . . meet these [new] demands . . . he knew little of the niceties of modern carpentry or iron-working; he knew practically nothing of mills and machinery."[37]

If there were a significant share of black craftsmen who were inefficient, an understanding of group profiling suggests that this would have a damaging effect on *all* black craftsmen. Without a cheap method of identifying qualified black applicants, employers would simply choose from among the many qualified white workers available. Indeed, this is exactly the way Du Bois describes the situation of black workers in Philadelphia: "Being few in number compared with the whites, the crime or carelessness of a few of his race is easily imputed to all, and the reputation of the good, industrious and reliable suffer thereby."[38]

Group profiling may explain why there was a disparity between the experience of blacks trained at noted schools like Tuskegee, Claflin, and Hampton, and the general situation of black workers. A Tuskegee instructor after summarizing numerous examples of requests from many corporations for black graduates noted: "There is beginning to be an earnest call for colored mechanics. . . . During the last three years we have been unable to furnish half of the colored youth called for in the mechanical engineering lines; and we are satisfied that they were not called to fill the places of strikers. In all cases the call came from men of standing who desired to give these opportunities to colored youth."[39] This suggests that when employers could identify qualified black applicants in a cost-free manner, many were willing to hire them. However, when this identification was costly, employers fell back on racial profiling, hiring only white workers.

The New Deal and Postwar Events

While many unions excluded black workers, they were not always able to exclude them from the work force. Some black workers were able to gain a foothold as longshoremen and railroad workers. They often organized separate unions and labor associations to further their access to employment in these areas. With the onset of the Great Depression, discriminatory actions by southern white workers intensified, typified by the slogan of the Atlanta Black Shirts— "Niggers back to the cotton fields, city jobs are for white folks."[40] White unions renewed their efforts to eliminate black employment. In particular, white unions in the railroad industry renewed their attempts to eliminate black workers. For example, they demanded that all railroads running through Memphis hire only white railroad workers. Black leaders of the Colored Trainmen of America demanded government intervention when vigilantes began maiming and killing black railroad workers, but federal officials turned a deaf ear. By 1940, thousands of black stokers, break and switch operators, and flaggers had been replaced with whites, remaining only in the lowest-paid and dirtiest jobs that whites rejected.[41]

Adding to these problems was a number of New Deal policies. The pressure of competition from southern factories bankrupted most New England textile mills. This mobilized the fears of northern workers and owners alike that low southern wages would lead to the demise of northern manufacturing. These groups sought ways to undermine the regional wage differential that they believed was the source of their problems. Under the guise of reducing competition among firms and maintaining worker purchasing power, the National Recovery Act (NRA) raised southern wages, reducing industry interregional wage differentials by one-third or more.

Black workers were doubly harmed by the NRA. The mechanization that it fostered eliminated unskilled jobs that had been a major source of black employment. By raising wages, these jobs became more desirable to white workers, further reducing black employment. The Cowles Commission found that directly and indirectly the minimum wage provisions of the NRA caused 500,000 blacks to go on relief, and for others, the restrictions on work hours had the effect of further lowering incomes. For these reasons, black newspapers derided the NRA as the "Negro Removal Act."[42]

When the NRA was terminated in 1935, it was immediately replaced by the Works Project Administration (WPA). This agency had as one of its objectives the reduction of interregional wage gaps. The WPA directly hired workers in construction and some manufacturing jobs at so-called prevailing wages that in 1935 were $19 to $21 per month in southern states but $40 per month in midwestern states. While the minimum rate paid in the Midwest remained at the same level, in the South it was raised in 1938 to $26 per month and in 1939 to $31.20 per month.

In 1938, national minimum wage legislation was enacted. Beginning at twenty-five cents per hour, it increased by five cents per hour in each of the next three years. Given the growing racist climate in the South, the employment repercussions of this legislation were predictable. The vast majority of southern industrial jobs became high-paying jobs reserved for whites. In the tobacco industry, where in 1930 two-thirds of the workers were black, the labor force was only one-fourth black by 1960.[43]

The Agricultural Adjustment Act (AAA) was another federal program that had adverse consequences for southern black workers. When cotton prices fell from twenty cents in 1927 to five cents in 1931, congressional representatives of the planters molded this federal legislation. The AAA paid cotton producers to keep some land out of production so that supplies were reduced, enabling the market price to rise. Payments to farmers went to the planters rather than their tenants or share-croppers.

Cotton acreage in production fell by 46 percent between 1932 and 1940, substantially reducing labor demand. The excess supply of agricultural workers enabled producers to implement unpopular labor policies. Mechanizing cotton production was technically feasible for decades but it would have required a shift away from tenancy and sharecropping to hired labor used only during the harvest season. In the recent past, the limited supply of harvest labor had made it impractical to mechanize. However, the AAA, by restricting cotton production, had reduced the overall demand for labor while at the same time expanding the number of workers available at harvest time. These changes made mechanization feasible. Cash transfers from the federal government and cheap credit further encouraged mechanization.

In the Mississippi Delta, tenancy went from comprising 81.9 percent of cotton production in 1930 to 58.2 percent by 1940. By 1936, 36 percent of owner-operator cotton acreage in plantations was picked by off-plantation labor. Many sharecroppers, who could not survive on their share, hired themselves or family members out during the picking season to earn supplemental income. As Wright notes, "So long as the relief administrators cooperated by clearing the rolls at harvest times, southern planters had 'labor for the picking' and were able to move toward pre-harvest mechanization even in the midst of the Great Depression."[44]

Southern black sharecroppers did not passively accept their fate. They organized the interracial Southern Tenant Farmers Union (STFU), which demanded that a greater share of government payment for crop reduction go to tenant farmers. In 1935, the STFU organized a strike of five thousand cotton pickers in eastern Arkansas, forcing planters to more than double wages. It was even able to convince a significant number of white tenant farmers to join. However, the planters were too powerful, and racism too entrenched, for these heroic struggles to be sustained. When strikes were staged in 1936, the planters evicted striking sharecroppers from plantation-owned housing, used physical violence, and obtained strikebreakers with the help of the Memphis Chamber of Commerce and WPA officials.[45]

The planters were united in their support of New Deal legislation, in marked contrast to the fragmented southern industrialists. Planters were also successful because state legislatures and Congress apportioned representation more favorably to rural than to urban areas; it was not until 1964 that the Supreme Court required each state and federal election district to have an equal number of people. In addition, employment was still dominated by agriculture. For example, in 1910, 62 percent of black men and 52 percent of white men were employed on farms as either operators or laborers while less than 20 percent of each group were employed by industry (mining and manufacturing). Only by 1940 were white southern male employment shares between industry and farming equalized.

The AAA had created a "planters' heaven."[46] Funds for mechanization and cheap labor enabled them to replace the tenant and sharecropper system. Since the burden of displacement fell on black workers disproportionately, with white workers increasingly obtaining the now high-wage industrial jobs, it is easy to see why at times many white voters in the South also supported the New Deal. This is most dramatically illustrated by the 1938 senatorial election victories of avowed New Dealers Lester Hill (Alabama) and Claude Pepper (Florida). Faced with support for the New Deal by planters and white workers, it was impossible for southern capitalists to forestall New Deal wage-setting policies even if they had wanted to.

The Postwar Actions of Southern Industrialists

Between 1920 and 1940 mechanization of the pre-harvest activities reduced the worker hours per bale of cotton from 269 to 191—a 29 percent decline. Not surprisingly, during World War II, the farm population declined by 22 percent. The most decisive effect of technological innovation on the demand for farm workers, however, came after the war with mechanization of the harvesting of cotton. The demand for agricultural workers declined from 150 million hours in 1947 to less than 25 million a decade later.

Postwar labor surpluses created a strong potential for southern industrial growth. In the past, this potential was stifled by the ambivalence of the planters since it would weaken their hold on agricultural laborers. With the dramatic decline in their labor needs, the planters were no longer antagonistic to industrial expansion. Southern industrialists were now able to advance strategies to attract northern capital, including lowering state corporate taxes. Wright notes that "between 1950 and 1978, the median corporate tax rate in the South went from 85 percent above, to 13 percent below, that of the rest of the country."[47]

In many communities, business leaders were willing to support desegregation policies in order to attract northern firms. Elisabeth Jacoway and David Colburn state:

> While the desire for new industry did not cause southern business leaders to become supporters of black protest or champions of civil rights, the articles in this volume suggest that it did lead to a willingness to modify southern race relations. . . . [T]hey used their influence in their communities to press for the alteration of southern racial patterns that they had come to believe were necessary. . . . In city after city, [they] consciously chose to abandon traditional racial patterns, even in the full knowledge that they were abandoning the old "southern way of life." . . . These articles demonstrate that southern business leadership . . . became a significant if oft-times reluctant element in the desegregation process.[48]

In a number of communities, including Atlanta and Birmingham, business leaders formed biracial communities to ease the movement away from the segregated past. Often these business efforts were initially unsuccessful due to the concerted effort of racist politicians and

Table 4.3 Growth of Manufacturing Employment, 1955–1967

| YEAR | TOTAL MANUFACTURING | | DURABLE GOODS | |
	South (000)	Midwest (000)	South (000)	Midwest (000)
1955	2,647	4,888	680	3,446
1958	2,665	4,261	758	2,869
1961	2,777	4,273	833	2,897
1964	3,107	4,622	1,057	3,416
1967	3,593	5,151	1,183	3,602

SOURCE: U.S. Bureau of the Census, *Census of Manufactures* (Washington, D.C.: Government Printing Office, various years).

citizens' groups. For example, in Birmingham business leaders reluctantly abandoned their biracial efforts when the White Citizens' Council successfully limited donations to the Community Chest and Red Cross. By the early 1960s, however, business leaders gained enough support to carry out desegregation policies in many southern cities; lunch counters were integrated in Tampa and hotels were desegregated in Dallas.

The Role of Northern Corporations

While willing to concede that "their belated support for concessions were of crucial importance," Wright rejects claims that southern capitalists were motivated by "the thought of gains in efficiency or a lowering of production costs." Southern capitalists might have been timid, but national corporations played a more prominent role. Racial employment practices became particularly important to national corporations when they began opening southern production facilities after World War II. This shift of production was aided by the building of a national highway system and government funding which brought electricity to rural southern areas.[49]

Most important, the strength of unions in the North and Midwest enhanced the incentives for southern manufacturing relocation. Between 1955 and 1967, manufacturing employment in the South expanded dramatically while it stagnated in the Midwest (see Table 4.3). Durable goods employment increased by 73.9 percent in the South but by only 4.6 percent in the Midwest.[50]

National unions were unable to extend their successful organizing efforts to the South due to racial divisions. For example, tobacco

Table 4.4 Black Employment in the Chemical Industry, 1940–1960

YEAR	TOTAL	BLACK	%
Leading northern states (NY, PA, IL)			
1940	140,356	3,409	2.43
1960	236,357	13,725	5.81
Leading southern states (VA, TX, TN)			
1940	47,693	7,669	16.11
1960	132,330	8,112	6.13

SOURCE: William Quay, *The Negro in the Chemical Industry* (Philadelphia: University of Pennsylvania Press, 1970).

firms were able to take advantage of racial tensions to thwart unionizing drives from 1946 to 1948—efforts that would have allowed for integrated unions. The resulting low labor costs were an essential factor in the decision of corporations to expand their southern facilities. One corporation opened eighteen of its twenty-six new plants in southern areas. Similarly, "Westinghouse chose remote, rural locations in order to tap available labor and also to enable it to pay lower wage rates."[51]

Though able to pay less than elsewhere, the wages southern firms offered were still quite high by local standards, and as a result they were expected to hire only white workers. As long as there was a surplus of southern white workers, national corporations continued to accommodate Jim Crow exclusionary laws. Corporate indifference to southern black employment was most apparent in the chemical industry. Between 1940 and 1960, the total southern employment of chemical workers nearly tripled but the employment of black workers was virtually unchanged (see Table 4.4). In contrast, during the same time period, while total northern employment of chemical workers doubled, employment of black workers quadrupled. While the chemical industry was quite willing to hire blacks in the North where they could easily do so, they were unwilling to confront the racist hiring practices in the South during this time period. Similarly, Scott Paper in Alabama hired blacks only for outside work and menial factory jobs but reserved all machine-operator jobs for whites.[52]

The situation was somewhat less accommodating in the automobile and electrical manufacturing industries. In particular, General Motors made a decision to hire blacks in a number of their southern plants despite protest from white workers. Similarly, the electrical industry began to promote equal opportunity in its plants during World War II and showed a willingness to confront the resistance of white workers and unions in some of its northern plants. After the war, these plants began actively recruiting black technical personnel. In 1947, General Electric president Charles Wilson issued a call for national equal employment legislation.[53]

Most of these national corporations joined an organization, Plans for Progress, which had as its stated goal "the integration of the corporate work force." They held meetings with local and national politicians, seeking reforms to further their goal. This general sympathy for equal employment did not translate, however, into a consistent black employment policy in the South. While in some areas, particularly the border states of Kentucky, Maryland, and Virginia, corporate members did confront white racism and aggressively hire blacks, in other areas they accommodated the local racial employment patterns.

Besides an unwillingness to challenge local racial hiring practices, researchers suggest that there were structural reasons why the southern black employment of national corporations did not grow more robustly during the 1950s. In the chemical industry, rising educational requirements limited the pool of qualified black workers. Also, national corporations were generally required to use state employment agencies when finding workers for their new southern plants. Since these agencies were notoriously racist, they referred only white applicants to these manufacturing firms.

By 1960, however, the surplus of white workers seeking manufacturing employment was eliminated in many southern states, particularly the Carolinas. Corporations became concerned that they would face rising labor costs in their southern plants if they maintained their current hiring practices. Since this conflicted with Jim Crow laws, these corporations began to rethink their accommodation to southern labor restrictions. At this point, many corporations realized that national legislation was necessary and, through Plans for Progress, began to support the civil rights movement. In the first year after Jim Crow ended, black manufacturing employment in South Carolina increased by over 50 percent when "entrepreneurs seized on the new federal legislation to do what they wanted to do anyway."[54]

To conclude, one decision made immediately after the Civil War was to have a crucial effect on southern living standards: the move to a system of production where the planters rented their land in various forms (tenancy and sharecropping) instead of hiring paid labor. This stifled mechanization so that in 1935 cotton was produced by essentially the same labor-intensive method as it was in 1865. Without mechanization, cotton farmers were doomed to low income. Since education and industrialization would provide alternatives which would limit the supply of individuals willing to labor in the cotton fields, planters discouraged both of these endeavors, further limiting the economic prospects for southerners. As a result, poverty was a persistent and widespread characteristic of southern life.

Southern poverty affected both white and black southern workers. During the latter part of the nineteenth century when cotton prices were depressed and fertility rates were high, many white southerners saw a deterioration in their standard of living, reducing the differences between white and black farmers. The similarity in standards of living was also due to the effects of agricultural labor markets on the wages of white workers, even those employed in the all-white textile industry. In addition, the lack of migration to the North had a crowding effect on southern labor markets, adversely affecting all wages.

At first, this growing commonality led many white farmers to forge a multiracial movement for the betterment of all farmers. To forestall this movement, the planters disenfranchised blacks and instituted Jim Crow regulations. While these actions enabled the planters to maintain political power, white workers attempted to shape the separate-but-equal doctrine to serve their economic interests by extending it to include exclusionary employment policies. While white and black farmers continued to suffer, these exclusionary policies did enable a modest share of southern whites to elevate themselves out of poverty through industrial employment. Exclusionary policies intensified during the 1930s, as federal minimum wage legislation made virtually all southern industrial jobs desirable.

Given the hostile southern environment blacks faced, a central question is why they did not move northward before World War I. The traditional view claims that racist practices of northern unions and indebtedness limited black mobility. This chapter presents the alternative revisionist view: Indebtedness did not reduce the ability of blacks to move, and northern employment prospects for black workers were quite favorable through the 1890s. Moreover, this argument maintains that the lack of northern movement reflected, to a substantial degree, the rising living standards experienced by former slaves and their unwillingness to move away from familial surroundings.

This chapter provides background to the pro-market thesis that exclusionary practices were unprofitable and, in the long run, would be opposed by capitalists. There was some evidence that when blacks could be hired at lower wages, many capitalists were quite willing to employ them. Without these wage differentials, however, there were few financial incentives, especially when cheap white labor was available. Educational disadvantages and lack of experience often made black labor less productive than white labor. In the South, this led employers to abandon efforts to integrate textile production. In the North, this led employers to engage in group profiling, adversely affecting all black workers, except those with credentials from training programs.

From the 1890s through the 1940s, broad sections of white society had a vested interest in maintaining racial divisions. For the agrarian elite, racial divisions enabled them to maintain political power and made available an expanding supply of farm workers willing to be sharecroppers. For nonfarm white workers, it enabled them to increasingly monopolize industrial and craft employment. Against this constellation of forces, southern capitalists before World War II were powerless to change employment practices even if they were so inclined.

Moreover, the higher production costs from accommodating Jim Crow employment practices were quite meager, as long as southern capitalists had a surplus of white workers available. This enabled capitalists to hire white textile workers in the postbellum period without the need for a wage premium. Even after World War I, when there was a modest wage premium, capitalists obtained indirect benefits: the ability to defeat unionizing efforts. Imbued with racist attitudes and wishing to protect their privileged access to industrial employment, white workers did not embrace union organizing efforts or fight against the adoption of anti-union right-to-work legislation. Southern capitalists evidently benefited from these anti-union efforts. Indeed, capitalist accommodation to Jim Crow exclusionary employment practices may be another example of the efficiency wage theory: Paying a wage premium to current workers can result in a lowering of overall labor costs.

When northern firms began to expand their southern production facilities and mechanization eliminated cheap labor concerns of the planters, the profit motive began to support integrationist efforts. Southern communities began to include in their calculations the impact of segregationist behavior on their ability to attract northern firms.

National firms also had to consider the impact of southern employment decisions on the uniformity of their hiring practices—how could they have one set of hiring practices in their southern plants and another set in their other plants? Finally, firms began to move toward nondiscriminatory hiring, attempting to undermine exclusionary employment practices.

These movements were gradual and timid. Southern capitalists feared political reprisals from racist whites and still feared unionizing efforts. Most northern capitalists were willing to implement Jim Crow practices as long as the white workers they were able to hire and the tax concessions they were able to obtain made the South an employers' paradise. This indecisiveness is most apparent in the actions of the Kennedy administration. President John Kennedy would continually try to dissuade Rev. Martin Luther King Jr. from taking an aggressive stance and would intercede only when forced.[55] Similarly, Plans for Progress was inactive throughout most of the civil rights period. Only when southern white labor became expensive, and the civil rights movement raised the political costs of Jim Crow, did capitalists begin to move more decisively against exclusionary practices. The struggle to end Jim Crow, the evidence argues, was only marginally aided by the actions of profit-seeking capitalists.

5

Gender before Class

Patriarchy, Capitalism, and Family

Patriarchy can be defined as a set of relationships that enable men to exploit women. Historically, the site of this exploitation has been the family. Religious, cultural, and government institutions have constrained the ability of women to reject the patriarchal family. Within the capitalist era, exclusionary employment barriers at first aided these institutions but, over time, increasingly displaced them as the principal obstacles women face.

The first wave of feminists struggled against the existing employment barriers. They demanded that women and men should be able to compete equally for available jobs so that productive merit alone determined employment. These feminists believed that employment equality would also liberate women from the patriarchal family. Thus, many activists, including Marx and Engels, foresaw that the entry of women into the labor force would fundamentally undermine the power that men had over them.

The entry of women into the labor market in the nineteenth and early twentieth century also affected the wages received and jobs held by men. In light industry, like garment, female labor was used so extensively that the threat of undermining male crafts was real. In heavy industry, like steel, male labor was more secure though new technologies, which reduced the necessary physical strength required, sometimes opened up the possibilities of increased female employment. Thus, male antagonism to female employment arose for two reasons:

(1) it would limit the ability of men to obtain preferred jobs; and (2) it would limit the patriarchal exploitation of women within the family.

While men might desire female exclusion, in capitalistic economies, the profit motive determines employment decisions. If exclusionary barriers persist, they must be in the interest of capitalists as well. Certainly, many feminists believe that patriarchy persists because it serves the interests of both men and capitalists. In contrast, an alternative perspective must be considered. Capitalists do not benefit from exclusionary barriers and accommodate them only when the losses are small and/or abandoning them would prove even more costly.

Finally, exclusionary barriers affect women quite differently than they affect blacks. The benefits white workers obtained from Jim Crow policies in no way benefited black workers. However, exclusionary policies that privilege men could indirectly benefit an important group—their wives. Thus, we might expect to find some female support for the implementation of labor policies that privilege men even if these policies made it more difficult for women to gain access to better-paying jobs.

During the late nineteenth and early twentieth centuries, the struggle for the family wage for married men and restrictions on female labor were the principal means by which the privileged position of men was advanced. How did capitalists respond to these demands? To what extent were these demands supported by women? By looking at these policy struggles in France and Great Britain, as well as in the United States, we can better understand when capitalists benefited from exclusionary policies and when they did not.

The last half century, however, has witnessed a dramatic increase in the ability of women to free themselves from patriarchal families and to compete for a wide range of available employment. Though male patriarchal privileges have been reduced, a substantial amount remains. New studies continue to document inequality within the home—for the typical married couple, husbands have five hours more leisure time than their wives, more than double the disparity a decade earlier.[1] The persistence of these inequalities suggests that the entry of women into the paid labor force is not sufficient to end the patriarchal privilege men enjoy. In order to better understand the factors that influence the patriarchal price married women typically pay, this chapter will develop a model of the marriage market.

Family Wage Struggles

Between the mid-nineteenth and mid-twentieth centuries, the main struggles of industrial workers, often voiced through their trade union representatives, were for better wages and better working conditions. In the United States, but even more so in France and England, these struggles were intertwined with patriarchal judgments concerning the appropriate role of women. Whereas today, in recognition of the growth of female-headed households, there is a strong *living* wage movement throughout the United States, a century earlier the demand was patriarchal: a *family* wage for married men.

Around 1980, a debate developed among feminists as to how these family wage struggles should be viewed. On the one hand, Heidi Hartmann claimed that they were patriarchal because, by focusing on male wages at the expense of female wages, the family-wage movement made it impossible for working women to survive materially without a male breadwinner. On the other hand, Jane Humphries argued that, though sometimes adopting patriarchal language, these struggles were primarily attempts to raise living standards.[2]

Great Britain

During the 1820s and 1830s, British technological innovations facilitated the entry of women into a number of trades. Fearing their replacement, male workers, including cotton spinners and tailors, struck against the introduction of female workers into their industries.[3] As more women and children became employed, it became easier to lower male wages since they were no longer the sole breadwinners. This trend was accelerated by the 1834 Poor Laws, which reduced government welfare by shifting the responsibility of supporting the poor to other family members.

Female labor continued to replace male labor throughout the nineteenth century in Great Britain. In the 1860s, when a new women's machine was able to compete successfully with the men's machine, the hosiery industry shifted to female labor. The same thing happened in the 1870s in the carpet weaving industry when new light and fast looms were introduced. Thus, the proletarianization of women was reducing the wages of some men rather than primarily increasing the economic well-being of the working class.[4]

Uncertainty and even fear crept into the minds of male workers who experienced no immediate threat from female labor. They, too, worried that technological innovations or financial imperatives would cause employers to undermine their wages and employment. Since attempts to exclude female workers for purely economic reasons were generally unsuccessful, it is not surprising that the fight for a family wage was adopted. Adopting this prospective as early as the 1820s, the *Trades Newspaper* stated: "Wages can never sink below the sum necessary to rear up the number of labourers capitalists want. The weaver, his wife and children, all labour to obtain this sum [whereas in the past] the blacksmith and the carpenter obtain[ed] it by their single exertions. . . . The labouring men of this country should return to the good old plan of subsisting their wives and children on the wages of their own labor."[5]

The vision of returning to the "good old plan" was false nostalgia. Prior to the Industrial Revolution, the social norm was for women to earn enough to at least maintain themselves. This was clearly true in agriculture but also in many pre-industrial trades in which women labored. Indeed, some early industrial enterprises used the family method of production, where women and children labored under the direction of the patriarch. Thus, the ideal that a man as head of a household was the sole breadwinner was a *new* concept which only gained acceptance gradually.

That the early nineteenth-century working class had not embraced this social norm was most clear when owners attempted to remove women from the coal mines. At the time, mines were often organized under the family labor method. Independent colliers would be paid at a fixed piece rate and were responsible for decisions on how to produce and whom to hire. Colliers almost always employed family members, enabling them to keep the entire sum paid by owners.

Beginning in the 1830s, technological advances enabled the digging of deeper shafts, the use of steam power for drainage, and transporting by railway tracks and ponies rather than sledge and baskets. These changes undermined the profitability of using independent trades people as intermediaries so that the family labor system was no longer desirable. As a result, coal owners began refusing to allow women and children to work in the mines.[6]

In virtually every mining area where the family system was used, the colliers and their families opposed these changes. However difficult the jobs were for women, they preferred them to alternative work as domestics. The colliers, too, rejected a change in their position in the production process. Thus, it was only when state laws were passed in 1842, outlawing female and child labor in mining, that owners were finally able to eliminate the family method of production.

That women should be full-time homemakers supported by working husbands became the prevailing view during the last half of the century. Benefiting from rising real wages, this cult of domesticity was embraced by a prospering middle class that sought Victorian respectability. In addition, the educational acts of the 1870s made it more difficult for women to work outside the home and yet fulfill their household responsibilities. Finally, within this environment, restive working-class men embraced this ideology which strengthened their bargaining position. Explaining why unions in 1877 supported exclusionary practices, a delegate stated: "It was their duty as men and husbands to use their utmost efforts to bring about conditions of things where their wives should be in their proper sphere at home, seeing after their house and family, instead of being dragged into the competition for livelihood against the great and strong men of the world."[7]

The attitude of British women was more complex. Hoping that it would raise living standards, "we look in vain for working-class women's objections to either the family wage system or to social provisions made through the labor market which assumed the existence of such a system."[8] It was only when the family wage was linked to exclusionary employment measures that working women balked.

By the end of the nineteenth century, the cult of domesticity was universally accepted. The share of married British women in the active labor market fell from 25 percent in 1851 to 10 percent by 1901. Those married women who worked faced "a labor market skewed against them and a dominant discourse of the deleterious effects of their work on the sobriety of their husbands, the health of their children, and their own morality."[9]

France

The conflict faced by working women—whether or not to support the family wage if it meant exclusionary practices— did not occur in France. Late nineteenth-century economic development there included a sharp rise in the demand for female labor. Between 1861 and 1911, the share of women in the French labor force rose from 30 to 37 percent. Most striking, in 1911, 48 percent of married French women were in the work force. Given this crucial role women played in the economy, French trade unionists primarily fought to raise female wages and for equal pay but not for a family wage.

Instead of demanding a raise in male wages, unions sought family allowances. These were supplements paid to married men, which varied depending on the number of children they had.

This movement was aided by declining birth rates and by notions of social justice. Between 1861 and 1911 the population of France grew by only 9 percent, whereas its growth in both Germany and Great Britain was over 50 percent. In response, child labor was restricted, health policies attempted to reduce infant mortality, and new policies enabled mothers to gain state welfare even if unwed or able-bodied. With a focus on aiding children, there was broad support for family allowances.[10]

These actions were supported by the Catholic Church, which believed that family allowances were an application of Pope Leo XIII's 1891 Encyclical, *De Rerum Novarum*. In it, the Pope stated: "[W]orkers and owners should as a general rule make free agreements [on wages;] nevertheless there underlies a dictate of natural justice more imperious and ancient than any bargain between man and man, namely that . . . a workman's wages be sufficient to enable him to maintain himself, his wife, and his children in reasonable comfort."[11]

At first, family allowances were given primarily to government and railroad workers. However, French capitalists also supported these family allowances since they were much less costly than alternative family wage provisions. Whereas family wage provisions required firms to pay *all* male employees a wage sufficient to support a normal-size family, family allowances were only given to men with children. Trade unionists generally supported family allowances because they enabled married men to regain a wage differential with single men that had eroded after World War I. Given this broad consensus, family allowance policies were quickly instituted without conflict throughout French industry, as well as in Belgium, Holland, and Germany.

Initially, these allowances were paid directly to qualifying workers as part of their individual pay. In some cases, owners did not see a problem: "[T]he slight difference in costs between married and single workmen was considered more than offset by the former's additional steadiness and extra value to the employer as belonging to the more peaceful strata of labor. The additional allowances per child were modest."[12] However, it was feared that competitive pressures would encourage many firms to hire single men rather than married men with large families. In response to these fears, family allowances were usually paid out of a common pool that was often citywide or industrywide. Thus, a system developed which "compensated parents for dependent children, but not men for women."[13]

Feminists and female trade unionists also found family allowance policies superior to family wage policies. Since allowances were given as supplements, the direct wages paid to men and women could be equalized. Some argued that these allowances were recognition for the valuable work performance by women outside the workplace. However, many feminists considered it an assault on "women's newly gained freedom" since it reinforced patriarchal notions of gendered divisions of labor. These critics were willing to support family allowances only if payments went directly to mothers and were not dependent upon their husbands' employment.[14]

Capitalists did not oppose family allowances as long as they controlled their distribution. As noted above, some capitalists saw family allowances as profitable since these policies enabled them to retain married men who were thought to be more productive and less inclined to militancy than single men. Allowances were also profitable in many communities where they allowed firms to suppress the wages of unmarried workers by more than the allowances paid to married men.[15] Contemporary feminist Michele Barrett contends that family-support policies pressured husbands into remaining docile politically. Moreover, she maintains that these policies encouraged workers to focus on their nuclear family, weakening class solidarity. Thus, Barrett believes that it was capitalists rather than workers who most advocated additional income for married men.[16]

United States

Given laissez-faire (and anti-Catholic) sentiment in the United States at the beginning of the twentieth century, there was no possibility that family allowances could have been instituted. Children, far from being educated and protected by their mothers, were sent into the labor force in early adolescence to help pay the bills. It would be seventy-five years, with the adoption of the Earned Income Tax Credit (EITC) program, before the government would provide family allowances to working families with children.

Among U.S. workers there was certainly interest in family wage policies. Throughout the nineteenth century, men often claimed that "if wives and children were forced to enter the labor market to supplement income, the status of the workingman would be degraded."[17] For a number of reasons, however, demands for a family wage were quite limited. Among native-born white Americans the cult of domesticity was the social norm. Through their writings, upper-class women argued that wives should engage in the homemaking professions since wives "were the natural keepers of this domestic sphere."[18] Facilitating the domesticity of native-born white women, immigrant women in the North and black women in the South allowed for a plentiful supply of domestic help at very low cost. Almost every young Irish girl who came to the United States spent some time in domestic service. Beginning work around age eleven, most left once they got married. More than one-half of all German and Scandinavian immigrant female workers were employed as domestic servants while, in 1900, 44 percent of employed black women were domestics.[19] Indeed, during the first half of the twentieth century, expenditures on domestic servants by lower-middle-class households was a priority—for each 1 percent rise in income, expenditures on domestic servants rose by 4 percent.[20] Thus, among the native-born, both husbands and wives embraced the cult of domesticity and generally had the income to realize this ideal.

Even among many immigrant households, when male wages were insufficient to support families, married women did not have to enter the paid work force. In 1900, only 4 percent of immigrant wives were in the active labor force.[21] Their families escaped poverty due to the ability of married women to provide family earnings without leaving the home. As a result of high rates of immigration from Europe and of migration from the South, there were a large number of single men and women who needed temporary housing. This enabled many married women to supplement family income by taking in paying boarders and lodgers. While some men lamented that this arrangement robbed them of "their sanctuary," these earnings moderated the need to press for a family wage.

The ability of U.S. male workers to act on their patriarchal desires was quite limited due to the low-level and weak position of unions. The major threat to unionized workers was not from female labor but from immigrants. Xenophobic sentiment, not the maintenance of patriarchal privileges, dominated the psyche of threatened male workers. As a result, the main legislative initiative of the American Federation of Labor was immigration restrictions not limitations on female employment. The demands of its president, Samuel Gompers, for a "growing minimum wage . . . sufficient to maintain [workers] and

those dependent upon them in a manner consistent with their responsibilities as *husbands, fathers, men* and *citizens*" took a backseat
to his attempts to limit immigration.[22]

In this environment, when family wage demands surfaced, they
were often directed against single immigrants. In the Pittsburgh steel
mills, the Chicago meatpacking plants, and the Pennsylvania anthracite coal mines, settled immigrants worked with an increasing number of single sojourners—immigrants who had no families and often
longed to earn enough to return to their homeland. Single sojourners
were much more willing to accept poor working conditions and low
pay than settled workers. Sojourners preferred long hours so that they
could earn as much as possible in a short period, while settled immigrants frequently complained about such conditions. Some unions
including the United Mine Workers distinguished between "good" immigrants—permanently settled family men—and "bad" immigrants—
sojourners or single men.

As sojourners undermined wages, some unionists raised the family wage demand. Since the conflict was with sojourners, not female
workers, the demands were overwhelmingly supported by their wives.
Indeed, during strikes in steel, meatpacking, and anthracite coal industries, wives "joined picket lines, organized strike commissaries,
formed women's auxiliaries, agitated for the union, vehemently attacked
scabs, and fought street battles with the police."[23]

For these reasons, nineteenth-century family wage demands in the
United States were more limited and less patriarchal than in Great Britain. However, in the twentieth century, these demands became widely
accepted through their endorsement by Progressive social reformers
and leading industrialists, including Henry Ford and John D. Rocke-
feller. This suggests that family wage policies might have been implemented because they were profitable to capitalists.

The prime example always cited by those who support Barrett's
viewpoint were the actions of Henry Ford. As discussed earlier, when
labor turnover became costly, Ford instituted a five-dollar-day pay scale
for qualifying workers. To qualify, a worker not only had to be employed for six months, but also had to meet personal conditions that
were patriarchal. Ford enlisted a team of investigators to determine if
the worker maintained a stable family life, including the support of
family members. Combined with a reduction in the workday from ten
to nine hours and the introduction of industrial safety standards, Ford's
jobs became most desirable.

While there is no question that these policies dramatically reduced labor turnover (and forestalled any unionizing efforts), there is some question as to whether the *patriarchal* requirements imposed by Ford were necessary. That is, would implementation of these changes in wages and working conditions alone, and the six-month employment provision, have been sufficient to accomplish the goal? If so, his patriarchal requirements would have had more to do with Ford's sensibilities than the profit motive.

That Ford's patriarchal requirements were motivated by personal values is seen by some of the other characteristics of his policy. Ford would not allow workers to qualify if they had paying boarders in their homes. He claimed: "We have to break up the evil custom among foreign workers of taking in boarders—of regarding their homes as something to make money out of rather than as a place to live in." To realize his goal that workers attain this middle-class form of family life, Ford provided lawyers to help workers secure credit and mortgages for new homes and boasted that through his efforts "eight thousand families have changed their place of residence . . . from poor and squalid to healthful, sanitary quarters, with an environment conducive to health, happiness, and comfort."[24]

Ford's patriarchal attitudes also led him to ignore the productiveness of his female work force. Only after being criticized did he extend the five-dollar day to female heads of households. Moreover, he was adamant against the employment of married women—not because of potential turnover—but because it went against his vision of family life. Whenever it was discovered that a woman had a working husband she was immediately fired. Since only 10 percent of his female work force qualified for the wage bonus, Ford sacrificed cost-savings policies when they conflicted with his patriarchal visions.[25] While other firms improved working conditions and benefits in order to reduce labor conflict and labor turnover, virtually none included patriarchal requirements.

Ford's willingness to impose his patriarchal vision on workers reflected a guiding principle of Progressives to change the lifestyle of immigrants—part of their Americanization project. His attitudes dovetailed with those of social reformers who advised that every means possible should be used "to make the wife see her duties as a homemaker [and] there should be no relaxation in the effort to make the man do his duty as breadwinner."[26] These reformers wanted a more child-centered family in which each member was said to have a proper

role. Homebound wives were required to nurture children and provide comfort to working husbands. Like Ford, these social reformers
believed that men must be able to earn a family wage, *and* they opposed families taking in boarders since their presence often led to "im-
proper" intimacy with wives and daughters.

Marriage Bars

After World War I, many social reformers supported
limits on the employment of married women with working husbands.
There was also widespread support for marriage bars within the trade
union movement, even among unions that aggressively supported female workers. For example, the Seattle trade union movement actively
supported the entrance of women into a range of nontraditional industries. They helped organize these new workers and fought to eliminate gender wage inequities. To accomplish these goals, the Seattle
Central Labor Council hired a full-time female labor organizer specifically to work among women. However, many of the leaders believed
that it was inappropriate for married women with working husbands
to seek employment. As a result, the Central Labor Council disquali-
fied two women from running for the organizer position simply because they were married.[27]

While the attitudes and actions of many trade unions were patriarchal, this had little to do with the implementation of marriage bars.
After World War I, there was a successful business and government
attack on unions, eliminating their ability to influence employment
policies. Even in Seattle, where union strength had been substantial,
the victory of capital was such that "the Seattle Central Labor Council could do little to discourage the continued increase in married
women's entry into the labor market during the 1920s."[28]

Whatever the sins of trade unions, there were only isolated instances of marriage bars in unionized sectors. They were, for example,
virtually nonexistent among firms hiring factory operatives. Instead,
marriage bars were instituted in nonunionized, white-collar occupations that almost always required a high school education. Moreover,
in most cases, these were female occupations so that marriage bars had
little effect on male employment. This suggests that marriage bars were
ideologically driven and focused on limiting the employment of educated, middle-class women.

The role of ideology is most apparent in the decisions of city governments. While in some cities marriage bars covered all government

workers, the primary focus was on schoolteachers. In 1928, 61 percent of school districts nationally did not hire married women, while 52 percent would not retain single women when they married. Government adoption of marriage bars would seem to be primarily a response to political demands. After all, having no profit motive, city governments can presumably ignore efficiency calculations and focus employment decisions solely on the views of voters. As the depression increased public demands to protect male employment, governments responded; by 1942, 87 percent of school districts barred the hiring of married women, while 71 percent would not retain single women who married.

Office work was the other major occupation in which marriage bars were extensive. In a 1931 survey of firms in New York City, Philadelphia, Chicago, and Hartford, the use of marriage bars was widespread. It found that 36 percent of office workers were employed by companies that refused to hire any married women, while another 16 percent were employed by companies that left this decision up to the discretion of individual managers. Almost 35 percent of office workers had employers that "would not retain them if they married as a condition of both policy and discretion."[29]

While not eliminating the role of personal prejudice, the economist Claudia Goldin believes that other considerations were paramount. In particular, she stresses that marriage bars were generally profitable for firms that had fixed salary scales with raises determined by seniority. She finds that this was the wage-setting pattern in the teaching and clerical professions, especially among the larger firms and school districts.

Economists contend that seniority-driven, fixed wage patterns almost invariably create a situation in which older workers receive annual pay increases greater than their annual productivity gains. During the first half of the twentieth century, there were no federal laws which would have restricted firms from firing older workers at will. If this was done on an individual basis, however, all workers would perceive future uncertainty which would be bad for morale. It would also undermine the corporate movement toward having regulated, uniform personnel policies. As a result, firms often instituted a mandatory retirement age. Goldin contends that in female-dominated occupations, such as office worker and public schoolteacher, the firing of female workers when they married functioned as the equivalent of instituting mandatory retirement age. By avoiding retaining workers whose wages had outpaced their productivity, firms benefited.

A different explanation is necessary to explain why firms refused to hire married women, who, since they were new hires, would receive low starting salaries. Goldin contends that the hiring bar was adopted because it was believed that many of these workers would be transient. As the profiling model presented earlier indicates, firms make hiring decisions based on group characteristics. Since more than 80 percent of working women left the labor market at marriage or soon thereafter, school systems and office managers feared that if hired, these married women would quit after working only a short period of time. In this case, it would be foolish to hire them and invest the necessary training costs.

Though the male breadwinner ideology was strong in the 1950s, marriage bars were virtually eliminated during that decade. Goldin contends that it was primarily due to changes in the relative supply of young single women. During the 1920s, young single women were plentiful, so school districts and offices could relatively easily replace their current employees who married. Moreover, relatively few married women entered the labor market, so that refusing to hire them was not costly. The situation in the 1950s was entirely different. Whereas in 1920 young single women, not in school, comprised 13 percent of all adult women, in 1950 they comprised only 6 percent. In addition, there was a large increase in the number of older married women who had entered the labor force. Thus, firms and school districts in the 1950s could no longer "bar the hiring of married women without placing formidable restrictions on their labor supplies."[30] So marriage bars were lifted and the participation of married women was no longer impeded by one of the most blatant forms of employment discrimination women have ever faced.

Inequality within Marriage

The male breadwinner model of family life posited a sexual division of labor: Men specialized in market production while women specialized in home production. Many sociologists have claimed that this sexual division of labor is crucial to family stability, allowing each spouse to have complementary rather than competitive roles. For these analysts, husbands and wives benefit equally from marriage so that patriarchal exploitation could not be the norm. Complementing these views, pro-market economists contend that this sexual division of labor is efficient because partners specialize in what they do best.[31]

Second-wave feminists reject this idyllic vision of marriage, questioning any notion that marriage had become nonpatriarchal. In the not-so-distant past, women were often forced to marry or remain under the authority of a father or a brother. Constrained access to well-paying jobs and societal pressures against unwed mothers had created a "reserve army" of women willing to marry at virtually any price. While during the second half of the twentieth century the situation in the United States has changed substantially, these feminists see no evidence that the patriarchal family has been eliminated. They continue to believe that in the marriage market women pay a patriarchal price.[32]

The Marriage Market

Let us define an equitable marriage as one in which intimacy and the allocation of household time and income are determined by each spouse's preferences and their relative skills in performing household services. In particular, a marriage would be equitable, even if the wife did the bulk of household services, as long as this allocation reflected genuine altruism or an acceptable compensation for services rendered.[33]

The actual services provided by each spouse in the typical marriage can deviate from those that should be provided in equitable marriages. Indeed, we would expect that "men's power, much like capitalists', enable them to extract economic benefits from the dependent group."[34] These economic benefits typically include a disproportionate share of "luxury goods, leisure time, and personal services."[35] Excess services may include ceding control of household income to husbands, requiring wives to do an excessive share of household production, and/or ceding to husbands excessive influence over the choice and frequency of sexual activities.

In our model, since women have some choice of living arrangements, their marriage decision is influenced by the degree to which marriages are equitable. Many women are willing to marry if marriages are equitable. However, if women must pay a price—the excess services provided—at least some would change their minds and choose not to seek marriage. As the marriage price rises, more women would opt for alternatives to marriage so that the number of women willing to marry declines still further. Similarly, the number of men willing to marry is influenced by the marriage price. If marriages are equitable, only a limited number of men might be willing to marry. However, if men are able to extract excess services, more would be willing to marry. Thus, the decision of both men and women is influenced by the level of excess services expected in the typical marriage.

As suggested, if the typical marriage is equitable, the number of men would be less than the number of women willing to marry. Facing this excess demand for men, some women would be willing to provide excess services in order to increase their chances to marry. As the marriage price rises, excess demand declines. Somewhat fewer women continue to seek marriage, while the number of men increases. Eventually, a marriage price is reached at which the number of men and women willing to marry is equalized.

This outcome reflects the marriage price paid by women in the typical marriage. The actual marriage price paid by any individual wife will deviate around this norm according to her bargaining power. For women who have particularly desirable traits to men, the marriage price will generally be lower, while women in poor bargaining positions will likely pay a higher price. These deviations from the social norm mirror the pattern in labor markets. There, the wage paid to individual workers deviates around the typical wage paid to the class of workers they belong to. Those who have somewhat more desirable traits—such as experience or competing job offers—can often negotiate above-normal wages, while other workers—those who are not as flexible in where they are willing to work—generally obtain a below-normal wage.

Until recently, these outcomes were also influenced substantially by cultural and governmental institutions. For example, Teresa Amott and Julie Matthaei point to the experience of Chinese women at the end of the nineteenth century. The U.S. Chinese Exclusion Act of 1882 created a severe shortage of Chinese women in the United States; thirteen men for every woman. Our model would predict that Chinese women living in the United States would be in a highly favorable situation. With a shortage of women, the marriage price they pay should be reduced substantially. However, few of these women benefited from their scarcity. The vast majority was forced into prostitution and the payments received were controlled by Chinese men. It was the patriarchal policies enforced by Chinese cultural institutions, not the imbalance between the number of men and women willing to marry, which primarily determined their situation.[36]

Similarly, west of the Mississippi River there was generally a shortage of women during the nineteenth century. In a few cases, this enabled white women to escape some of the limitations of patriarchy. For example, western states were the first to allow women to vote. However, the shortage of women did not necessarily lower the patriarchal marriage price. Instead, cultural institutions often enabled men to import women. Dorothy Smith notes that in Canada, as competition lowered the price farmers received for their output, it became necessary to lower labor costs: "Women's labor is substituted for hired labor in working the land and in the production of subsistence for the family. . . . Increased inputs of her labor compensate for the lack of money at every possible point in the enterprise. Her time and energy, indeed her life, are treated as inexhaustible. . . . Women were virtually imported into Canada in this period to serve these functions."[37] Thus, even in the rare situations in which there were shortages of available women, cultural institutions often enabled men to continue to extract a substantial patriarchal price.

More generally, at the turn of the last century, social norms made it difficult for unmarried women to live outside the supervision of family members. In addition, government regulations concerning inheritance, property ownership, and work regulations limited the ability of women to gain financial independence. As a result, even when cultural norms did not limit the living arrangements, low earnings usually forced single women to remain at home. Just as importantly, prevailing social norms made it virtually impossible to consider giving birth and raising a child outside of wedlock so that motherhood required marriage. For these reasons, few men would consider an equitable marriage since the typical woman would be willing to pay a high patriarchal price to marry.

Over the past century, the power of social norms and the use of government regulations to limit the choices available to single women have declined substantially. Freed from the social stigma of unwed motherhood, freed from government regulations which limited their ability to attain better-paying jobs and wealth, women have more choices available, and this has had a predicted effect on their attitude toward marriage. Many women are no longer willing to pay as high a patriarchal price as before.

The declining ability to find women willing to pay a high patriarchal price has changed the marriage behavior of men. Realizing that they would not gain as many privileges as before, men have reduced their willingness to marry. As Elaine McCrate noted, "Men may be abandoning marriage rather than adjusting to women's new demands."[38] Thus, while the typical marriage is more egalitarian, the marriage rate has declined.

Persistence of the Marriage Price

Despite this progress, the marriage price remains substantial. Researchers continue to find that inequities are greatest with respect to household activities that have historically been assigned to women (cooking, cleaning, child rearing, etc.). They find that in households where both husbands and wives are full-time, year-round workers, over 70 percent of these household tasks are done by wives, and the number of hours husbands spent on them has been unchanged since the 1960s.[39]

Men continue to exert power over their wives in other ways. Among college daters, men compensated for lack of power in other areas by seeking greater control over the behavior of their girlfriends. For men, this control is especially important in areas characterized as sex-affective production: the fulfillment of human needs for affection, nurturance, and sexual expression. Patriarchal power often enables men to dictate the forms of intimacy allowed or the beauty styles that are acceptable.[40]

We might ask, "Why does patriarchy persist despite the ending of many of the institutional and cultural constraints women had historically faced?"

The Persistence of Patriarchal Social Norms. Social norms continue to constrain women. This was most visible after World War II. As a result of the war effort, female labor was needed in industry. Articles and stories championed the value of day care and the benefits of paid work for women. Firms also provided day care and expressed a willingness to hire women in nontraditional occupations, thus creating such phenomenon as "Rosie the Riveter." With their patriarchs at war, women were less constrained and there was a dramatic increase in female labor force participation. With the ending of the war and the return of men, opinion changed. Now it was found that absent mothers were responsible for juvenile delinquency and that certain jobs detracted from femininity. Firms eliminated day-care facilities and again refused to hire women for certain jobs. Men began to reinforce their desire for women to be full-time mothers and housewives. Many women left the work force, resigning themselves to becoming "happy homemakers."[41]

While not as powerful, a similar movement arose in the 1970s in response to the feminist movement. Led by Phyllis Schlafly, this movement reaffirmed that the preferred way to raise well-adjusted children was for mothers to be full-time homemakers. Her efforts were supported by 1977 survey data that indicated a majority of women believed "married women's paid work was discretionary and should not come at the expense of men's paid work."[42]

Initially, some feminists were hopeful that there would be a genuine change in male attitudes since the traditional patriarchal family "deprived men of significant access to their children." There was a hope that "marriage is being transformed from a complementary relationship, based on masculinity and femininity, to a symmetric one, based on a new kind of personhood." This hopefulness was soon abandoned, however, when such an intense backlash occurred that it was viewed by many as an "undeclared war against American women."[43]

The ambivalence society feels toward married women working when they have children is still significant. A 1991 poll found that 88 percent of working mothers felt that "if I could afford it, I would rather be home with my children," while 82 percent of the American public believed it is best for "young children to be cared for by one or more parents or by extended family members."[44] Today, the Moral Majority continues to decry the decline of traditional family values, while the Promise Keepers promote the reestablishment of patriarchal families, led by caring and sensitive men.

The latest wrinkles on this theme have been recent studies that seek to explain variations in the earnings of men. Holding productivity factors constant, husbands with working wives earned on average 10 percent less than those whose wives were full-time homemakers. Husbands with working wives were somewhat less willing to relocate, to work overtime, or to take on special projects. These studies reinforced traditional notions that career women sacrifice the interest of all members of their families—husbands and children. This stigma continues to burden women in ways that limit their earnings and independence and in ways which enable men to maintain patriarchal relations within the family.

Policies to Increase Female Willingness to Marry. Many traditionalists believe that the marriage rate decline is due to changing female behavior. If women are the culprits, government should undertake social policies that increase female willingness to marry. One such policy, known as Bridefare, was enacted by the Wisconsin legislature in 1994. It allowed the welfare department to raise monthly benefits from $440 to $531 for recipients who marry. To the extent this policy increased the willingness of unwed mothers to marry, it increased the marriage price they offered. Fearing this harmful outcome, Wisconsin state representative Gwendolyn Moore stated: "The Bridefare program . . . may place battered women in more danger. . . . Aid to Families with Dependent Children (AFDC) has traditionally been one way that women could escape from abusive situations that were dangerous for them or their children. Let us not begin telling battered women that if they do not marry, they and their children will be thrust deeper into poverty."[45]

Dismissing the seriousness of the harm bad marriages can do to poor women, traditionalists blame welfare for the decline in marriage rates among poor women. As welfare became more generous, they maintain, women increasingly "traded dependence on man for dependence on the government."[46] The problem with this thesis is that the growth in caseloads occurred during the 1980s when the value of welfare declined. However, there is no question that as more women have recently been pushed off welfare, many have been forced to seek male partners, raising the patriarchal price they must pay.

Changes in Male Preferences for Marriage. As has been noted, in response to the lowering of the patriarchal price they obtain, the number of men willing to marry has declined. However, some observers argue that there has been a more fundamental change in male marriage behavior—fewer would choose marriage even if the excess services provided to them had remained the same. They point to statistics that indicate that the percentage of married men has declined even when the patriarchal price they could obtain remained high. For black men with stable employment, almost one-half of those twenty-five to thirty-four years old were unmarried; for those sixteen to twenty-four years old, more than 80 percent were unmarried.[47]

Barbara Ehrenreich traces the change in male marriage preferences to the 1950s. Historically, male self-image was derived from men's ability to be the family breadwinner. Men were expected to marry young and focus on providing for their family. Patriarchy allowed men to be "king of their castle," but it required them to seek fulfillment through the financial support provided, not personal activities. For many men, this social norm was a heavy burden. Trapped in joyless marriages, sacrificing their happiness for the family good, these men did not feel that these patriarchal rules served their interests.

Ehrenreich believes that this explains the meteoric rise in circulation of *Playboy* magazine. It now became more acceptable for middle-class men to seek gratification outside of marriage, to no longer suppress their desires. Rather than marrying their high school or college sweethearts, more men began to delay marriage until they had spent time being free of familial responsibilities. This new male attitude, she maintains, was one of the reasons that the Frank Sinatra, Las Vegas "Rat Pack" had such mass appeal. After all, these were men who rejected the "home life" and, instead, sought hedonistic pleasures. Through them, middle-class men could live vicariously.[48]

Ehrenreich believes that the 1960s counterculture movement accelerated this "flight from commitment." Women were attracted because it allowed them to rebel against oppressive sexual mores. Men were attracted because it freed them from traditional male responsibilities: getting a steady job so that they could marry and support a family. Indeed, Ehrenreich believes that female rejection of patriarchal sexual mores, however justifiable, reinforced male devaluation of marriage. These changing male values help explain why the marriage price has remained.

The Growing Scarcity of Marriageable Men. William Wilson has emphasized that low marriage rates among poor women reflect the declining number of marriageable men available.[49] Due to rising incarceration rates, an increasing share of poorly educated men are not available for marriage. This is particularly the case in the black community where in some regions there are 20 percent more black women than black men in the noninstitutionalized population. The wages of low-skilled men have not kept pace with inflation. As a result, the share of male workers who work full-time year-round but do not earn enough for a family of four to escape poverty rose from 9 to 13 percent between 1979 and 1994.[50] Kathryn Edin found that poor women were very conscious of the employment record of the men they chose to partner with. As one of her respondents offered: "If after I lived with him for a couple of years and I see that nothing's gonna change in the relationship, then maybe I'll marry him. But he's gotta be somebody that's got [enough] money to take care of me."[51]

However, Edin's study indicated that the reluctance to marry available black men went well beyond income calculations. Just as our model predicts, these women realized that given the shortage of available men, they face a high marriage price. As another respondent stated, "There's a shortage of men so that they think, 'I can have more than one woman. I'm gonna go around this one or that one, and I'm gonna have two or three of them.'"[52] Many of these women feared that they would become their husband's personal slave, cooking their meals, cleaning their house, and doing their laundry. They lamented, "A man gets married to have somebody to take care of them 'cause their mommy can't do it anymore."[53] They expected that their husbands would feel free to spend money on personal leisure activities rather than on family necessities. As one respondent recounted: "I gave my child's father the money to go buy my son's Pampers. He went on some street with his cousin and they were down there partying, drinking, everything. He spent my son's Pamper money on partying."[54]

Moreover, since welfare was never enough to allow women to escape poverty, they were often forced to maintain relationships with men who abused them. This has been particularly the case with teenage black mothers. One recent study found that over one-half of these women had experienced domestic violence from their partner in the last year. The financial support is, however, quite meager since one-half of these men were high school dropouts, and only 48 percent were currently employed.[55]

Many of these black men realize that they don't have much to offer and cannot really support their partner or their children. They are worried that women will leave them and, therefore, become super jealous and possessive and use violence to keep the women with them. A significant proportion of these young men consciously sabotage the ability of teen mothers to gain additional education or outside employment. One study found that "three times as many abused women as nonabused women (39.7% as compared with 12.9%) reported that their intimate partner actively prevents their participation in education and training."[56]

While Edin does not dismiss the need to improve the employment and earnings of low-skilled men, she points out that marriage rates will remain low (and domestic violence high) as long as male behavior toward women is unchanged. Thus, the high marriage price poor women already face has increased still further due to callous welfare policies.

The Tax System. While paid work is not sufficient to end patriarchy in the home, for many women it is a precondition. As a working-class Mexican woman recounted:

> Of course it is important because if you can earn your own money, you yourself distribute it and you do not have to beg for it. You buy food or a dress for your daughter, the socks for your son. He used to tell me, "You must wait, because I do not have enough money this month." But he would never do it, neither today, nor tomorrow. Now I want to buy it, I buy it. If he gives me money, fine. If not I buy it myself. And one feels fine and useful with one's own money. Also, in case of an emergency, an accident, if I have my own money I can fetch a taxi and take the child to the hospital. And it is money well spent *because I earned it myself.* Otherwise he would tell me, why didn't you take a bus, why did you spend on a taxi.[57]

Traditionalists have consistently used the federal tax system to discourage middle-class women from working. Beginning in 1948, except in specific situations, married couples have been required to file joint returns. This joint return requirement, which traditionalists have consistently defended, continues to be a major impediment to the ability of married women to gain from paid employment. A numeral exercise will demonstrate this point.[58]

Let us assume a simple married tax schedule with rising marginal tax rates: The first $15,000 of adjusted gross income is untaxed; the next $25,000 is taxed at 15 percent; any subsequent income is taxed at 30 percent. Now let us look at the situation of more than 80 percent of married couples where husbands earn more than their wives. Specifically, let us assume that the husband earns $40,000 while his wife earns $25,000. In this situation, it is reasonable to assume that the wife is considered the secondary wage earner in the household.

Let us look at the economic consequences of the wife's decision to work. If she chooses not to work, household income is $40,000 and its tax liability is $3,750—15 percent of the last $25,000 the husband earns. If the wife chooses to work, her income is added on and is taxed at the higher 30 percent rate. Thus, $7,500—30 percent of $25,000—of her income would go to federal taxes. If we add on social security and state taxes, close to one-half of her income would be lost to taxes. If we then add on the child-care and business expenses incurred, the net additional income to the household would be quite small. This could easily discourage the wife from working, resulting in a strengthening of the patriarchal family.

The simplest way to solve the secondary wage earner problem is to eliminate joint returns, forcing all households to file individually. (This would also solve the marriage-penalty problem many households face.) Eliminating joint returns is unpopular with traditionalists for two reasons. First, by raising their net earnings, it would induce more married women to work. Second, it takes away the current benefits accruing to households where one spouse has very little income. Indeed, the reason that the joint return was instituted in 1948 was to enable middle- and upper-income married households with one wage earner to reduce their tax liabilities by having the husband's income taxed at the joint tax rate that was lower than the single tax rate.

The secondary wage earner bias could also be reduced if the highest tax rate is lowered. Since this is the tax rate at which the wife's income is taxed, it would increase the net income she receives. With more net income, more married women would find it profitable to work. This was exactly the outcome in the 1980s when the highest tax rate was reduced from 70 to 28 percent. Married women, especially those whose husband's earnings placed them in the 70 percent tax bracket, had little to benefit financially from working before the rate reductions. Once rates were lowered, many entered the labor force. This solution, however, increased income inequality.

Another possibility is to reduce the tax rate on secondary wage earners. This can be accomplished by eliminating a certain percentage of the wife's income from taxation. In our example above, suppose that only 60 percent of the wife's income is taxable. In that case, she would add only $15,000—60 percent of $25,000—to the household's taxable income. Thus, the household's taxes would rise by only $4,500—30 percent of the $15,000; a tax savings of $3,000.

Traditionalists also strongly oppose this proposal. They argue that it would undermine the notion that households with the same income should be taxed the same. In particular, households with adjusted gross income of $65,000 but where wives have no income would not benefit from this proposal and would be paying $3,000 more taxes than households where husbands earn $40,000 and the wives $25,000. When Congress enacted a modest version of this proposal in 1981, traditionalists were taken by surprise. Over the next few years, they fought for its repeal which was incorporated in the 1986 tax reform bill. When this proposal was being discussed again in 1999, traditionalists responded immediately. They again voiced their opposition because of the inequity it would create between married households with and without working wives.

A final way to increase the benefits to married women who work is through child-care credits. Federal taxes could be reduced to offset child-care expenses. If the credit is 40 percent, the household's taxes would be reduced by $2,400 if $6,000 is spent on child care, again improving substantially the benefits from work.

Traditionalists have responded in two ways. First, they made sure that the child-care credit is available to households with taxable income, whether or not both spouses are working. In this case, the credit is not linked to work and, at least for some married women who already have their children in day care, this policy does not increase the benefits from work.

Second and more important, traditionalists have fought attempts to increase the generosity of this policy. Instead, they have lobbied for tax relief through a child credit program. This program, which was a centerpiece of the Republican Contract with America, was enacted in 1998. It allows households to subtract four hundred dollars from their tax liabilities for each dependent child. Since this shifts income to households with children whether or not the secondary wage earner is working, it has no affect on their benefits from work. Married women still face higher marginal tax rates and still are discouraged from working, sustaining patriarchal relations within the family.

Special Needs of Women. As long as women have primary responsibility for child rearing, they will not attain labor market equality. Many jobs are structured by patriarchal notions of the family. Employees are expected to sacrifice household responsibilities if they conflict with corporate needs. If the firm requires overtime, unexpected rescheduling of work hours, or other adjustments, spouses are expected to adjust their schedules. As long as many jobs are structured in this way, job applicants who do not have a spouse willing to accommodate to the firm's prerogatives are at a disadvantage. Patriarchy posits that women be the accommodating spouse. Thus, even if firms are genuinely nondiscriminatory, without a change in job requirements, women will continue to be at a disadvantage.

The most visible example of the dilemma professional women face has been their experience in major law firms. These firms pay high salaries but also require long hours. Moreover, to gain partnership, junior lawyers have to further extend themselves by networking in order to demonstrate an ability to draw customers to the firm. This networking can often require attendance at professional and social events on top of the long hours at the office. Not surprisingly, many women find it impossible to balance these demands with those of their family. In recognition, law firms began developing what became known as "mommy" tracks. Women would have the option of working shorter hours but would sacrifice upward mobility within the firm.[59]

For these reasons, there should be a greater focus on public policies that limit the conflict between work and home faced by working mothers. There are two models that can accomplish this. On the one hand, most consistent with first-wave feminism is the *universal* breadwinner model. This model emphasizes providing services, particularly quality day care, which free women from child-rearing responsibilities. On the other hand, second-wave feminism stresses the *caregiver* model, emphasizing policies that allow women to fulfill their child-rearing activities without sacrificing their earnings potential. These policies include flextime without prejudice and more generous family leave policies.[60] In the past decade, many companies have adopted one or more of these policies, enabling women to break through previous glass ceilings. However, as long as these policies are not universally required, many women will be unable to compete on an equal basis with men, reinforcing the patriarchal family.

In summary, beginning in the late nineteenth century, marriage began to be idealized in a neo-feudalistic manner—recreating the lord-serf "partnership" in the family. Each partner in the relationship was predestined to his or her situation, which was sanctified by religious dogma, with each having an ethical obligation to their partner. Like feudal lords, men were obligated to protect their families from adversity, which was interpreted as providing them with a rising standard of living. Like serfs on the manor, wives had to submit themselves to the desires of their lords, providing household services and intimacy.

This ideology was promoted by middle-class social reformers during the nineteenth century and in some cases led to the adoption of the family wage. In Britain, the working class supported the notion of a family wage at first but resisted eliminating married women from the labor force. However, as more male jobs were threatened by female labor, men began to embrace the notion of a "moral" economy with a male breadwinner. By 1900, this cult of domesticity was widely accepted in Great Britain so that few married women remained in the work force.

Policies evolved differently in France. Due to a desire to increase population growth and to support working families, the Catholic Church, unions, and government agreed on a family allowance policy. Supplements were given to married men to support children, not wives. Capitalists supported family wage policies because these policies often allowed them to lower wages of single men by more than the family allowance paid. Moreover, as long as it was under capitalist supervision, workers would be reluctant to militantly oppose their bosses. As a result, labor tranquillity reigned and married women maintained a sizable presence within the labor force.

In the United States, native-born workers were primarily concerned with the threat posed by immigrants rather than that from female workers. As a result, the family wage was an ideal held by social reformers and some unionists rather than a policy that was widely implemented. Citing the actions of Henry Ford, some observers contend that family wage policies were implemented because they were profitable to capitalists. However, a more detailed assessment of Ford's policies seems to indicate that the patriarchal requirements he attached to his five-dollar-day plan were a result of his social reform desires rather than any attempt to maximize profits.

To some, marriage bars were a logical extension of the struggles of male workers for a family wage. However, male unionists could not be responsible; their unions were too weak and virtually all the bars were in female white-collar occupations. As a result, these employment barriers must have been instituted because they served the interests of capitalists.

Generally, capitalists do not benefit from exclusionary employment barriers because of their adverse impact on labor supplies. However, there have been countervailing factors. In particular, marriage bars were instituted in industries that had fixed wage patterns tied to seniority. As a result, older workers tended to have wages that outpaced their productivity. Similar to mandatory retirement policies, marriage bars enabled firms to eliminate workers whose pay exceeds their productivity.

This policy made sense in the 1920s and 1930s when a growing supply of educated young women could easily replace terminated married women who were employed as teachers and office workers. However, in the 1950s, when the number of young women declined and the number of available married women was substantial, firms could no longer profitably maintain marriage bars. The neo-feudalist family became untenable, and the male breadwinner model had declining support. Not surprisingly, both men and women adopted the same behavior in their approach to marriage as in their market relationships: individualistic and utilitarian. For each partner, marriage would be "purchased" as long as the benefits to the individual outweighed the cost. As benefits and costs are altered, the decision whether or not to seek marriage changes. While personal ethics might still play some role, it no longer remained the decisive factor governing marriage decisions.

The marriage market has biases similar to the labor market. In capitalism, workers and owners do not necessarily negotiate from an equal position. As long as there is substantial unemployment, workers must adapt to the desires of capitalists if they wish to avoid poverty. Similarly, men and women do not necessarily enter the marriage market from equal positions. Only if women have equality in the labor market, can they bargain effectively. As long as women cannot earn a decent living, they must adapt to male desires if they wish to avoid poverty.

This marriage model emphasizes how market forces, not inherent traits, determine behavior. When we find capitalists paying their workers starvation wages, we don't argue that those who become capitalists have inherently different values than those who remain workers. Instead, we focus on the market forces that compel capitalists to act that way. Similarly, men take advantage of the marriage market by extracting the available patriarchal price from their spouses. We should not consider men to be inherently different from women—men are from Mars, women are from Venus. Instead, we should realize that they are simply responding to the market outcomes available to them. Change the marriage price and men will respond differently.

Movements toward equality would be accelerated if men rejected the benefits they can obtain from market forces. Just as Ebenezer Scrooge was transformed from responding solely to market forces, during the 1970s, men's groups attempted to change male values so they, too, would not simply accept the benefits of the "market." Dickens's *A Christmas Carol* suggests that ethical personal values can overcome market forces. Historically, these personal values were embedded in religious dogma. Since most religions are strongly patriarchal, however, this vision does not seem realistic. As a result, we must rely on secular solutions to patriarchy that rely on changing market relationships.

Women must have the same alternatives as men, which, at a minimum, requires full gender equality in the labor market.

Finally, there is a downside to this secular solution to patriarchy. It risks dramatically devaluing children. They are increasingly viewed as burdens, diminishing the ability of men to partake in hedonistic activities and constraining the occupational mobility of women. Michael Males captures this danger: "Maybe America, for all its prating about family values, hates its children. What else can explain the cruel abandonment of so many kids to such wretched circumstances: bad schools, poor health care, deadly addictions, and crushing debts— and utter indifference?"[61] Unless market systems find a way to socialize the cost of child rearing, harming children may be one unfortunate legacy of the quest for gender equity within capitalist societies.[62]

6 The Immigration Controversy

Who Wins and Who Loses?

As we've seen previously, broad-based movements defended racial and gender exclusionary barriers on the basis of both economic and social considerations. White southerners argued that Jim Crow employment laws were necessary both because they protected white living standards and because they sustained a morally desirable social order. At the same time, northern male workers defended barriers to female employment, claiming they were part of a moral economy. This chapter will identify similar positions among opponents of unrestricted immigration: Continued immigration undermines wages and working conditions of native-born workers and, by changing the racial composition of the United States, undermines core American values.

The cultural arguments presented by immigration opponents will be examined in the following pages. However, the focus will primarily be on the conflicting claims concerning immigration's impact on the well-being of native-born and immigrant workers. These conflicting assessments were highlighted by Ric Burns's 1999 documentary on the history of New York. He chose to use the 1911 Triangle shirtwaist factory fire, in which 146 workers lost their lives, as a context for his discussion of the economic consequences of immigration. Michael Wallace, in his Pulitzer Prize–winning book, *Gotham: The History of New Yor*[illegible]-grants were hapless [illegible]n in brutal, dehumanizing garment factories; the fire was laissez-faire competitive capitalism at its worst. This provoked the *New York Times* television critic John Tierney to write a column entitled "A 1911 Fire as Good TV, Bad History," characterizing the program as "a documentary not burdened with the less vivid facts."[1] Tierney presented the views of pro-market economists who claim that New York City immigrant garment workers were generally treated fairly and did not undermine the wages or working conditions of native-born workers. Moreover, whereas Burns's documentary asserted that government regulations were necessary and effective instruments in improving the welfare of workers, the pro-market economists Tierney quoted reached the opposite conclusion: Government legislation was unproductive and threatened the welfare of workers.

These assessments are not solely of historical interest. The current wave of immigration has unleashed the same antagonisms and the same set of competing claims. The Republican candidate, Pete Wilson, made opposition to immigration the centerpiece of his successful 1994 California gubernatorial campaign. Eliminating financial aid to immigrants was a prominent component of the 1996 Welfare Reform Act. The reappearance of sweatshops and the potential threat immigrant labor poses to native-born workers, particularly blacks with limited education, have also fueled the same debates. Does immigration undermine wages of native-born workers? Does it enable capitalists to exploit powerless immigrants?

The pro-market view provides some useful insights. However, we will see, once again, that when profits from fair employment are modest, social attitudes may play a decisive role in explaining discriminatory behavior. The substantial differences between the two waves of immigration will also be explored, particularly two features that are distinctive to the current wave—illegal immigration and utilization of government welfare programs by immigrants.

Measuring Immigration Flows

During the first major wave of immigration, 1880–1925, working-aged immigrants increased the U.S. labor force by an average of 2 percent each year. By 1890, 14.7 percent of the total U.S. population was foreign-born and remained at that level for two decades. The immigrant share of the population began to decline after World War I and more dramatically after restrictions were enacted in 1923. With passage of new immigration laws in 1965, a second immi-

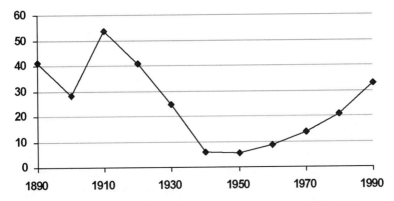

Figure 6.1 Immigration as a Share of Population Growth, 1890–1990. *Source: George Borjas, "The Economics of Immigration,"* Journal of Economic Literature *32 (December 1994): Table 1.*

gration wave began, but by some measures does not appear to be as substantial as the first wave. For example, only 7.9 percent of the population was foreign born in 1990.

Due to the declining birthrate of native-born women since 1970, however, new immigrants have become a significant portion of our population growth, reaching 33.1 percent by 1990. Since 1990, the level of immigration has increased substantially. Whereas between 1980 and 1985 immigration averaged about 550,000, during the 1995–1997 period, it averaged over 800,000. As a result, during the 1990s, immigration accounted for close to 40 percent of the U.S. population growth, just about the same as during the 1890–1920 period (see Figure 6.1).[2]

While comparisons of legal immigration can be useful, they are incomplete. Whereas during the earlier wave all immigration was legal, during the current wave there is substantial illegal immigration. Estimates of illegal immigration are often extrapolated from the number of illegal entrants caught by government Immigration and Naturalization Service (INS) agents. A widely accepted assertion is that for every illegal entrant caught, two others successfully enter the country. Accepting this relationship, annual illegal immigration during the 1980s was 2.5 to 3 million and has risen steadily until in 1997 it was estimated by the INS to be close to 5 million. If we added these illegals into our figures, the rate of immigration rivals that of the first wave.

The effect of immigration on labor markets cannot be judged, however, by simply measuring the number of new arrivals. Suppose that we expect one million immigrants to arrive annually over the next decade and obtain employment. The long-term effect on labor markets differs dramatically depending upon whether these immigrants become permanent residents or are sojourners. If all are sojourners, returning to their country of origin after only one year, *net* immigration equals zero. Each year's immigrants replace the previous year's immigrants in one million jobs. In contrast, if all become permanent residents, at the end of the decade, 10 million U.S. jobs are filled by recently arrived immigrants.

Though today as many as 5 million illegals may be entering the United States annually, probably close to 90 percent are sojourners. Sojourners were also a substantial component of first-wave immigration. Between 1890 and 1920, 18.3 million aliens arrived in the United States but departures equaled 8.8 million.[3] Thus, net immigration must be emphasized in order to accurately assess the long-term impact of immigration on labor markets.

An Urban Institute report that derived net immigration estimates for the entire twentieth century states that for the peak decade in the first wave (1901–1910), *net* immigration equaled 4.7 million, which was just over 5 percent of the 1910 U.S. population. For the decade ending in 1990, 8.2 million net legal and illegal immigrants arrived, which was just over 3 percent of the U.S. population. While somewhat less than the peak decade of the earlier immigration wave, net immigration during the 1980s was probably about the average rate for the entire first-wave period, 1875–1925.

Besides legal and illegal immigration, temporary employment visas aid those employers seeking foreign-born workers. Whereas in 1985, 75,000 workers entered through temporary work permit programs, by 1996 their numbers had reached 227,000.[4] The two principal temporary work programs are H1–B visas, which allow U.S. companies to hire foreign workers who possess special skills for up to six years, and L-1 visas that allow foreign-based companies to fill positions in their U.S. plants with foreign workers for six-month intervals.

In 1998, responding to intense lobbying pressure from business groups, the annual quota for H1–B visas was increased from 65,000 to 115,000 for a three-year period. In 2000, Congress passed legislation introduced by Judiciary Committee chairman Orrin Hatch and Immigration Subcommittee chairman Spencer Abraham that would further increase the H1–B visa annual quota to 195,000. In addition, for the first time H1–B workers who received at least a master's degree from a U.S. college or university, or who work for a U.S. institution of higher education, would be exempted from the quota. This legislation will greatly expand the number of "guest workers" employed in technical labor fields.[5]

Temporary visa workers can cause more harm than just replacing native-born workers. After mastering key elements of the work process at U.S. firms, L-1 visa holders return home to train others to do the same work. This then facilitates the export of jobs abroad by American firms seeking low-cost, high-tech labor. India is a fertile ground because of its English language school systems and educational emphasis on mathematical skills. Experienced programmers can be hired in India at one-fifth to one-third their cost in the United States. In 1995, over 75,000 programmers in India were employed by U.S.-based companies.[6]

During the 1990s these visa programs were even utilized by firms seeking low-waged labor. For example, a used clothing recycling company was allowed to hire twenty-two H1–B visa workers for $4.50 per hour after it found that Cambodian immigrants were "unsatisfactory." Most telling was the case of Robzen Inc., a Scranton, Pennsylvania, meatpacking company. When an INS raid removed two-thirds of Robzen's workers who were illegal aliens, the company petitioned successfully to be allowed to hire thirty foreign-born workers at $5.50 per hour through the H1–B visa program. In a Labor Department inspector general's report, it was found that in the vast majority of cases where companies apply for visa workers, they had made no meaningful attempt to hire U.S. residents; they had either rejected all applicants regardless of qualifications or discouraged applications through deceptive advertising.[7]

Trade Union Hostility toward Immigration

By increasing labor supplies, many workers fear that immigration causes wages to decline. This view has been widely accepted within the trade union movement. Indeed, the first president of the American Federation of Labor (AFL), Samuel Gompers, led his organization on a thirty-year crusade for the enactment of immigration restrictions. During this time, he was unwilling to aid the immigrant community, even refusing to support the unionizing efforts of Jewish immigrant garment workers in New York or Philippino farm workers in California.

At that time, the AFL represented skilled craft workers. In many of the industries in which these unionized workers were employed, the majority of workers were nonunionized immigrants. Even in these situations, where their own members would be directly affected, the AFL refused to organize immigrant workers. As a result, many craft unions were unsuccessful when companies attacked them since the nonunionized workers were unwilling to come to the unions' aid. Moreover, companies often reorganized their production system, firing craft workers and replacing them with nonunionized immigrant workers.

The most famous example of this deskilling process occurred in the steel industry. When the industry began to grow rapidly during the 1870s, skilled unionized workers had a central role in the production process. Eventually, however, the factory owners, led by Andrew Carnegie, sought to undermine the power of their craft workers. This led to major conflicts, culminating in the defeat of the steelworkers union in the Homestead (Pennsylvania) Lockout of 1892. Afterward, the factories were reorganized, replacing unionized craft workers with nonunionized immigrant workers. It was forty-five years before steelworkers were again able to mount successful unionizing efforts in their industry.

During the most recent period, immigration has played a somewhat different role. Today, most skilled native-born workers have been shielded from competition with immigrant workers. Instead, the competition is most intense within low-waged labor markets. Since 1980, over 40 percent of *legal* immigrants (sixteen years and older) have less than a high school education compared to 20 percent for the native-born population. The potential divisiveness created by such a large influx of low-skilled immigrants may be quite modest, however, since most are employed in establishments that are ethnically homogeneous.[8]

Interestingly, it may be high-skilled rather than low-skilled immigrants who create divisiveness. Recent revisions of immigration policies have focused on increasing the share of immigrants with high skill levels. As a result, during the 1990s, 23 percent of all legal adult immigrants—40 percent of adult Asian immigrants—had college degrees. For many of these college-educated immigrants, English skills and licensing requirements exclude them from employment as managers, government workers, or service professionals. In response, many shift to entrepreneurial activities. In many poorer black neighborhoods, immigrant firms dominate.[9]

This growing gap between immigrant and black ownership has

become a divisive element within urban America. In virtually every city that has a large immigrant population, activists have focused black resentment on immigrant-owned businesses. In New York, Los Angeles, and Miami, black protesters have committed violent acts against immigrant-owned businesses in their communities. For example, the 1992 Los Angeles rebellion after the acquittal of police officers for the beating of black motorist Rodney King focused on Korean merchants. In New York City, a boycott of immigrant businesses in Brooklyn and later Harlem resulted in six deaths. Similar incidents have occurred over the years in the Overton section of Miami.

Some researchers question the degree to which immigrant entrepreneurship is harmful to the black community. First, it may very well be that despite the visible nature of immigrant businesses in the black community, these firms primarily have a white or immigrant clientele. Moreover, it is not necessarily the case that their presence in black communities reflects a displacement of black firms. Finally, there is some evidence that immigrant businesses tend to revive areas that are in decline, improving the situation for both themselves and the community.

Whatever the effect of these immigrant businesses, they have fomented ethnic antagonisms, similar to those that occurred during the first wave of immigration. Rather than uniting to demand better social services from government and better employment opportunities from corporations, immigrant and black groups dissipate their political energies fighting each other. As documented earlier, corporate taxes have declined as have government expenditures on urban infrastructure and social services.

Anti-Immigrant Ideologies

Beginning in Darwin's time, racial ideologies developed, promoting the view that northern and western Europeans—Aryans—were genetically and culturally superior to southern and eastern Europeans, as well as nonwhites. This racial ideology was embraced by elites throughout Europe and the United States. While not developed to rationalize exploitation of workers, this ideology did help to justify the colonization of Africa and Asia and the continued victimization of blacks. Racial ideologies fomented anti-immigrant attitudes in California that created a small conflict for profit-maximizing capitalists there. In particular, the Chinese exclusion laws of 1882 did somewhat limit labor supplies, making California labor more expensive.

However, this racial ideology was not strong enough initially to undermine the European immigration that capitalists favored.

These racial notions were embraced by a wide variety of political leaders. When comparing African natives with African Americans, Booker T. Washington wrote:

> The natives have never been educated by contact with the white man in the same way as has been true of the American Negro. . . . their ambitions have never been awakened, their wants have not been increased, and they work perhaps two days out of the week and are in idleness during the remaining portion of time. . . . How different in the Southern part of the United States where we have eight million of black people! . . . these people have not by any means reached perfection but they have advanced on the whole much beyond the condition of the South Africans.[10]

To explain why African Americans were the most advanced blacks in the world, Washington believed that the Negro did gain certain benefits from slavery: self-discipline and future-oriented values. While slavery improved blacks, he believed that they still were not the equal of whites at the time of emancipation. As a result, Washington considered the Reconstruction era to be an inappropriate preparation for an "ignorant and inexperienced" black population.[11]

Similarly, John Dewey, in his attempt to promote more public funding of education, and Margaret Sanger, in her attempt to promote family planning, both embraced the racial anti-immigrant attitudes then prevalent in public discourse. Following the pronouncements of the labor economist John R. Commons, the AFL leadership also supported the view that the newer immigrants were culturally inferior. Even President Theodore Roosevelt promoted racial anti-immigrant notions. When addressing the graduating class at Wellesley College in 1903, he lamented that Aryan women were having smaller families compared to non-Aryan women. President Roosevelt feared that unless native-born women rededicated themselves to having large families, the Aryan composition of America would decline, undermining Western values.

Like Commons, the influential economist Irving Fisher demonstrated the way in which even those who sympathized with the plight of workers could be infected with racial anti-immigrant notions. He was appalled by the treatment of industrial workers and favored the use of scientific management as a means of bettering their conditions.

However, he also feared "race suicide," which he associated with the decline in the Aryan component of the U.S. population.[12]

Similar notions underpin one segment of the contemporary anti-immigration movement. For example, Peter Brimelow points to the impact new immigration is having on the future ethnic composition of the United States: "Now American Anglos are reproducing below replacement levels. . . . So post-1965 Second Great Wave immigrants are having a proportionately much higher demographic impact on America than the pre-1925 Great Wave."[13]

He contends that post-1965 immigration accounts for one-half of the population growth between 1970 and 1990. This is substantially higher than the estimates shown in Figure 6.1 where new immigrants during those two decades accounted for about 28 percent of population growth. Brimelow obtains higher figures since he includes not only the new immigrants arriving, but also the children of immigrants (and their children) who were born in the United States *regardless* of the race or ethnicity of their spouse. He projects that immigrants and their *offspring* will make up two-thirds of the population growth during the 1990s and virtually all of the population growth thereafter. Echoing the race suicide arguments of the earlier period, Brimelow asserts: "Immigration policy is quite literally driving a wedge between the American nation, as it had evolved by 1965, and its future."[14]

A second staple of contemporary racialists is that government policies are favoring nonwhite immigrants over native-born Americans: "No matter how new, all immigrants from the right 'protected classes'—black, Hispanic, Asian—are eligible for preferential hiring and promotion. They are counted toward government quota requirements that were allegedly imposed on employers to help native-born minorities."[15]

Third, racialists condemn the contemporary multicultural movement because it is a barrier to the cultural assimilation that they believe is crucial to American society. Brimelow contends that the ability of the United States to prosper from the first wave of immigrants was a result of the Americanization process that encouraged assimilation. Similarly, Thomas Sowell contends that the Americanization process had a powerful affect on the Irish American community, causing "one of the great transformations of a people."[16] For Sowell, "The Irish who are accepted today may be very different from the nineteenth-century emigrants from Ireland whose personal behavior would still be wholly unacceptable to others today, including today's Irish Americans."[17]

Racialists fear that if this multicultural view triumphs, it will eliminate any notion of a culturally unified nation. They suggest that the United States could disintegrate like Lebanon under the weight of the disunifying effects of separatist cultural values. Since non-European immigration strengthens the power of the multicultural movement, for racialists, this further justifies dramatically changing immigration policies.

The politician most associated with this racial anti-immigrant ideology is Pat Buchanan. In his 1996 Republican presidential campaign, Buchanan stressed a nativist theme, articulating views which he had voiced for sometime. For example, in 1993 Buchanan wrote: "By 2050, according to the Census Bureau, whites may be near a minority in . . . America. . . . By the middle of the next century, the United States will have become a veritable Brazil of North America. If the future character of America is not to be decided by our own paralysis . . . we must begin to address the hard issues of race, culture, and national unity."[18]

Echoing anti-immigration contentions concerning Jewish and Italian behavior a century earlier, Buchanan focused on the alleged criminality of the Latino immigrants and blacks. He stated, "[F]our in ten felonies in San Diego County are the work of illegals. While white-on-black crime has become relatively rare . . . black criminals now choose white victims, in rapes and muggings, 50 percent of the time."[19]

Buchanan also linked the issue of national unity with the dangers of multiculturalism: "And demands are growing that our heritage of individual rights be superseded by a new system of racial entitlements. . . . On college campuses, there are new demands for all-black dorms and all-black cultural centers; blacks, whites, Hispanics and Asians tend to congregate, more and more, only with each other."[20]

Racialists hold these views despite demographic evidence that many immigrant groups do not remain culturally isolated. Almost 80 percent of all Asians are part of a multiracial kinship network, with about 50 percent of the second generation marrying a non-Asian. Second-generation Latino immigrants have similar outmarriage rates. Even marriage rates between blacks and whites have become substantial. In 1993, of the total number of marriages involving blacks and whites, 12.1 percent were interracial, up from 2.6 percent in 1970.[21]

This evidence brings into question the 2050 projections. In particular, to make its projections, the Census Bureau assumed that a child born to an interracial couple today will take the race of the mother and in the future there will be no further interracial marriages. That is, the child of a white male and Latino female is considered Latino and projections assume that the child will marry a Latino as will all future generations. Thus, these projections for the racial composition of the United States should not be taken seriously. At best, they project that in 2050 a slight majority of the U.S. population will have *some* nonwhite ancestry.

Immigration Restrictions

When capitalists have a decisive stake in legislative debates, they generally have the power to determine the outcome. This certainly seemed to be the case during most of the first wave of immigration when, given the size of the immigrant flows, immigration restrictions would have had a substantial adverse affect on labor supplies. After World War I, however, the benefits to capitalists from open immigration waned for a number of reasons.

Czarist Russia had been the major country of origin of Jewish immigration. Both the Soviet Union and the newly independent Poland offered hope that Jews would no longer suffer from virulent anti-Semitism. Moreover, the newly independent countries in eastern Europe created rising expectations for other ethnic groups so that after World War I immigration from this region lessened substantially. As a result of these and other factors, the annual rate of immigration for 1919 to 1923 was about one-third its pre–World War I level. These lower rates reduced the value to capitalists of open immigration.

Second, the triumph of communism in the Soviet Union and the attempted revolutions in Hungary and Germany generated political anxieties in the United States. Since immigrants were perceived as most susceptible to revolutionary policies, politicians joined in attacking them as threats to the "American way of life." Thus, capitalists became less sanguine that continued open immigration was in their political interest.

Third, the post–World War I anti-immigrant hysteria intensified anti-Semitic attitudes. Henry Ford published the fabricated "Protocols of the Elders of Zion" in his *Dearborn Press*, which promoted the idea of an international Jewish conspiracy. Senator Robert La Follette assigned responsibility for World War I to Jewish international bankers. The liberal Catholic publication *World's Work* complained that Jewish immigrants were draft dodgers and war profiteers.[22]

As anti-Semitism grew, capitalists felt compelled to adopt exclusionary policies. In 1910, only 0.3 percent of employment advertisements specified Christians and no colleges had restrictive entrance policies. By 1920, 10 percent of employment ads specified Christians, rising to 13.3 percent by 1926. In addition, many prestigious universities, including Columbia and Harvard, adopted restrictive admissions policies that were intended to limit Jewish students. These exclusionary policies, in turn, made it more difficult for capitalists to condemn immigration restrictions.

Fourth, in industries where capitalists had eliminated unions completely, they began to use black workers to create another wedge. These racial divisions enabled capitalists to undermine steel- and metalworker organizing drives, causing frustrated immigrant workers to attack black communities in St. Louis and Chicago in 1919. Seizing on the anticommunist hysteria, police rounded up immigrants who were often union activists, deporting tens of thousands of them during the infamous 1919 Palmer Raids. As a result, unionizing efforts were thoroughly defeated, and capitalists found that black workers could serve the same purpose as immigrant labor. This turn of events further weakened the need for maintaining open immigration.

When capitalists have a limited financial stake, racial ideologies may dominate political and economic decision making. Earlier, this thesis was offered to explain why the baseball industry did not integrate more rapidly after Jackie Robinson broke the color line in 1947. It was also offered to explain why national capitalists were not more supportive of federal legislation to end Jim Crow until the post–World War II era. Similarly, cultural arguments became decisive in legislative debates when corporate benefits from immigration waned. As a result, the eugenics movement faced little opposition when it sponsored a racist immigration bill during the 1920s. This bill, which was approved in 1923, limited future annual immigration from any country to no more than 2 percent of the number of individuals from that country who resided in the United States in *1890*. Since the vast majority of eastern and southern European immigrants had come after 1890, the quotas from these regions were quite low, virtually eliminating any immigration from outside western and northern Europe.

In the recent period, it is more difficult to measure the gains to capitalists from legal immigration. The economist George Borjas has estimated that there would be a $120 billion shift from nonwage to wage income if immigration were eliminated.[23] His calculation, however, was based on a labor demand response which most other researchers believe is unrealistic. Critics suggest that a much lower estimate is warranted since legal immigration probably put downward pressure only on the wages of the least-skilled workers. For example, a National Research Council report found that immigration had virtually no impact on the total wages of the native-born workers, primarily redistributing income "from the poor and unskilled to skilled workers and owners of capital."[24]

Another factor that must be taken into account is the prominence of the firms that would be adversely affected by immigration restrictions. At the beginning of the twentieth century, immigrant labor was crucial to the growth of major industrial corporations, particularly those in the steel and railroad industries. As a result, *powerful* capitalists had a substantial financial stake in open immigration. In contrast, in the contemporary era, major telecommunications, media, durable goods, and computer corporations hire very few immigrants. Immigrant labor is primarily hired by small-scale producers in light manufacturing and the service sector. Thus, open immigration may not concern the politically most powerful capitalists today as much as it did comparable capitalists at the beginning of the twentieth century, especially if temporary employment visas are available.

The Economic Welfare of Native-Born Workers

Let us look more closely at the conflicting estimates of the effect of immigration on the earnings and employment of native-born workers. Clearly, immigration increases the supply of workers. However, we cannot determine its impact on wages or employment without making some judgment on its impact on labor demand. In the zero-sum model, immigration is assumed to have no effect on labor demand; for every job taken by an immigrant, there is one less job for native-born workers.

The zero-sum model generally captures the situation in many technical fields. Immigrant labor does lower the wages paid to engineers. However, engineering labor costs comprise a very small share of the total costs. As a result, their salary reductions will have virtually no effect on the prices these companies can charge so that they will have no effect on total sales or employment. Thus, the entrance of foreign engineers has simply enabled firms to keep wages down by substituting foreign for domestically trained engineers.

Supporting this position, journalists Donald Bartlett and James Steele note: "Between 1990 and 1995, the total number of engineers employed in the United States increased by 72,000. During those same years, 388,000 students were graduated from American colleges and universities with bachelor's degrees in engineering. A total of 178,000 received master's degrees in engineering. A total of 36,000 received doctorates. And 237,200 foreign engineers came into this country to work 'temporarily.'"[25]

A second major area in which visa holders substantially expand labor supplies is the computer industry. Despite unprecedented growth in the computer industry, visa holders have kept wage increases down for programmers to between 7 and 8 percent annually during 1997 and 1998. During this period, in contrast to what you would expect if workers were scarce, firms hired only about 2 percent of their software applicants and made job offers to no more than 25 percent of those they interviewed. Indeed, this data led the Department of Commerce in 1999 to retract its 1997 assessment that there was a substantial shortage of information technology workers.[26]

A similar situation exists in hospitals where nursing costs have very little influence on the demand for medical services. Increases in acute care raised the demand for nurses. This should have increased their wages and improved their working conditions. However, hospitals responded by increasing the supply of nurses recruited from training programs overseas. In addition, hospitals shifted a number of responsibilities from registered nurses to nurse's aides, similar to the deskilling process which occurred in the steel industry in the late nineteenth century. As a result, nursing wages and working conditions did not improve substantially.

Even if total labor costs are significantly affected by immigration, total labor demand may be unaffected. Consumers may not change their demand substantially and firms might not be able to shift between domestic and overseas production in response to changing wage levels. This reflects the situation in meatpacking where Marc Cooper documents the adverse impact of immigrant labor. He states, "In 1980, the meatpacking industry was unionized and the industry's hourly pay, including benefits, peaked at $19. By 1992 it was below sixties levels at $12 an hour, and it has continued to fall."[27]

Many supporters of open immigration deny that immigration adversely affects native-born workers. They emphasize situations in which immigrants take jobs that native-born workers seem to be unwilling to seek. But they rarely ask why native-born workers shun certain jobs. In meatpacking, nursing, and engineering, firms face labor shortages only when wages are low. If immigration was eliminated, native-born workers would be encouraged to seek engineering, nursing, and low-wage production jobs in response to the improved wages and working conditions employers must offer. Thus, labor shortages may be a signal to improve wages and working conditions rather than a signal to allow immigration to fill business needs.

It is certainly possible that immigration expands labor demand so that at least some immigrant employment does not come at the expense of native-born workers. In industries where labor is a significant share of total costs, immigration can lower prices and, hence, stimulate total sales and employment. In the 1970s, Michael Piore suggested that the remaining vitality of garment districts in Los Angeles and New York City was primarily determined by their ability to utilize illegal immigrants who kept costs low enough to maintain profitability in the face of growing competition from imported goods.[28] Indeed, Thomas Muller suggests that it is only the continued infusion of cheap foreign-born labor that enables older urban areas to maintain any economic vitality:

> Older American cities in particular would have difficulty with the concentrated production of capital-intensive goods, which require high technology. Most of these cities are not considered by investors as potential sites for new industry. . . . For any stagnating urban economy, any productive economic activity is a plus. A Newark, NJ is not likely to attract large research laboratories and certainly not a Japanese automaker. But with both commercial space and immigrant labor available at low cost, older cities can attract labor-intensive manufacturing and service industries.[29]

Muller points to the prosperity of the shoe industry in Los Angeles: "Without these immigrants . . . local shoe manufacturers would find it difficult to survive. Unskilled blacks could not fill the role of these immigrants, who had extensive shoemaking training in Mexico and were accustomed to working for rock-bottom piece rates."[30] Muller notes that probably close to 40 percent of workers in apparel, leather and footwear, and canned foods and vegetables were held by illegal workers.

Measuring the Wage Effect

To measure the wage effect of immigration, most studies compare wages across a set of urban areas. Presumably, if immigration has an adverse influence, urban areas with a larger share of immigrants in their labor force should have lower average wages than urban areas with a smaller share of immigrants in their labor force. In a representative study, Robert LaLond and Robert Topel found that immigration had no effect on the average wage received by Latino and African American workers. In another study, David Card looked at the impact of the May 1980 Mariel boatlift that brought Cuban refugees to Miami, increasing its population by 7 percent. He found that this sudden increase in Miami's labor supply had no effect on the employment or earnings of either black or non-Cuban Latino workers.[31]

A number of researchers believe, however, that comparing wage differences across urban areas underestimates the impact of immigration. Suppose that we begin with a fairly uniform wage nationally. Immigration to particular urban areas might lower the wages of native-born workers there to below the national average. Just as firms, native-born workers are mobile. Since the wages they are obtaining are now below the national norm, some begin to move away. This reduces labor supplies in areas where immigrants settle, raising somewhat the wages there. The local labor supply could decline until wages increased back to the national norm. This could explain why statistical studies did not find wage differentials between high and low immigrant urban areas.

While this *mobility effect* is theoretically possible, the empirical evidence is uneven. However, a recent study of migration trends by William Frey seems to strongly support the mobility thesis. He found that the six states with the highest number of immigrants—California, New York, Texas, Illinois, New Jersey, and Massachusetts—had undergone major outmigration of the native-born population. As the mobility thesis would predict, this outmigration was disproportionately high among groups which face particularly strong competition from immigrant labor: high school graduates, high school dropouts, and low-income residents.[32]

Even if we ignore the mobility effect, there are other reasons why many studies found a limited adverse wage effect. Immigration might have had a substantial *service effect*. Immigrants add to the total population so that they induce a growth of government services and infrastructure. If these services and infrastructure expenditures are net additions, they generate additional employment and production in the local economies in which immigrants settle.

The service effect increases the employment of white-collar workers and professionals who provide these services: social workers, educational personnel, and medical providers. This expansion may also provide some upward mobility for production workers, further reducing the displacement effect described above. For example, Roger Waldinger found that during the 1970s, black workers left the garment industry for expanded government employment.[33]

Since 1980, the service effect has lessened considerably. While the demand for social services has increased, government expenditures have not been as responsive. For example, "Between 1985 and 1992, the number of limited-English-language proficient children in the nation's schools rose by 65 percent, to about 2.5 million. During the same period, federal spending on bilingual education rose by only 4 percent."[34]

Michael Piore and Thomas Muller suggest that there are additional benefits from the employment expansion created by immigration. The growth caused by immigrant labor will also increase the demand for goods produced by firms that do not use immigrant labor. In particular, the additional workers hired will buy more consumer goods creating a *multiplier effect*. The multiplier effect also includes increased capital investment, reflecting immigrant home buying and business formation. Indeed, if the multiplier effect is robust enough, total employment may rise sufficiently to offset the initial adverse wage effects.

The multiplier and service effects suggest that the earnings and employment of most native-born workers are enhanced by immigrant labor. Many of these workers also benefit from a *consumer effect* since they are often direct consumers of services provided by immigrants. Almost 60 percent of employed Salvadoran women in the Los Angeles area are private household workers.[35] As a result, immigration lowers the cost of household child-care and cleaning services. In addition, home-care attendants for the elderly are disproportionately immigrant women. Without this supply, many more of the elderly could not afford to stay in their homes and would be forced to choose alternatives which they consider inferior, such as nursing homes or residence with other family members.

The service, multiplier, and consumer effects suggest that only a limited share of native-born workers—those in direct competition— are harmed by immigration. Though immigrants are less than 10 percent of the overall labor force, between 1979 and 1997, their share of high school dropouts, ages twenty-five and older, rose from 15.7 to 23.4 percent. For this reason, a number of researchers have focused on measuring the effects of immigration on the wages of unskilled workers, and their studies have found that immigration has a significant dampening effect on wages in this labor market. For example, the 1997 National Science Council report found that while immigration has benefited the vast majority of native-born workers, it has caused the wages of native-born dropouts to decline by 5 percent.[36]

A study by the economist Cordelia Reimers suggests that the adverse effect on native-born dropouts is not uniform. She found that negative effects were concentrated on native black and white male dropouts who were earning above-average wages, given their educational attainment. Apparently, immigration harmed primarily those dropouts who were benefiting from unionization and seniority. In contrast, she found that native Mexican American dropouts benefited, probably because they are bilingual so that they can serve as supervisors of the Spanish-speaking new immigrants.[37]

In his study of Los Angeles labor markets, the sociologist Roger Waldinger also found that black dropouts were harmed by immigration. He claims that "the story of black displacement in restaurants and hotels can be traced not to [black] skill upgrading, but rather to competition with a rapidly growing immigrant population." Similarly, economists David Howell and Elizabeth Mueller identified the adverse effects of immigration on black employment in New York City. They identified the twelve largest employment niches for African American men and African American women. For each group, these jobs provided about 20 percent of their total employment in New York City. In virtually all of these twenty-four job niches, the share of immigrant workers doubled between 1980 and 1990, suggesting increased competition and declining earnings. This evidence led the *New York Times* to editorialize against extending citizenship to illegal immigrants who they argued were responsible for "the widening of the gap between the wages of high school dropouts and all other workers."[38]

The Economic Welfare of Immigrants

When assessing the situation of immigrant workers, two major issues emerge: (1) judging the fairness of the wages and working conditions they obtain; and (2) estimating their utilization of social welfare programs.

Immigrant Workers: Wages and Working Conditions

Unions often argue that capitalists benefit from immigration because it enables them to exploit defenseless workers. Unions point to the lack of safety regulations and the resulting indus-trial accidents in sweatshops during periods of high immigration. Ac-cording to Vernon Briggs, a leading proponent of this viewpoint: "The alien workers are also frequently victimized by employers who know of their vulnerability to detection. Accounts of alien workers . . . being personally abused are legion. For as one government official who de-cried the exploitation of alien workers exclaimed, 'Nobody gives a damn, since aliens are nobody's constituents.'"[39]

In contrast, the business community generally rejects any notion that capitalists profit from their ability to employ workers unfairly. They even contend that government-imposed industrial safety require-ments often harmed immigrant workers. Let us detail the basis for these competing assessments of the impact of government intervention on immigrant workers.

Earlier we examined Paul Krugman's dismissal of claims that transnational corporations exploit workers in developing countries. Instead, he argued that workers were the main beneficiaries of unregu-lated capitalist enterprises, and they would be harmed if U.S. poli-cies restricted their employment. Similarly, pro-market economists contend that safety regulations are another example of how govern-ment policies harm groups by restricting employment. Whereas gov-ernment restrictions on the labor practices of transnational corporations would harm workers in developing countries, safety regulations harm U.S. workers by restricting the employment choices available to them (see Figure 6.2).

The wage-offer curve *ABC* plots all the combinations of units of safety and wage rates at which a typical firm obtains "competitive" profits—profits similar to those normally earned in most industries. One combination the firm can offer and still obtain "competitive" prof-its is a wage rate equal to $6.75 per hour and four units of safety. Since this competitive firm has no excess profits, it can provide additional units of safety only if workers are willing to accept wage cuts sufficient to pay for them. For this reason, the wage-offer curve is downward sloping: There is an inverse relationship between the wages these com-petitive firms are able to offer and the safety which they can profitably

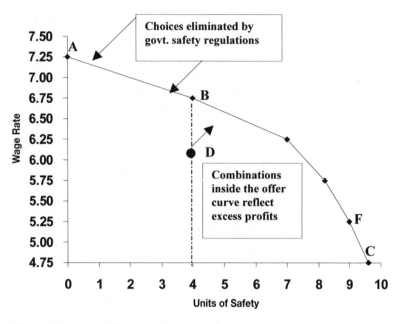

Figure 6.2 Wage Offer Curve for Firms in Competitive Industries.

provide. If workers desire nine units of safety, they must accept a $5.25 wage rate (combination *F*).

Combinations on the wage-offer curve are the *maximum* offers firms would be willing to make. What if firms were able to obtain excess profits by hiring workers at wage and benefit packages inside the wage-offer curve? For example, suppose that firms in the industry were able to hire workers for only $6.25 per hour while supplying four units of safety—combination *D*. According to the pro-market model, this situation could not persist. Since firms would be obtaining excess profits, this encourages new firms to enter the industry. If labor was fully employed, these new firms must offer improved wages and benefit packages to attract workers away from their present employment. Older firms must follow suit or risk losing their best workers. New firms would continue to enter the industry with more generous wages and benefit packages until all firms obtain only "competitive" profits. Thus, the invisible hand of competitive markets—not unions, not government intervention—eliminated the exploitation workers experienced.

Moreover, it is workers who determine the actual benefit package they receive by weighing the value of additional units of safety against the necessary wage reduction. Workers who place a high value on safety would choose more safety and lower wages than workers who place little value on safety. At one extreme, workers who place a very low value on their safety might prefer $7.25 per hour with no safety (combination *A*).

Now suppose that the government decides it must protect workers from unsafe conditions by requiring firms to provide at least *two units* of safety. This would adversely affect those workers who prefer fewer than two units of safety. After the imposition of government safety standards, firms can no longer offer these workers their preferred choice.

Using this model, Thomas Sowell contends that turn-of-the-century immigrant workers gained from the lack of safety provisions. Sowell builds on studies that claim that immigrant workers had poor skills and that only by trading off safety were they able to earn *barely* sufficient income to provide for their families. In support of this viewpoint, data collected in 1908 by the U.S. Immigration Commission found that garment wages were 8 percent above average and nearly equal that of native-born workers.[40]

Though their incomes were low, an environment conducive to upward mobility was created. With livable wages and stable employment, workers could master skills that eventually raised their wages and provided the social infrastructure for the upward mobility of their children. In contrast, any safety requirements would have forced immigrant workers to receive lower wages, undermining the employment and family stability necessary for advancement. Thus, claims that low-waged workers require government intervention are not only misguided but could harm the intended beneficiaries.

The same perspective is found in contemporary writings. Similar to Sowell, Borjas rejects the claim that illegals are exploited. He states,

> These individuals obviously benefit from being in the United States, for otherwise they would simply return to their country of origin where they could avoid the exploitation and stigma attached to illegal status. . . . In fact, after controlling for [age, English proficiency, and skills], illegal aliens have essentially the same wage rate as legal immigrants. . . . Therefore, despite the frequent claims of exploitation, the available (though limited) evidence suggests that U.S. labor market . . . operated in a way that did not penalize illegal aliens. . . . Illegal aliens in the United States have lower wages than legal

immigrants not because they are illegal, but because they are
less skilled.[41]

As just presented, the pro-market model infers that workers in early
twentieth-century sweatshops were not exploited by their employers,
nor are contemporary workers who are employed in meatpacking, clothing, and shoe industries. However, these claims should not be accepted
uncritically. Relative wage data only prove at best that garment workers were paid as fairly as other low-waged (noncraft) manufacturing
workers during the first wave of immigration; that low-waged illegals
are paid as fairly as legal low-waged workers during the current wave.
However, the evidence cited is still consistent with the thesis that *all*
low-waged workers are underpaid in an environment where there are
excess workers available.

Just as the Ric Burns documentary claimed, with the presence of
large numbers of immigrants, wages and working conditions were bid
downward. If an especially restricted labor force is available—children
in nineteenth-century England or illegals in late twentieth-century
America—workers are allocated to the most dangerous jobs. However,
in the early twentieth century, with open immigration and child labor laws enforced, U.S. owners had to pay a modest wage premium
to attract workers to the most dangerous jobs—not as much as they
would have had to if labor markets were fully employed. It was little
consolation that the benefits from this exploitation accrued to consumers.

Similarly, during this current immigration wave, the wages and
working conditions of all low-waged workers fell dramatically. For
example, between 1973 and 1995, the hourly wage of the lowest-paid
20 percent of male workers fell by over 18 percent after adjusting for
inflation. It has only been since 1996—when unemployment rates fell
to historic levels—that wages for this group of workers have risen relative to inflation. Thus, critics contend that immigrants remain vulnerable to exploitation when labor markets are unregulated and there is
significant unemployment.[42]

Immigrant Workers: Government Transfer
Programs

In 1970, legal immigrants had a lower participation rate in social welfare programs than non-immigrants. However, over the next two decades this situation changed dramatically. Despite changes in the U.S.
economy, more than one-third of all immigrants twenty-five years and

older continued to have less than a high school education. Moreover, the number of parents of U.S. citizens admitted annually through family unification provisions doubled between 1980 and 1990. Low levels of education and an increased number of dependent parents had a dramatic impact on poverty rates among immigrant households. Between 1979 and 1997, their poverty rate grew from 15.5 to 21.8 percent while it remained constant at 12 percent among native-born households. As a result of family unification, from 1986 to 1996, the number of noncitizens receiving Supplemental Security Income (SSI) benefits increased about 230 percent. By 1995, slightly more than half the SSI benefits provided to the elderly were collected by noncitizens.[43]

To understand more clearly the fiscal impact of immigration, the National Research Council estimated the taxes immigrants in New Jersey and California paid and the government expenditures they received in 1995. In both states, immigrants paid slightly more federal taxes than the federal expenditures they received. However, state and local expenditures on immigrants far outpaced state and local taxes collected. As a result, immigrants imposed an added tax burden of $232 on each native household in New Jersey and $1,178 in California.[44]

Pro-immigration economists contend that these numbers overestimate the financial problems caused by immigrants. Poverty rates and tax-benefit estimates are dominated by the experience of the most recently immigrated households who are underpaid relative to their skills. For example, at time of entry, immigrant workers in 1990 earned about 25 percent less than comparably skilled native-born workers. It is therefore quite likely that initially these immigrants will experience above-average poverty rates and pay less taxes than the value of the benefits they receive from social programs. However, economic studies generally find that immigrants, as they gain language skills, reduce the earnings gap over time.[45] Given their expected relative earnings growth, it is likely that over their lifetime of residency in the United States, most immigrants will pay more total taxes to fund government social services than the value of total benefits received.

Also, immigrants are no more likely to be on welfare or other social programs than other residents of the *state* they live in. Immigrants have a higher national participation rate because they disproportionately live in states that have above-average welfare participation rates. Economic studies demonstrate, however, that immigration location is not based on the generous welfare certain states provide but on their high average incomes and job potentials.[46]

Table 6.1   Welfare Participation Rates by National Origin Group, 1990

REFUGEE-INTENSIVE COUNTRIES		ABOVE AVERAGE NON-REFUGEE-INTENSIVE COUNTRIES	
Cambodia	48.8	Dominican Republic	27.9
Laos	46.3	Ecuador	11.9
Vietnam	25.8	Mexico	11.3
U.S.S.R.	16.3	China	10.4
Cuba	16.0	Philippines	9.8

SOURCE: George Borjas, "The Economics of Immigration," *Journal of Economic Literature* 32 (December 1994): Table 1.

Finally, poverty rates and tax-benefit estimates do not distinguish immigrants who came as refugees seeking political asylum from other immigrants. This distinction becomes important when we look at the 1990 welfare participation rates of countries with rates above the average for all immigrant-headed households (see Table 6.1). A refugee-intensive country was defined as a country in which more than two-thirds of immigrants were admitted because they were fleeing political persecution. Refugee-intensive countries have much higher rates of utilization of social programs than other countries. Although refugee-intensive countries contributed only 11 percent of immigrants during the 1980s, they accounted for 39 percent of immigrants from that decade who were receiving welfare benefits at the time of the 1990 census. Whereas 9.7 percent of immigrant households were receiving welfare that year, the proportion of welfare immigrant households from all nonrefugee-intensive countries was only 6.7 percent—below the participation rate for native-born households (7.4 percent). Since entry of refugee groups is based upon humanitarian concerns, they should not be included when evaluating legislative policies that affect other immigrants.[47]

Public Policy Implications

Immigration has generated antagonistic relationships between native-born and immigrant groups. During the first wave, the AFL leadership fought for legislation to restrict immigration and was unwilling to seek unity within the workplace. In contrast, during the second wave, the conflict arises most visibly between native-born small business owners and their immigrant competitors rather than among production workers. These antagonistic relationships have been amplified by anti-immigrant ideologies. During the first wave these ideologies claimed that the newer immigrants were from a distinct and inferior white race. This viewpoint was embraced by liberal social reformers and union leaders. Today, anti-immigrant ideology generates fears that nonwhite immigration will undermine important European values.

Capitalists have at times embraced and promoted these racial ideologies. However, anti-immigration movements have been successful only when the benefits capitalists obtain from open immigration begin to wane. This occurred after World War I, leading to the passage of the 1923 Immigration Restriction Bill. Today, it is unlikely that capitalists have a strong stake in maintaining current *legal* immigration levels. The largest capitalists hire few legal immigrants so that they are more concerned with protecting temporary visas to hire foreign-born professional workers than legal immigration. The smaller capitalists have low-wage labor-intensive production so that they are probably more concerned with the supply of illegal than legal immigrants.

There is growing evidence that native-born production workers and some technical-support professionals have been adversely affected by immigration. Initial studies did not identify this impact because of the mobility effect: the moving of native-born workers away from areas in which immigrants located. Moreover, during the 1970s, many native-born production workers, who were initially displaced by immigrant labor, found new employment as a result of the service and multiplier effects. It is in the more recent period when the service and multiplier effects have become quite small that the adverse consequences may have become more substantial.

Whatever the adverse effects have been on production workers, the majority of native-born workers and households benefit from current immigration. Due to language and credential barriers, most native-born workers have jobs which are complementary rather than in competition with immigrant workers. In addition, the service and multiplier effects substantially increase professional employment. Finally, consumers have benefited from immigration since it has lowered the price of many goods, especially household services.

For all of these reasons, it is unlikely that racialists will be successful in restricting immigration. The 1996 welfare bill was a substitute for a restrictive immigration bill. Given the tremendous desire to enter the United States, it did not reduce legal or illegal immigration;

both grew substantially and were about one-third higher than 1980s levels. Instead, these changes—which were repealed in 1998—simply reduced temporarily the social wage that immigrants can expect to receive, becoming even more underpaid.

There does seem to be increasing concern with the impact immigration is having on less-educated native-born workers. Some are forced to move away from immigrant areas to avoid job competition. Immigrants also may have absorbed government resources that might otherwise have been used to service the needs of native-born poor households. In particular, financial resources are stretched in high immigrant areas, diluting the quality of social service and educational resources provided.

It would be a mistake, however, to focus solely on the impact of immigration on low-wage labor markets and government services. There are more serious issues created by the influx of high-skilled immigrants through new quotas and temporary visa programs. These immigrants may be quite damaging to the upward mobility of native-born workers. As long as foreign-born workers provide a cheap source of technical labor, corporations have little concern for upgrading educational institutions, and stagnating salaries discourage native-born workers from entering these fields.

This certainly is the view held by many witnesses before congressional immigration hearings. They note that almost all the claims of severe shortages of technical labor are based on studies done by the tech companies. These witnesses cite the selectivity of the tech companies who are unwilling to hire thousands of trained U.S. applicants who are underemployed. Silicon Valley headhunter Linda Tuerk believes that companies are doing this because they can save a substantial amount of money. "Companies are firing older, more expensive workers—people making 80 grand—and they can turn right around and hire two people right off the plane for 45 grand each," Tuerk said.[48] Therefore, it might be more advantageous for immigration opponents to focus on the temporary visa programs rather than being sidetracked into attacks on the most vulnerable immigrants.

7

The Rise of Working Women
Race, Class, and Gender Matters

Over the last thirty years, the situation of women has been radically transformed. Family television sitcoms of the 1960s seem distant from our reality. Today, the idea of living their lives through the exploits of other family members is foreign to the vast majority of women. While they may lament the strains of leading double lives, most women with children now also work outside the home.

Historically, women were excluded from a majority of occupations. Working-class women labored in low-waged light manufacturing industries, like textiles and electronics, or as sales and clerical workers. College-educated women dominated the nursing, librarian, and teaching professions. By increasing labor supplies and competition for employment in a narrow band of occupations, wages were lowered, increasing the gender earnings gap. As more and more women entered the labor force, and occupational crowding decreased, the wage gap between men and women lessened. This breaking down of occupational barriers has been crucial to the economic advancement of women. However, we will find that substantial barriers still persist in occupations that do not require a college education so that, in this labor sector, significant gender earnings disparities remain.

The persistence of exclusionary barriers is just one reason why women continue to earn only 75 percent as much as men. Many women who have gained access to better-paying professions do not earn as much as their male counterparts because of the glass-ceiling phenomenon: the inability of women to advance due to discriminatory promotional procedures. At least part of the gender earnings gap, however, reflects the higher wages men receive for greater work experience, longer hours worked, and accepting unfavorable working conditions. These disparities often reflect the constraints child-rearing responsibilities place on women rather than direct labor market discrimination. The extent to which the gender earnings gap is due to discrimination rather than these other factors will be detailed below.

Finally, it would be inappropriate to discuss gender issues without including a discussion of class and racial differences among women. There has been a growing gap between the earnings of college and noncollege graduates. In 1967, college graduates earned almost 50 percent more than workers with only a high school degree. By 1995, college graduates earned 70 percent more than high school graduates.[1] This growing earnings gap exists just as much for women as men, making it increasingly necessary to analyze gender earnings differences in these two distinct labor markets separately. Similarly, there is no reason to believe that black and white women have had similar labor market experiences. As labor market barriers to women have begun to crumble, they have done so more rapidly for white women than for black women, especially when the role of affirmative action employment waned in the 1980s. The decline in government welfare programs has also had a disproportional effect on low-waged labor markets where black women are more heavily concentrated. Thus, class and race issues must be an important part of our inquiry.

The Changing Position of Women in the Labor Market

The clearest indicator of the evolving position of women is the change in labor force participation rates. At any point in time, the labor force participation rate (LFPR) estimates the percentage of the noninstitutionalized population that is either working or actively engaged in job search. In 1959, for workers sixteen years or older, there was a 46.6 percentage-point gender gap, meaning that 83.4 percent of men but only 36.8 percent of women were in the active labor force (see Figure 7.1). Forty years later, the gender gap had been reduced to 14.7 percentage points. The most telling change, however, has been for married women with children. Their LFPRs increased from 27.6 percent in 1960 to 71.1 percent by 1997, virtually the same as

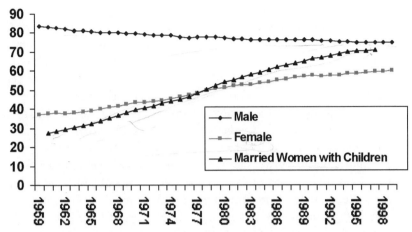

Figure 7.1 Labor Force Participation Rates, 1959–1999. *Source: U.S. Bureau of Labor Statistics, Employment and Earnings (Washington, D.C.: Government Printing Office, January 2000).*

for comparably aged women without children. Thus, at the beginning of the new millennium, women with and without children are deciding to work at the same rate and that rate does not significantly differ from that of men.

While female LFPRs increased in a relatively continuous fashion from 1959 forward, increases in the ratio of average female to male earnings—the gender earnings ratio—did not really begin until the late 1970s. This reflected the way in which the expanding female labor force was integrated into the economy. During the first decade after World War II, the female LFPR increased from 30.8 to 36.9 percent. This increase was disproportionately among older and less-educated women. While the majority was absorbed in clerical labor markets and expanding service industries, many went to work in manufacturing, especially as machine operators.[2]

Since the rapid expansion crowded most women into traditional female occupations, wages in those jobs stagnated. In addition, their employment expansion in the manufacturing sector was disproportionately in nonunionized companies so that female operators were less well paid than their unionized male counterparts. As a result, between 1955 (the first year for which the rate was tabulated) and 1961, the gender earnings ratio among full-time year-round workers *declined* from 63.9 to 60.8 percent.[3]

To a large extent, this pattern continued through the 1960s with the next major shift occurring during the 1970s. At the time, most women still considered paid employment only when household finances required it. Most striking was the low LFPR of white women with a college degree. Whereas the 1970 participation rate of black female college graduates twenty-five to fifty-four years old was 92 percent, it was only 59 percent for white female college graduates.[4]

As new white female college graduates raised their participation rates, it did increase the gender earnings ratio substantially for younger workers, aged twenty-five to thirty-four years old, from 64.9 to 68.5 percent between 1970 and 1980. However, there was only a modest change in the pattern of exclusionary employment practices so that most older women were still trapped in traditional occupations. As a result, the gender earnings ratio for workers aged forty-five to sixty-four years old declined from 57.7 to 53 percent, while the overall gender earnings ratio was virtually unchanged.

Between 1980 and 1990, when measured by the usual weekly wage, the gender earnings ratio for full-time workers rose from 64.4 to 71.9 percent. To some extent, this reflected the breaking down of exclusionary barriers as women entered higher-paying occupations. Unfortunately, however, it also reflected the decline in male wages as a result of the disappearance of high-waged unionized manufacturing jobs, disproportionately held by men.

The gender earnings ratio rose to 77.1 percent by 1993, as male wages continued to decline. Afterward, male wages began to increase and the gender earnings ratio was essentially unchanged, equaling 76.9 percent in 1999. If younger workers are excluded and those working less than full-time are included, there was a small rise after 1993. However, the overall evidence suggests that a plateau had been reached where the typical female workers received only three-quarters as much as the typical male worker.

Given the lack of significant overall improvement, let us look more closely at the impact of the 1990s economic boom on various groups of female workers. The labor market can be subdivided regionally and into two distinct sectors: those occupations that require some college and those that do not. In every region, between 1991 and 1997, the gender earnings ratio in the college-required sector increased at least 1.7 percentage points and more than 3 percentage points in New England, Mountain, and Pacific regions—regions in which there was particularly large reductions in occupational segregation (see Figure 7.2). In contrast, in the Mid-Atlantic, Midwest, and Plains regions—the re-

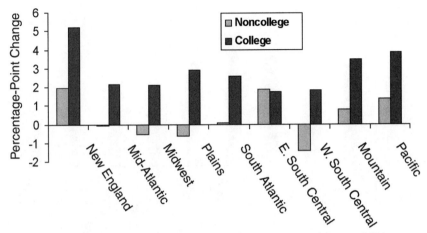

Figure 7.2 Changes in Gender Earnings Ratio by Occupational Sector, 1991–1997. *Source: Heather Boushey and Robert Cherry, "The Economic Boom and Women: Issues of Race, Class, and Regionalism," manuscript, 1999.*

gions most associated with the older goods producing industries—the gender earnings ratio in the noncollege sector declined. This seems to indicate that a substantial share of the rising regional gender earnings ratios was the result of relative wage gains made by women in the college-required sector.[5]

One might conjecture that the three regions that had the largest increase in gender earnings ratios—New England, Mountain, and Pacific—might have done so because of a particularly large increase in the share of women in the college-required sector. In every region, there was a substantial increase in the share of all women who were employed in the college-required sector but these three regions were not among those with the greatest increases (see Figure 7.3). To some degree, what distinguished the three regions was the lack of growth of the male work force in the college-required occupations. Indeed, New England and the Mountain regions were the only two regions in which the share of men in the college-required sector declined.

If we define the class ratio as the ratio of the average wage paid in the noncollege sector to the average wage paid in the college-required sector, the smaller the ratio, the larger the class gap. During the expansion, the wages of women grew more in the college-required than the noncollege-required sector, creating a growing class gap among women in eight of the nine regions. In contrast, the economic expansion was relatively favorable for working-class men so that, in most

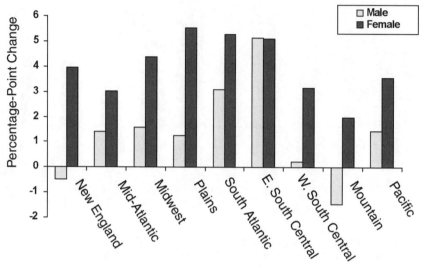

Figure 7.3 Changes in Share of Women and Men in the College-Required Sector, 1991–1997. *Source: Heather Boushey and Robert Cherry, "The Economic Boom and Women: Issues of Race, Class, and Regionalism," manuscript, 1999.*

regions, the class gap among men declined. As a result, by 1997, the class gap was larger among women than among men in every region.[6]

Measuring Labor Market Discrimination

While the movement of women into college-required occupations have been substantial and earnings inequities in that labor sector have declined, disparities between the average earnings of men and women persist. Since women have at least as many years of schooling as men, educational differences cannot explain these remaining disparities. However, there are other factors affecting productivity that must be accounted for. In particular, a significant number of women have historically had discontinuous labor market experience due to their child-rearing responsibilities. As a result, as men and women age, their years of work experience diverge. In 1989, men and women had, on average, 17.4 and 12.7 years of full-time work experience, respectively. Correcting for this difference would have raised the gender earnings ratio from 72.4 to 79.6 percent.

In addition, men and women tend to work in different industries. In 1989, 42 percent of men but only 15 percent of women worked in mining, construction, durable manufacturing, and transportation. These are industries that require substantial physical exertion and an increased safety risk. As a result, workers should legitimately receive higher wages to compensate them for these onerous working conditions. These are also industries in which the average workweek of full-time workers is substantially higher than that in the white-collar and service industries where women are concentrated. Finally, these are industries that are the most heavily unionized. If men and women worked in the same industries and had the same level of union representation, the gender earnings ratio would have increased still further to 86.9 percent. The remaining gap suggests that, even in occupations where men and women are equal in numbers, women still have a lower probability of ascending to the higher-paying job categories. These barriers are referred to as the glass ceiling.

Occupational Segregation

The sex dissimilarity index measures the level of gender imbalances in the labor market. Using a variety of occupational groupings, studies estimated the index to be about 60 percent in 1960 and 1970. This means that 60 percent of women would have had to change occupations in order to bring about full gender occupational equality. At that time, pro-market economists claimed that this imbalance was a matter of personal choice. Gary Becker reasoned that "women spend less time in the labor market than men and, therefore, [they] have less incentive to invest in market skills." Moreover, he argued, that since "women want their investment to be useful both as a housewife and as a participant in the labor market," they will naturally choose occupations which mirror household activities: nursing, teaching, and other helping professions.[7]

For much of the next decade, sex dissimilarity indexes declined modestly; only during the 1980s did they fall substantially. This was primarily due to the movement toward equality within *expanding* occupations, like retail sales, where women had already gained a *significant* foothold. About 31 percent of all male workers were in these occupations in 1978, as compared to 15 percent of all female workers. In 1988, the share of all male workers had increased only slightly to 32 percent but the share of female workers had increased to 25 percent. In contrast, there was little change in blue-collar occupations in which less than 5 percent of female workers were employed. Over 35 percent of all men worked in these job categories. Segregation declined

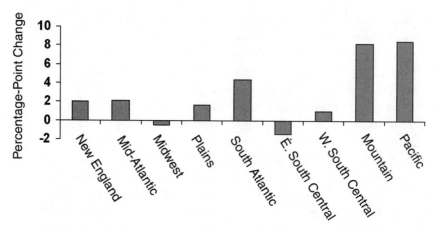

Figure 7.4 Reduction in Sex Dissimilarity Indexes, 1991–1997. *Source: Heather Boushey and Robert Cherry, "The Economic Boom and Women: Issues of Race, Class, and Regionalism," manuscript, 1999.*

primarily in those labor markets in which some college education was required. For workers with no more than a high school degree, sex segregation actually increased.[8]

There were substantial changes in the sex segregation index across regions for the period 1991 to 1997 (see Figure 7.4). The dissimilarity index declined by almost 5 percent in the South Atlantic region and by over 8 percent in the Mountain and Pacific regions, where production and employment opportunities were growing rapidly. More generally, the sex dissimilarity index seems to have declined more in regions associated with the new information-age industries than in regions associated with the old goods-producing industries.

While the overall reduction of sex segregation has been modest, there have been important breakthroughs for female college graduates. In the 1960s, Becker's thesis had some credibility. At that time, women comprised less than one-seventh of the majors in computer science, architecture, natural and physical sciences, economics, and business.[9] However, Becker failed to acknowledge that these choices often reflected adaptation to employer discrimination, as well as the obstacles female undergraduates faced when they attempted to major in male-dominated fields. Regardless of the reasons, however, it is true that women did not have the same careers as men did.

By the 1990s, the situation had changed dramatically as women comprised about 30 percent of computer science, architecture, natu-

**Table 7.1 Percentage of Females in Selected Professional
Occupations, 1970 and 1999**

OCCUPATIONS	1970	1999
Architects	4.0	15.7
Computer Systems Analysts	13.6	28.5
Economists	15.9	51.2
Lawyers	4.9	28.8
Management Analysts	10.3	43.2
Market, Advertising, and Public Relations Managers	7.9	37.6
Physicians	9.7	24.5
Purchasing Managers	8.5	47.4

SOURCES: U.S. Bureau of the Census, *Detailed Occupations of the Experienced Civilian Labor Force,* Supplemental Report PC80–S1-15 (Washington, D.C.: Government Printing Office, March 1984); and U.S. Department of Labor, *Employment and Earnings* (Washington, D.C.: Government Printing Office, January 2000), Table 11.

ral and physical science, and economics majors and almost one-half of all business majors. Moreover, there was a dramatic change in female enrollment in postgraduate programs in high-paying fields. In 1969, women represented 3.2 percent of the MBA students, 3.8 percent of law students, and 6.7 percent of medical students. By 1993, women comprised 34.6 percent of MBA students, 42.5 percent of law students, and 37.7 percent of medical students.[10] These educational changes dramatically altered the occupational choices of women (see Table 7.1).

However, the crowding of women into the lowest-paid white-collar and professional fields, such as pre-school teachers, still exists. And as long as there is a greater supply of applicants, wages in these occupations will be depressed relative to male-dominated occupations. In 1999, for each additional percentage point a managerial or professional occupation was male, the usual weekly wage increased by $4.30. For example, an occupation that is 60 percent male would be expected to have a usual weekly wage $86 more than one that is only 40 percent male. Similar disparities occur in technical, sales, and administrative support occupations. In these fields, the average weekly wage increases by $3.25 for each additional percentage point the occupation was male. Thus, even in occupations where physical exertion, occupational safety, and overtime play no role, the more men employed, the higher the average wage.[11]

Glass-Ceiling Effects

While some occupational barriers persist in the college-required sector, only 15 percent of gender wage disparities in this sector reflect differences in wages across occupations. Since the vast proportion of the gender earnings gap reflects wage disparities within occupations, glass-ceiling effects are clearly a major barrier professional women face. Studies have consistently documented the inability of women to progress professionally at the same rate as comparable men.

At the beginning of this book it was noted that the 1995 salaries of men who matriculated at the most selective colleges in 1976 were 65 percent higher than the salaries of female matriculants after adjusting for class rank.[12] A more extensive study followed the careers of men and women who graduated the University of Michigan's Law School in the early 1970s. At the beginning of their careers, there were little earnings differences between men and women. However, after fifteen years, women earned only 60 percent as much as men. Some of the difference reflected the shorter hours women tended to work. However, after controlling for this and other skill factors, women would still have earned 20 percent less.[13]

The lack of upward mobility is most apparent at the senior management levels. Indeed, in many fields in which women represent a majority of the profession, men dominate the senior positions. For example, this was true in many of the health fields for a long time. Directors of speech and hearing clinics or nursing departments at hospitals were invariably men, even though the vast majority of practitioners in both fields were women. In public school after public school, the principal was male even though the vast majority of primary and secondary schoolteachers were women.

The differential ascendancy to top positions is not a matter of job tenure—the number of years working for the same company. Among college-educated individuals, men and women have about the same turnover rate.[14] However, men have a substantially higher return to job tenure than women. Economists Joyce Jacobsen and Laurence Levin estimate that in 1991, after ten years of work with the same employer, white male college graduates would be earning 50 percent more than their starting wage level whereas white female graduates would be earning only 35 percent more. These differential gains do not necessarily reflect discriminatory procedures. Men continue to be more likely to obtain advanced education credentials, such as doctorates, that are often used as requirements for senior positions.[15]

Social factors are also an important reason for career advancement disparities. Women have more difficulty balancing career and family because they still take on more of the family burden than men. It continues to be more acceptable for men to use evenings to further their careers by improving their educational credentials, working overtime, or undertaking social networking. Thus even without overt discrimination by employers, many women are still unable to gain the added credentials and experience necessary for leadership positions.

Child rearing continues to be primarily the responsibility of mothers. However, men who seek a more active role in family spheres are also penalized. When their wives work, these men sometimes have to sacrifice work effort to care for sick children and often do not volunteer for assignments that would take too much time away from household responsibilities. Studies find that the average wage of professional men who have working wives is 10 percent lower than equally skilled men whose wives do not work. While family standards of living are improved when both spouses work, child-rearing responsibilities limit their career advancement.

The lack of women in leadership positions is most striking in the corporate world. In 1990, only 2.6 percent of the officers of Fortune 500 companies were female; in only the apparel industry did it rise above 10 percent. Over the next nine years, the picture changed. By 1995, 8.7 percent of all Fortune 500 officers were female, rising to 11.9 percent by 1999.[16]

In 1999, forty-one companies filled one quarter or more of their corporate officer positions with women, up from twenty-five in 1995. In 1990, only 1.5 and 5.1 percent of corporate officers in transportation equipment and publishing, respectively, were women. In 1999, about 25 percent of the corporate officers in both industries were women. Thus, while women continue to be underrepresented, there seems to be substantial improvement.[17]

A study done by Catalyst, a Wall Street consulting firm, found that women face barriers to entry well beyond their ability to balance family and work. For example, women have to adopt male management styles to make men feel comfortable. This often requires learning about sports and being able to play golf. In addition, women have less access to mentors without whom corporate advancement is virtually impossible.

As a result, women are less likely to be elevated to major policy-making positions. For example, in 1991, women held only 5.1 percent of "clout" positions, such as chief operating officer, president, or chair. Similarly, women represented only 3.3 percent of the top earners—the five highest-paid officers in each of the Fortune 500 companies.[18]

Pay-Equity Proposals

In attempting to close the gender earnings gap between men and women, most economists have focused on increasing the educational attainment of women so that more could enter professional employment. This strategy has been largely successful. Women have increased their representation in professional occupations, and because of equal employment opportunity policies, many barriers to the highest-paying fields have been broken down. As a result, occupation segregation and earnings disparities have been substantially overcome in professional labor markets. This contrasts with the noncollege sector where in 1997 more than one-third of the gender earnings gap was due to women and men being in different occupations.[19]

In an ideal world these disparities would be eliminated as the number of workers seeking employment in the lower-paying field declines while those in the higher-paying field increases. As long as there are no barriers to movement into the higher-paying fields, this process of adjustment can be relied upon. In many blue-collar occupations, however, historic barriers are not easily overcome and the ability to monitor individual hirings may be limited. As a result, many male-dominated blue-collar occupations have been resistant to female entry.

The persistence of these exclusionary barriers led many feminists to recommend that, in the noncollege labor sector, direct government intervention to promote "pay equity" was necessary. Beginning in the 1970s, they demanded that comparable-worth studies, rather than prevailing market conditions, should determine wages in traditional female occupations. This approach underpinned President Clinton's 2000 recommendation to create government wage guidelines.

Comparable-worth proposals assume that objective measures would allow investigators to compare the productive worth of different occupations. Each occupation would be evaluated and allocated a number of points based upon the following: (1) required knowledge and skills; (2) mental demands; (3) accountability; and (4) work conditions. Occupations that scored the same number of total points would be considered equivalent and thus receive the same salaries.

Beginning in the 1970s, many governmental units began to explore using comparable-worth evaluations to determine wage scales. A comparable-worth study in the state of Washington found that women received 20 percent lower pay than men for jobs requiring equal skill and responsibility. For example, on all four components of the job evaluation scale, registered nurses received higher scores than higher-paid civil engineers. Once the state of Washington enacted comparable-worth legislation, the gender earnings ratio rose from 76 percent in 1980 to 86 percent in 1986. In Minnesota, implementation of comparable-worth policies resulted in a similar increase in the gender earnings ratio, from 74 to 82 percent between 1980 and 1986.

Pro-market economists were quick to point out the problems that occur when government imposes wage structures. Comparable worth raises labor costs since female job categories have their wages raised to match their comparable male job categories. This might cause some firms to reduce female employment. Also, efficiency losses occur since wage incentives cannot be used to adjust to growing demand for certain jobs. Without raising wages to remain competitive where qualified workers are scarce, employers would be forced to hire unqualified applicants. For these reasons, government adoption of comparative-worth guidelines may raise the cost or reduce the quality of services provided.

Staffing problems in high schools and colleges highlight the potential harm that can result from comparable-worth policies. All public high schools have fixed pay schedules that are independent of specialty; English teachers are paid the same as math teachers with the same years of schooling and job experience. However, math teachers have skills that are more highly valued in the private sector than are the skills of English teachers. As a result, most urban school districts have difficulty recruiting math teachers and an oversupply of English teachers. School systems adapt by lowering their hiring standards for math teachers. This might help explain the poor performance of public school students on nationwide math tests.

Similarly, universities often have salary structures that require classics and finance faculty to be paid salaries based only upon professional qualifications. However, finance instructors have higher-paying private-sector employment alternatives than do classics professors. As a result, most colleges find it difficult to recruit finance instructors while they have no trouble obtaining first-rate classics instructors. These distortions do not occur at colleges where faculty pay is not constrained by notions of comparable worth. In these institutions, a finance instructor just out of graduate school may earn as much as a classics or philosophy professor with twenty years of solid experience. While humanities professors may lament the vocationalization of academe, these adjustments are necessary to maintain quality instruction in applied areas where instructors have lucrative private-industry alternatives.

Finally, some female workers may actually be harmed by comparable-worth policies. In response to the anticipated rise in wages of female job categories, firms may shift away from the use of this labor by accelerating the automation of those functions. Indeed, studies find that the growth of employment in female job categories was less in states that had comparable-worth guidelines. Governments also might attempt to circumvent guidelines by contracting with the private sector to supply services provided by female job categories. For example, public hospitals could contract out custodial and dietary services if comparable-worth guidelines raise the cost of internally providing these services relative to private-sector costs. This was the approach taken by the automobile, chemical, and electronics industries after WWII, when they shifted production to the South in response to the high wages they had to pay in their unionized northern and midwestern production facilities.

Government-legislated wage guidelines can be useful when setting *minimum* pay scales. They would eliminate much of the gender wage disparities without limiting completely the ability of firms to use incentives to attract new workers. Moreover, to the extent these guidelines are implemented nationwide rather than simply in the nonprofit sector, market distortions could be minimized. Indeed, this seems to be the result in Australia where national minimum wage standards were enacted in 1975. Immediately, the gender earnings ratio increased to 84 percent from 65 percent five years earlier. This change did not appear to create any significant market distortions or efficiency losses, so we should not expect the U.S. economy to be harmed if such a policy were implemented here.

In general, the pro-market concern that pay equity will create substantial distortions and inefficiencies is unfounded. Historically, most large corporations developed internal wage structures that often substantially deviated from prevailing wages. Sometimes this was intended to limit turnover—the efficiency wage theory—but often it was based upon an understanding that their workers expected intra-firm wage differentials to reflect social norms.

During the 1930s, Westinghouse conducted comparable-worth studies at a time when job categories were completely gendered. The company found that workers in some female job categories were more skilled and more valuable to the company than workers in some male job categories. However, Westinghouse instituted an internal wage structure where all male job categories received higher pay than all female job categories. Westinghouse did this because it understood that social convention required companies to pay all men more than all women. If instead it used merit to determine the relative wages of various occupations, men would have balked at being paid less than women, creating labor dissension that the company decided to avoid.

In 1999, on average, the wages paid in any given occupation in the motor vehicle manufacturing industry was 32 percent higher than those in a benchmark industry. Why do auto companies choose to pay their accountants, secretaries, and other office personnel so much more than prevailing wages? Part of it may be that these companies benefit from having workers with above-average skills and from low turnover rates. However, these decisions also reflect their sensitivity to the social norm that white-collar staff should be paid more than blue-collar production workers. As a result of union bargaining power, auto assembly-line workers are paid a wage substantially above that of other semi-skilled manufacturing workers. If the automobile industry paid its white-collar workers their prevailing wage, many would earn less than these assembly-line workers. This would harm office morale to the degree that the companies calculate that it is cost-effective to maintain the socially expected white-collar, blue-collar pay differentials found elsewhere. Since U.S. automobile manufacturers have had record profits throughout the 1990s, this suggests that national comparable-worth legislation might not substantially adversely affect the profitability of businesses that would be subject to this policy.[20]

While supporting comparable-worth legislation, I am concerned with its potential effects on notions of gender roles. Recall that second-wave feminists focus on policies that would enable women to more easily maintain their traditional "feminine" roles and responsibilities. They support parental leave and flextime proposals that would allow women to more effectively balance work and family responsibilities. Like Becker, many believe that the choice of helping professions by women does reflect a natural preference. They reject, however, Becker's belief that the resulting occupational wage disparities are fair.

For many second-wave feminists, comparable worth is one way to combat unfair gender earnings inequities while supporting the so-called nurturing qualities of women. These feminists reason that if the nurturing professions like teaching, nursing, social work, and child-rearing service providers were paid more, fewer women would leave them for the higher-paying male-dominated professions. Consistent with this view, a number of studies found that the two economies that are most associated with raising the pay in traditional female occupations—Sweden and Australia—have high levels of occupational sex segregation. For example, the economist Joyce Jacobsen estimated that dissimilarity indexes for Sweden and Australia were about 20 percent higher than for the United States.[21]

I recoil from the thought that financial incentives will govern who enters helping professions and long for a time when they are populated by caring individuals. However, if the only way to maintain some semblance of humanity in these professions is to enshrine women with an abundance of nurturing instincts, we risk too much. We must support the goals of comparable worth without abandoning the belief that values are socially constructed. It is our job to restructure the messages both young girls and boys receive so that all develop nurturing values.

Tensions have arisen in Europe where some feminists are promoting government legislation that would provide basic incomes to all parents caring for dependent children. The feminist economist Ingrid Robeyns fears that such legislation would weaken the upward mobility of many young women as employers would be less willing to risk providing them with on-the-job training for fear that they will soon leave the labor market. She expects that, if implemented, it would reinforce traditional stereotypical attitudes "instead of challenging and changing them."[22]

Racial Wage Disparities among Women

One of the great myths of the late twentieth century was that, as a result of the demands of affirmative action, employers were eager to employ black women since both racial and gender diversity would be improved. Black women continue to face extreme prejudice in the labor market. Lawsuits continue to show egregious treatment, as in the case of Ms. Kimberly Orton mentioned at the beginning of the book. Recall that at Coca Cola she spent years training and supervising white employees who made more than she did. In April 2000, W. R. Grace and Company settled a lawsuit filed against one of its food-processing subsidiaries where it was found that four plant managers and two nonsupervisors had engaged in systemic sexual harassment that included requiring at least twenty-two female workers to perform sexual acts in order to maintain employment. All of these women were nonwhite.[23]

Maybe there was a kernel of truth to the pro-market view in the mid-1970s when the average hourly wage of black and white women was virtually the same. Indeed, in 1975, among recent college graduates, black women earned over 10 percent more than white women. Beginning in the late 1970s, however, the wages of black women did not keep pace with the wages of white women. By 1991, black women earned 14 percent less than white women and 10 percent less among recent college graduates.[24]

Between 1973 and 1991, the racial earnings ratio among women declined by 0.625 percentage points annually. This was partially the result of the decline in the real wages in the noncollege labor sector. Since black women were employed more heavily than white women in this sector, it caused the racial earnings ratio among women to decline. Black women were also harmed by the movement of manufacturing jobs out of central cities. In the Midwest, the percentage of black women employed in manufacturing declined from 28 to 9 percent, whereas the decline among white women was from 29.1 to 18.8 percent. Not only did black women lose employment disproportionately, they were increasingly relegated to the lowest-paying manufacturing jobs.[25]

In addition, black women were disproportionately employed in unionized jobs during the 1970s, but this advantage had disappeared by the end of the 1980s. Finally, black women are employed in the lowest-wage jobs, where pay scales are quite sensitive to the minimum wage. Between 1981 and 1989 the minimum wage was frozen at $3.35 per hour, adversely affecting the lowest-paid workers. Together all of these factors explain almost one-half of the growth of the racial earnings gap among women.

The weakening of the job market for black women was also reflected in the growing divergence of their work experience from that of white women. In 1970, black women were much more likely to be in the active labor force than white women; their LFPR was 11

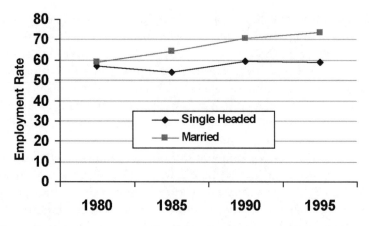

Figure 7.5 Employment Rates for Women with Children Six to Seventeen Years Old, by Marital Status, 1980–1995. *Source: U.S. Bureau of Labor Statistics,* Employment and Earnings *(Washington, D.C.: Government Printing Office, January 2000).*

percentage points above the white rate. By 1995, the black rate was 1.5 percentage points higher than the white rate so that, on average, black women now had a weaker labor market attachment than white women. However, white rates only exceeded black rates for women with no more than a high school education. Among female college graduates, the black rate was 8.4 percentage points higher than the white rate. Moreover, the rate among married women, especially those with children, remained substantially higher for black women than for white women. Thus, the relative deterioration was concentrated among black women with limited education who were single householders.[26]

The Plight of Female Householders

In 1980, the employment rates of single and married women with children six to seventeen years old were virtually the same (see Figure 7.5). By 1995, however, the rate for single mothers had risen only slightly, but for married mothers it had risen dramatically, creating a fourteen percentage-point gap. This growing gap created resentment among married mothers who became less willing to support nonworking female householders through government welfare programs.

Resentment grew as the welfare population increased. After remaining stable for over a decade, the number of welfare families rose from 3.8 to 5 million between 1989 and 1993. Not surprisingly, there was broad support for a reversal of welfare policies. Beginning in 1994, the federal government allowed states to experiment with various reforms, all focused on reducing the number of recipients. Midwestern states were particularly aggressive in adopting new welfare procedures. Building on these state experiments, in 1996, federal legislation enacted lifetime limits on the number of years welfare could be obtained. As a result, by 1999, the welfare population was halved.

The reduction in the number of recipients was disproportionately larger among white than black women. Whereas in 1994 slightly over one-half of all recipients were either black or Latina, by 1998 they represented two-thirds of the recipients. This disproportionate white decline was especially the case in larger urban areas. In New York City, there was a 57 percent decline in the number of white recipients but only a 30 and 7 percent decline for black and Latina recipients, respectively. In Los Angeles, the white decline was 40 percent but only 16 and 24 percent for black and Latina recipients, respectively.[27]

This disproportionate white decline should not be surprising. On average, white recipients had somewhat higher levels of education and previous work experience and tended to have fewer family health problems or other barriers to employment. Studies have found that these impediments have a predictable impact on the probability of employment. Using a set of sixteen employment barriers, including lack of a high school degree, limited work experience, no access to an automobile, drug dependence, and child health problems, researchers at the University of Michigan found that the probability that a black recipient would gain employment was 82 percent if she had no barrier but dropped to 41 percent if she had four barriers.[28]

The Michigan researchers found that 27 percent of all recipients possessed four or more employment barriers. Recall that when a significant share of a group has negative characteristics, employers will engage in profiling and reject *all* applicants from that group whenever possible. As a result, recipients were at the end of the job queue. Reflecting this pattern, the unemployment rate for female householders remained at over 15 percent throughout the 1990s boom.

The welfare stigma has had a particularly harmful effect on the employability of black recipients. In a study conducted during 1994 and 1995, 78 white employers were interviewed concerning the difficulty they had finding qualified workers. Almost one-half mentioned parenthood, family, or both when discussing female applicants, but rarely when discussing male applicants. The tendency to discuss motherhood was more prevalent when these employers discussed the hiring of black women and, most important, one-third of the respondents referred to black women by using the image of the single mother. In contrast, only 12 percent of the respondents mentioned single motherhood when discussing either white women or women in general. In these firms, 20 percent of black but only 6 percent of white mothers were single householders. However, the use of this stereotype stigmatized all black mothers, including the 80 percent who were living with a spouse or partner.[29]

Most employers believed that mothers, especially single household heads, were employment risks because they would have to take time off to care for their children. Indeed, one employer lamented that because of federal laws he no longer could ask applicants if their children became sick, "Do you have someone who can take care of them?" However, surveys of these firms' employees found that employer perceptions were generally unfounded. Even though black women were disproportionately single householders, they had a lower rate of absenteeism or lateness due to concerns about child care than white mothers. Interestingly, 30 percent of black male employees and 40 percent of white male employees indicated that over the previous year they had been either late, had to change hours, or been absent because of child-care responsibilities. Indeed, the white male rate was slightly higher than the black female rate.

How can employers maintain stereotypes that are inconsistent with their own experience? If one embraces a stereotype, it distorts the way observations are processed. When black mothers are absent, the employer might immediately project that regardless of the reason given, they must have been taking care of their children. In contrast, a male worker's explanation will be taken at face value. In addition, when men are absent because of family responsibilities, it might be viewed as an exception whereas when black women give this reason, it confirms the stereotype.

This study was done before welfare policies changed. As a result, the sample may have disproportionately included single black householders who were able to balance work and family; those who could not were on welfare. In this case, we might expect that once welfare no longer remained an option, more black women with employment barriers, including child-care problems, would enter the market. This would make subsequent data consistent with the stereotype. Indeed, this was expected when recipients with limited work experience began to enter the labor market in the mid-1990s.

Between 1994 and 1999, among those twenty-five to fifty-four years old, the LFPR of black women increased from 73 to 79 percent. Facing the racial stigma, employment difficulties arose for this group, particularly in New York City where the economic boom was weakest. Owing to anemic job growth, the New York City employment rate of black women declined between 1994 and 1997, causing their unemployment rate to increase from 8.6 to 15.2 percent. However, throughout most of the nation, where tight labor markets were the norm and there was a large demand for workers, it was no longer possible for most employers to engage in profiling. This was especially the case beginning in 1997 when national unemployment rates fell below 5 percent.[30]

When firms began hiring former welfare recipients, it appeared that the traditional stereotypes were true. The Michigan research team reported that many recipients lost their jobs because "they failed to understand the importance of punctuality, the seriousness of absenteeism, and resented or misunderstood the lines of authority and responsibility in the workplace."[31] Over time, however, it became clear that former recipients became valuable employees. In a large survey of major corporations, researchers found that to their surprise, former recipients stay on the job longer, with less turnover, than other employees. Borg-Warner, Giant Food, Marriott International, Salomon Smith Barney, Sprint, United Airlines, United Parcel, and Xerox found that they retained a larger proportion of former recipients than other entry-level employees. Typical was United Airlines, where after one year, of the 760 recipients hired, 70 percent were retained, whereas the retention rate for others hired at similar jobs was only 40 percent. At Giant Foods, 100 welfare recipients had been hired as cashiers, clerks, and assistants. The retention rate after ninety days was 79 percent, whereas it was only 50 percent for other employees in similar jobs.[32]

Part of the reason for the success rate at these large corporations is that often support services were in place. Indeed, government and nonprofit agencies had recruited and trained many of the welfare recipients. Recipients were also given access to job training, child care, and transportation services that were unavailable to other new hires. This suggests that barriers to employment can be overcome with modest support. Continued tight labor markets may allow more women who have been stigmatized to enter the workplace and, through their efforts, the stereotypes that have victimized them for too long will break down.

Table 7.2 Eleven Leading Occupations for Black Women, 1996 (in thousands)

OCCUPATIONS	EMPLOYED
1 Nursing Aides, Orderlies, and Attendants	536
2 Cashiers	359
3 Secretaries	290
4 Personal Service Occupations	268
5 Retail Sales Workers, excluding Cashiers	191
6 Janitors and Cleaners	176
7 Cooks	160
8 Maids	158
9 Registered Nurses	157
10 Elementary School Teachers	151
11 Social Workers	151

Source: U.S. Department of Labor, Bureau of Labor Statistics, tabulations from the *Current Population Survey, 1996 Annual Averages* (Washington, D.C.: Government Printing Office 1996).

Impact of the 1990s Economic Expansion

While the economic boom has enabled former welfare recipients to enter the workplace, we must also assess its overall impact on the relative earnings of black and white female workers. Earlier we found that sex segregation was an important reason for the gender earnings gap as women were crowded into lower-paying occupations than men. Similarly, racial earnings disparities among women reflect the crowding of black women into the lowest-paying occupations. Of the eleven leading occupations for black women in 1996, the first eight are among the lowest-paying noncollege occupations, while the last three are among the lowest-paying college-required occupations (see Table 7.2). In 1996, more than one in three black female workers were employed in these eleven occupations, whereas less than one in five white female workers were.

Let us assess the impact of occupational differences and the economic expansion on racial earnings disparities among women by looking more closely at the Midwest and South Atlantic regions where more than one-half of all black workers live. In both regions, black women were overrepresented in the eleven lowest-paying noncollege occupations. During 1995–1997, 17.5 percent of white women and 21.9 percent of black women were employed in these job categories in the Midwest. In the South Atlantic region, the disparity was even greater;

**Table 7.3 Decomposition of Changes in the Black-to-White Female
Earnings Ratio by Region, 1992–1994 and 1995–1997**

REGION	RACIAL EARNINGS RATIO		DECOMPOSITION INTO:			
	1992–1994	1995–1997	Total change	Sector shares	College wage	Noncollege wage
South Atlantic	89.49	86.72	-2.77	0.66	-3.99	0.56
Midwest	104.00	99.27	-4.73	-0.78	-3.05	-0.90

SOURCE: Author's calculations from U.S. Bureau of the Census, Current Population Survey Outgoing Rotation Group Files (Washington, D.C.: Government Printing Office, 1992–1997).

only 14.9 percent of white women but 24.4 percent of black women were employed in these occupations.

On average, black women work more hours per week than white women. This helps explain why in the Midwest there was racial earnings equality among women. The heavier concentration of black women in the South Atlantic region in the lowest-paid occupations helps explain why the racial earnings ratio among women there was substantially lower than in the Midwest region (see Table 7.3). Interestingly, while the Midwest region exhibited a *higher* degree of racial equality, it had the *lowest* gender earnings ratio of any region nationally.

The racial earnings ratio declined by 2.77 and 4.73 percentage points in the South Atlantic and Midwest regions, respectively. The *sector-shares* effect measures how much of these changes derive from changes in the distribution of black and white women within the college-required labor sector. If black women disproportionately shifted to the college-required sector, this would increase the racial earnings ratio, even if there were no changes in earnings inequality in either labor sector. That is, even though the level of inequality individual black women would face would be unchanged, because relatively more black women were in the higher-paying college-required sector, the average black wage would rise, raising the racial earnings ratio.

Of course, the racial earnings ratio could change because of changes in the racial earnings of female workers in either the college-required or noncollege labor sectors. The *college wage* effect measures how much the change in the racial earnings ratio is the result of changes in the average wage of black and white women in the college-required labor sector. The *noncollege wage* effect measures how much of the change in the racial earnings ratio is the result of changes in the average wage of black and white women in the noncollege labor sector.

By pinpointing the sources of changes, we can better understand the reasons for changes in the racial earnings ratio among women and to what degree discriminatory barriers have been broken down. In particular, the sectoral-shares effect indicates that the racial earnings ratio can increase without changing the level of inequality in either of the two labor sectors. This can give a false impression that gains against discriminatory practices within occupations have been made.

To some degree, sectoral shifts rather than a lessening of discriminatory practices within labor markets explained much of the increase in the racial earnings ratio among men during the 1960s. During that decade, black men moved outside the South, where the racial earnings ratio was about 60 percent, to the Midwest and Northeast, where the racial earnings ratio was about 80 percent. Without any change in regional racial earnings ratios, this population shift alone would have caused the national racial earnings ratio to increase substantially, giving the false impression that racial labor market discrimination had lessened substantially. Indeed, once the migration ended, increases in the national racial earnings ratio among men stalled since there was no lessening of racial wage inequality within regions.[33]

Our data indicate that the racial earnings ratio among women declined in both regions primarily because of an adverse college wage effect: In the college-required sector, the wages of white women increase much more rapidly than the wages of black women. This alone would have caused the racial earnings ratio among women to decline by 3.99 and 3.05 percentage points in the South Atlantic and Midwest regions, respectively.

The decline was only 2.77 percentage points in the South Atlantic region, however, because of the favorable sector shares and noncollege wage effects. South Atlantic black women comprised an increased share of workers in the college-required sector, and their wages increased more than white women's wages in the noncollege sector. In contrast, the racial earnings ratio declined by 4.73 percentage points in the Midwest region because of adverse sector shares and noncollege wage effects. Midwest black women comprised a smaller share of workers in the college-required sector, and their wages increased less than white women's wages in the noncollege sector.

Why didn't black women in the Midwest appear to shift as rapidly as white women into the college-required sector? Why didn't wages of black women in the noncollege sector increase as rapidly as white women's wages? During 1992–1994, the employment rate of black women was 20 percent lower in the Midwest than in the South Atlantic region. To a large extent, more generous Midwest welfare payments had allowed more women there to remain outside of the low-wage labor market than in the South Atlantic region. The economic expansion and changes in welfare policies pulled and pushed less-educated midwestern black women there into the labor market so that, by 1995–1997, the gap between the two regions was halved. The entry of so many less-educated black women lowered the average wage paid to black women in the noncollege sector in the Midwest and also reduced the share of black women who were employed in the college-required sector there.

As already noted, by far the major influence on racial earnings ratios among women were changes in the average wages in the college-required sector (Table 7.3). In both regions, there was a much more rapid increase in the average white than black wage. This alone would have caused racial earnings ratios to decline by more than 3 percentage points, dwarfing the impact of the other two effects. A more detailed evaluation of the employment and earnings changes within the college-required sector finds that white women were much more able to break down exclusionary barriers and enter the higher-paying professions than were black women. White women experienced a more dramatic shift out of the lower-waged technician categories than did black women. In addition, only white women significantly increased their representation in mathematical and hospital administration occupations that are among the highest-paying, college-required occupations for women. In contrast, black women lowered their representation in hospital administration by almost as much as they increased their representation in lower-paid management categories.

The differential advancement among professional black and white women is also apparent when looking at glass-ceiling problems. In a 1999 report, Catalyst found that if white women face a glass ceiling, women of color face a "concrete" one. Women of color represented only 11.2 percent of female officers in the 340 companies that provided data on race/ethnicity. One-half of all women-of-color managers at these companies believed that corporate diversity programs have been less than effective in dealing with issues of subtle racism, while only one-quarter believed that career development has been an important part of their company's diversity program.[34]

Concluding Remarks

During the 1990s, the movement toward gender inequality became more uneven. While progress continued in the college-required sector, gender earnings gaps changed little in the noncollege sector. Not only did the class gap between working-class and professional women grow, so too did the gap between black and white women. In addition, it appears that female advancements in both earnings and the breaking down of sex segregation were more substantial in regions associated with the new service economy than those associated with the older goods-producing industries.

The more limited advances in the noncollege sector have led to a resurgence of interest in pay equity legislation and government programs to aid the ability of working women to balance market employment and child-care responsibilities. While flextime, parental leave, comparative-worth, and basic income policies are valuable, we should be vigilant and not allow them to relegate women to "mommy" tracks and trap them in traditional female occupations or as child-care givers. Our efforts should enhance the nurturing values in both men and women, not simply help women balance careers and family.

There are other general policies that should be part of efforts to close the gender earnings gap in the noncollege sector. The minimum wage has historically been an important method of reducing wage disparities. Since the early 1970s, however, it has not kept pace with inflation and wage inequality has grown. Not surprisingly, wage inequality grew the most during the 1980s when the minimum wage was unchanged for eight years. During the 1990s, low-paid workers have benefited from two increases in the minimum wage. In addition, a number of cities have adopted legislation that requires firms that do business with the government to pay a living wage—generally two dollars per hour above the minimum wage—to their employees.

We have also found that black women faced a stigma as employers increasingly stereotyped them as single householders. When changes in welfare policies forced many black women into the labor market, this stigma threatened to undermine welfare-to-work strategies. Fortunately, very tight labor markets changed the behavior of employers. With no alternative sources of labor, firms began to hire former recipients and, to their surprise, found that they could be valuable additions to their work force. In addition to the economic gains, the Minnesota welfare-to-work program also found that increased employment is associated with an 18 percent reduction in the domestic violence experienced.[35] Unfortunately, there is a danger that these social and economic benefits will be lost if labor market tightness disappears. For this reason, it is crucial that tight labor markets persist even if it requires allowing inflation rates to rise.

Another policy that has aided the welfare-to-work adjustment of single householders has been the Earned Income Tax Credit (EITC) program. The EITC provides government-funded income supplements to poor and near-poor working families with children. In 1999, a family with two dependent children received a credit as high as $3,816. For a single householder earning $12,500, her disposable income was increased by 32 percent. Unfortunately, the EITC does not aid most low-paid workers in married households with two wage earners. These families have family incomes that disqualify them from receiving a significant amount of credits. By expanding the EITC program so that these households are aided, income inequality can be reduced. The concluding chapter will detail the advantages of maintaining tight labor markets, raising the minimum wage, and expanding the EITC and living wage programs.

8 | Jobs for Black Men
Missing in Action

When civil rights legislation was passed in the 1960s, many advocates hoped that there would be racial equality within a generation. This optimism, however, was dashed during the next decade when it became clear that, among other things, black and white men experience vastly different treatment in the labor market. Over a twenty-four-year period, 1974–1997, the black unemployment rate was never lower than 10 percent, while the white rate was almost never higher than 7 percent. In general, the black rate was at least double the white rate. Interventionists consider these disparities prima facie evidence that strong discriminatory employment practices persist, justifying continued government policies. In contrast, pro-market proponents believe that the racial disparities overwhelmingly reflect skill differences.

The high rate of unemployment over a generation made it difficult for young black men to maintain any confidence that through their efforts they could enter the mainstream of American society. When Federal Reserve chair Paul Volker engineered a deep recession in the early 1980s, raising black unemployment rates to depression levels, despair deepened. Not surprisingly, many turned to drug use and crime. Rather than showing compassion and understanding, state and federal governments reacted in a vengeful manner. Civil liberties were reduced, allowing law enforcement more leeway in fighting crime. Stiffer sentencing led to a quadrupling of the prison population so that by the early 1990s, more than one-half of all central-city black men, aged eighteen to thirty years old, were either in jail, on parole, or awaiting trial.

The widespread approval of this get-tough strategy led Republicans to use the image of the black criminal in the 1988 presidential campaign—the infamous Willie Horton ad. Willie Horton killed a woman while on a work release program from a Massachusetts prison. Republicans seized on this tragedy to damage the Democratic candidate, Massachusetts governor Michael Dukakis. Hoping to avoid a similar Republican effort to paint him weak on crime, William Clinton interrupted his presidential campaign in 1992 to fly back to Arkansas to oversee the execution of a mentally retarded black man.

The 1990s economic expansion renewed hopes that racial employment and earnings disparities would be lessened, and indeed, by 1997, official statistics seem to indicate that there has been a modest improvement for adult black men. This assessment was critically dependent, however, on the unemployment measure used. The official unemployment rate of black men had declined not so much because of gained employment but because fewer unemployed black men were included in the official count. Moreover, the racial earnings gap among men did not change significantly, even increasing in some parts of the country. Only when the national unemployment rate fell below 5 percent in 1997 did tight labor markets induce a modest decline in racial earnings and employment disparities.

Given the persistence of racial disparities, it becomes important to determine their source: labor market discrimination versus racial skill differences. Assessments are sensitive to the measurement of skills, work experience, educational attainment, and earnings used. In addition, labor market discrimination will vary across educational groups and regions.

Trends in Black-White Earnings Disparities

For most of the last thirty years, the official unemployment rate of black men has been deplorably high. After six years of economic expansion, the 1990 black unemployment rate stood at 10.6 percent. Similarly, after six years of economic expansion, the 1997 rate stood at 10.1 percent. Most troubling, however, was evidence that the unemployment rate was becoming a misleading measure of the labor market difficulties of black men.

During the 1990s expansion, a significant portion of the unemployment decline of black men was due to their withdrawal from the labor market. Between 1994 and 1997, the white male labor force participation rate was unchanged but the black rate declined. Researchers claim that at least one-half of that disparity reflects black workers who had given up using formal job searches because of a lack of employment prospects. Suppose that we assume the "true" participation rate of black men is the same as the white rate. An adjusted black unemployment rate, calculated under this assumption, declined slightly from 19.8 to 19.1 percent between 1994 and 1997, while the official rate dropped from 12 percent to 10.1 percent. This indicates that most of the decline in the official rate reflected the withdrawal of black men from the labor force. In the subsequent two-year period, 1997 to 1999, there was a robust drop in black unemployment rates by both the official and the adjusted measure. However, it is important to note that though the official rate fell to 8.2 percent in 1999, the adjusted rate was still 16.8 percent.[1]

Moreover, even this adjusted rate understates the underemployment of black men. Due to high incarceration rates and undercounting by the census, black men are more likely than white men to be missed in official counts of the noninstitutionalized civilian population. For example, in 1990 among those twenty to sixty-four years old, the female-male ratios for the noninstitutionalized civilian and military populations were 1.189 and 1.017 for blacks and whites, respectively. Only a small fraction of this racial disparity reflects differential death rates. Since the vast majority of black inmates and those missed by the census and employment surveys would be unemployed, their exclusion from the active labor force further understates black unemployment.

While employment rates are important, there is little progress if employment gains are not matched by earnings gains. In 1980, the black-white earnings ratio, measured by annual income for full-time, year-round workers, stood at 70.4 percent (see Figure 8.1). A decade later it had risen to 71.1 percent and by 1999 to 73.9 percent. One clear reason for the lack of substantial improvement has been the occupational disparities that persist. In January 1999, 29.7 percent of working white men but only 17.8 percent of black men were employed as managers and professionals. Instead, 30 percent of black men but only 19.6 percent of white men were employed as operators, fabricators, and laborers.

Notice that the racial earnings ratio for *full-time* male workers ac-

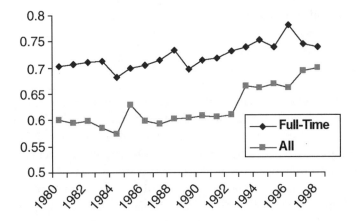

Figure 8.1 Black-White Earnings Ratio, 1980–1998. *Source: U.S. Bureau of Labor Statistics,* Employment and Earnings *(Washington, D.C.: Government Printing Office, January 2000).*

tually declined after 1997 just when tight labor markets were able to help close the racial employment gap. Results are different, however, when *all* male workers are included. Between 1980 and 1990 this racial earnings ratio was virtually unchanged, rising from 60.1 to 60.7 percent. However, during the next decade, it increased substantially. Indeed, between 1997 and 1999, it rose from 66.1 to 69.9 percent. The rise in the racial earnings ratio for all male workers during these two years suggests the following: An important component of the employment expansion was the ability of low-paid black men to move from part-time and/or part-year employment to full-time, year-round employment.

Data on the employment changes among workers with low educational attainment confirm this shift. In a study conducted in Boston during 1994, economists Barry Bluestone and Mary Stevenson found that black and white men with no more than a high school education were just as likely to have worked sometime in the previous twelve months. However, the expected number of hours worked differed dramatically. Black men averaged 1,327 hours over the previous year, while white men averaged 2,020 hours. National data also show similar disparities. Among noncollege-educated men, the 1994 probability of full-time employment was 59 percent higher for white men than for black men. As the economic boom tightened labor markets, however, the share of both black and white men with low educational attainment who worked full-time rose. Additionally, this increase was more substantial for black men so that, by the end of 1999, the probability of white men working full-time was only 37 percent higher.[2]

The recent closing of racial disparities in employment and earnings gives us hope for more change. However, our optimism must be tempered by the evidence that during the first six years of the expansion benefits were much more modest. Moreover, even when benefits from tight labor markets kicked in after 1997, racial gaps remain substantial. To understand why these disparities persisted, let us focus more closely on two factors. The severe stigma attached to young black men, especially those with low educational attainment, suggests that we should assess separately how the 1990s economic expansion affected their earnings and employment. And the fact that black men are more heavily concentrated in the noncollege labor sector while white men are more heavily concentrated in the college-required labor sector also makes it worthwhile to assess to what degree black men progressed in these two distinct labor markets.

Black Youth Employment Problems

The employment situation of black men under twenty-five years old has been the subject of many studies because of their high rate of joblessness and the social havoc that this can create. The research, however, is complicated by two factors: the inadequacy of the official unemployment measure and distinguishing between those in and those out of school. The inadequacy of the official unemployment rate became apparent during the deep 1980 to 1982 recession. The already high black youth unemployment rate did not rise substantially and, more puzzling, statistics indicated that the vast majority of young black men had very short official spells of unemployment; more than one-half left the unemployment roles within one month.

The ending of spells of official unemployment, however, did not occur because black youths found jobs. Black youth either became discouraged and stopped searching or began to use job search activities that did not meet the government's criterion. Among twenty- to twenty-four-year-old black men, the average duration of joblessness was more than six months for high school graduates and more than ten months for dropouts. During the 1980–1982 recession, 21 percent of all black men between the ages of twenty and twenty-four years old who were out of school had *no* work experience in the previous year. This rate was triple the white rate (7.2 percent) and almost double what the black rate had been a decade earlier (12.8 percent). However, this joblessness did not show up in official unemployment statistics because most of these young men did not meet the government criterion for job search so they were not considered part of the active labor force.[3]

Many researchers dismissed any focus on the unavailability of jobs. Instead, they claimed that unemployment problems were caused by the refusal of black youths to accept low-paid employment. Economists Harry Holzer and Kip Viscusi claimed that "outside income generated by illegal activities" was an important reason black youths shun low-paid jobs. Sociologists Christopher Jencks and Elijah Anderson claimed that the civil rights movement had generated a new consciousness that considered these jobs degrading. The political scientist Andrew Hacker believes this explains why black men reject jobs as taxicab drivers that recent immigrants take. Given this viewpoint, it was not surprising that there was broad indifference if not support for increasing the severity of penalties for criminal behavior, which culminated in the explosion of black incarceration rates.[4]

The sociologist William Julius Wilson claimed that the environment faced by low-income black youth also deteriorated as a result of demographic changes. As middle-class blacks moved outside the inner city, black urban ghettos began increasingly to contain only the poor. He suggested that this reduced the presence of role models and middle-class culture available to inner-city black youths, making it less likely that they would develop and maintain the proper behavioral traits necessary for permanent employment. According to William Darity and Samuel Myers, "[The] control and institutionalization of unwanted, superfluous inner-city residents, creat[ed] further marginalization of many young black males, thereby increasing observed pathologies like crime and violence."[5]

Beginning with the 1980–1982 recession, employers were swamped with job applicants. Focusing on the worst jobs advertised, economists Kim Clark and Lawrence Summers found an average of fifteen to twenty responses within two days of an ad's placement. In order to avoid spending substantial personnel resources on interviewing so many applicants, firms increasingly relied upon recommendations from present employees and neighbors. Given segregated housing patterns and little black business ownership, black youths suffered when jobs were filled through informal networks.[6]

The employment difficulties of young black men were particularly severe in older urban areas in the Midwest and Mid-Atlantic regions. The interstate highway systems enabled trucking to replace railroads as the principal means of transporting goods. In order to avoid traffic congestion, many manufacturing firms relocated to suburban industrial parks adjacent to interstate highways. Moreover, the growing use of assembly-line techniques, which require one-floor operations, made central-city multifloor industrial buildings unsuitable. This further increased the incentive for firms to move to suburban industrial parks.

This relocation of manufacturing production was devastating to black workers. Due to housing market barriers, black workers had difficulty moving close to these new locations, making it more costly to commute and more difficult to obtain information on new job openings.

Between 1975 and 1989 the share of young black men employed in durable manufacturing fell from 40 to 12 percent. By contrast, among young white men, the drop was only ten percentage points. Economists John Bound and Richard Freeman suspected that "an important part of this differential change [was] the closing of older plants in the central cities of the Midwest."[7]

Informal hiring networks continue to dominate the hiring process in low-wage labor markets. They accounted for approximately 35 to 40 percent of new hires in four major metropolitan areas surveyed between 1992 and 1994. In contrast, newspaper advertising accounted for less than 30 percent of new hires. More than one-half of all new hires for low-skilled blue-collar jobs were filled through informal methods.[8] In his more recent work, Wilson found that employers who use these informal networks embrace the notion that black youths tend to have more dysfunctional behavior than white youths.

Wilson found that "roughly two-thirds of the city employers who placed ads in newspapers did so in ethnic, neighborhood, or suburban newspapers instead of or in addition to the metropolitan newspapers." Many of those firms readily admitted that they selectively advertised job openings to avoid having to deal with inner-city black applicants. Not surprisingly, this selective advertising had an impact on hiring practices. Wilson noted: "City employers who placed ads only in local or neighborhood papers, not likely to circulate among inner-city residents, averaged 16 percent black in their entry-level jobs, compared to an average of 32 percent black for those who placed ads in the metropolitan papers."[9] After documenting this racial profiling, Wilson concluded, "Employers make assumptions about the inner-city black workers in general and reach decisions based on those assumption before they have had a chance to review systematically the qualifications of an individual applicant. The net effect is that many black inner-city applicants are never given the chance to prove their qualifications on an individual level because they are systematically screened out by the selective recruitment process."[10]

Harry Holzer found similar patterns of behavior. He notes that employers preferred Latino workers even though they tended to have less schooling and weaker language skills than black applicants. Holzer suggests that these preferences reflect employer perceptions that Latinos would work for lower wages and have better work ethics. His view builds on the work of Joleen Kirschenman and Kathryn Neckerman, who found that employers perceive blacks to be more troublesome and less compliant than Mexican Americans.[11]

Most striking was the broad black acceptance of these stereotypes. In Chicago, black as well as white employers used racial profiling to exclude young black men living in public housing projects. Even many black workers embraced negative black stereotypes. As one black resident told Wilson:

> I say about 65 percent of black males, I say, don't wanna work, and when I say don't wanna work I say don't wanna work hard—they want a real easy job, making big bucks—see? And, and when you start talking about hard labor and earning your money with sweat or just once in a while you gotta put out a little bit—you know, that extra effort, I don't, I don't think the guys really wanna do that. And sometimes it comes from, really, not having a, a steady job or, really, not being out in the work field and just been sittin' back, being comfortable all the time and hanging out.[12]

Similar viewpoints were depicted in Spike Lee's film *Do the Right Thing*. Lee portrays the black pizza worker, Mookie, as an irresponsible employee who takes time off to have sex with the mother of his child whom he is unwilling to support. He also contrasts the lack of industriousness of three black men, who consistently hang out on the street corner, with hard-working Asian shopkeepers.

Some data from the early and mid-1990s did suggest that a permanent black underclass has been created. In 1989, the employment rate of young black men equaled only 48.5 percent, well below the white rate of 68.0 percent. By the trough of the cyclical employment downturn in 1992, both employment rates had fallen, but the black rate more dramatically. Whereas the white rate was 94 percent of its peak rate, the black rate was only 85 percent.

It was in this environment that Wilson researched poor black Chicago neighborhoods for his book *When Work Disappears.* "The disappearance of work and its consequences for both social and cultural life," he wrote, "are the central problems in the inner-city ghetto." Wilson was not surprised that ambitious programs like Head Start generally have no lasting impact. He pointed to the inadequate public schools that poor inner-city black children must attend. However, it was the joblessness that is most decisive. When a majority of adults in many inner-city neighborhoods are jobless, social engineering is doomed.[13]

Typical of the men Wilson interviewed was a father of one child from a high-jobless neighborhood who explained why he began to sell drugs to augment his income from part-time work: "Four years I been out here trying to find a steady job. Going back and forth all these temporary jobs and this 'n' that. Then you know you gotta give money at home, you know you gotta buy your clothes which cost especially for a big person. Then you're talking about my daughter, then you talking about food in the house too, you know, things like that."[14]

The economist Chinhui Juhn documented the growing joblessness of black men, especially those with limited education and work experience. She found that on average at any moment during the 1994–1996 time period, about one out of every four black men was not employed. The nonemployment rate among the lowest-paid workers was nearly 50 percent. Juhn found that the nonemployment rate rose primarily because of longer spells of joblessness among a relatively small group.[15]

After an initial spurt upward during the early stages of the expansion, black employment rates fell back again so that in 1997 one could easily begin to view high black youth unemployment as permanent. Clearly, it appeared that the group profiling that Holzer and Wilson documented was taking its toll on black youth as long as employers believed that they had enough white (and Latino) youths available. Indeed, while black rates rose when labor markets tightened, they were no higher in 1999 than they were five years earlier.

These national figures, however, include both the employment situation of those in and those out of school. Over the last decade the proportion of young black men in school has increased. Since those in school tend to work less than those out of school, this shift alone would have caused the overall employment rate of young black men to decline. While the overall black employment rate was unchanged between 1994 and 1999, it increased substantially for those not in school—from 56.6 percent to 61.4 percent. Moreover, there was an even greater increase in full-time employment. The share of young black men, not in school, who held *full-time* jobs, rose from 43.8 percent to 53.4 percent. Thus, there were two opposing trends among those who were working less than full-time, year-round: One group was able to shift to full-time, year-round employment, while Juhn's evidence indicates that another smaller group became more detached from the labor market.

Tight labor markets aided not only employment, but also wage growth. During the first years of the economic expansion, 1992 through 1996, wages after adjusting for inflation declined for young noncollege-educated black and white men. However, once labor markets tightened, real wages increased dramatically. As a result, for the entire expansion through 1998, real wages increased by 5 and 10 percent for young noncollege-educated white and black men, respectively. This was above the 4 percent real wage increase for all male workers—the first increase in real wages in over twenty-five years.[16]

The impact of tight labor markets on the real wages of young noncollege-educated black men was most apparent when comparing different urban areas. Among areas where the unemployment rate was below 4 percent throughout the entire expansion, real wages for young noncollege-educated black men *increased* by 11 percent, while in areas where unemployment remained above 7 percent throughout the expansion, real wages *declined* by 5 percent. In areas where there was a rapid unemployment rate decline, real wages *increased* by 15 percent.[17]

A typical example of this striking improvement is Brian Bennett. Bennett graduated from an inner-city high school in Raleigh, North Carolina, in June 1997, when the local unemployment rate was 2.2 percent. After working at a series of temporary jobs for a year, he landed a full-time position as a front-desk clerk at an Embassy hotel. Planning to study hotel management part time with tuition help from his employer, Bennett said, "The sky is the limit, no one can hold me back but me."[18]

The manager of the Raleigh Employment Security Commission office said, "Employers are hiring people that two, three, five years ago they weren't hiring." In the early 1990s, four hundred black men between the ages of nineteen and twenty-five from the local area used to take part in a midnight basketball league where networking and interviewing tips were as much on the agenda as foul shots. However, by 1999, there was increasing "difficulty getting enough people to play because they [were] in the job market."[19]

Despite the earnings and employment benefits of tight labor markets, difficulties persist. In 1999, 19 percent of all black men between ages sixteen and twenty-four were neither in school nor at work, higher than during the peak of the previous expansion. Clearly the situations Wilson documented in the early 1990s and Juhn documented for the mid-1990s have not been eliminated. Most disheartening, black teenagers and students continue to have extreme difficulty obtaining employment. Only about one-quarter of black teenagers are employed compared to one-half of white teenagers. Among those sixteen to twenty-four years old, 50.7 percent of white students but only 28.6 percent of black students are employed. The gap is even larger in the cities in which poor blacks are concentrated.[20]

Employment is crucial for teenagers and college students. With the growing expenses of attending even public colleges, they need to accumulate personal funds in order to enter and remain in school. If black youths are unable to work, it is less likely that they will become college graduates. For those black teenagers who do not attend college, employment is crucial if they are to avoid racial profiling.[21]

In localities where the economic boom has not created tight labor markets, the situation of young black workers has remained dismal. This has been particularly true in New York City where more blacks—2.1 million—live than anywhere else in the United States. After seven years of economic expansion, the 1998 New York City unemployment rate stood at 8 percent, almost double the national rate. This contrasted with the peak of the previous expansion when New York City's unemployment rate was below the national rate.

With such a weak general labor market, black workers fared quite poorly. In 1998, black workers had an 18 percent unemployment rate in New York City, well above the 10 percent rate that was typical of other large cities. Indeed, Boston, Dallas, Atlanta, and San Francisco had rates of 6 percent or lower. The New York City employment rate for black men was six percentage points lower than other large cities. Among young black men in school, the New York City employment rate was 12.1 percent, whereas it was 20.7 percent in other large cities.

Most troubling, it does not appear that additional education alone will solve black employment difficulties in New York City. Among college-educated adults, black New Yorkers' 1998 unemployment rate of 9.8 percent was twice the U.S. black average and three times higher than the white rate nationally. Indeed, the poverty rate for New Yorkers with some college stood at 17 percent, up from 7.6 percent a decade earlier; among college graduates, the poverty rate increased from 3.5 to 6 percent. Thus, in the absence of tight labor markets, young black men continue to be at risk.[22]

Regional and Class Differences in Racial Disparities

Discrimination is a particularly important issue in the South Atlantic and Midwest regions since the majority of black workers live in these two regions. Furthermore, the historical importance of these regions cannot be underestimated: The history of slavery and Jim Crow in the South and the Midwest's importance as the primary destination of the black exodus indicate that the trajectory of discrimination in these regions is essential for understanding racial inequality in America. This section will present results from a study that analyzed changes in the racial earnings ratio in these two regions over the first five years of the 1990s economic expansion.[23]

The share of black and white workers can be placed into three occupational groupings: (1) fourteen college-required occupations in which at least 70 percent of those employed have some college education; (2) ten manual noncollege occupations that require physical labor and are low-paid; and (3) twenty-one noncollege skilled occupations (see Table 8.1). In order to have a sufficient sample size, data were combined for three-year time periods, 1992 to 1994 and 1995 to 1997.

As noted earlier, nationally black men are overrepresented in blue-collar employment and underrepresented in managerial and professional occupations. The degree of over- and underrepresentation seems to vary substantially among regions. In the Midwest, at the beginning of the expansion 21.54 percent of black men but 25.42 percent of white men were employed in the college-required sector so that black men were 85 percent as likely to be employed there as white men. However, South Atlantic black men were only 54 percent as likely as white men to be employed in the college-required sector in that region. In the manual occupations, South Atlantic blacks were twice as likely

Table 8.1 Male Occupational Employment Shares by Race

	BLACK (%)		WHITE (%)		BLACK-TO-WHITE RATIO	
	1992– 1994	*1995– 1997*	*1992– 1994*	*1995– 1997*	*1992– 1994*	*1995– 1997*
South Atlantic						
College	15.81	18.19	29.47	30.79	0.54	0.59
Skilled	55.54	55.65	56.77	55.81	0.98	1.00
Manual	28.65	26.16	13.76	13.40	2.08	1.95
Midwest						
College	21.54	22.28	25.42	26.68	0.85	0.84
Skilled	55.58	56.26	60.05	59.92	0.93	0.94
Manual	22.88	21.46	14.53	13.40	1.57	1.60

SOURCE: Author's calculations from the U.S. Bureau of the Census, Current Population Survey Outgoing Rotation Group Files (Washington, D.C.: Government Printing Office, 1992–1997).

to be employed as whites but only 57 percent more likely in the Midwest.

This more favorable black Midwest occupational distribution, however, was at least partially due to a selectivity bias. Our data included only those who are working. At the beginning of the economic expansion in 1992, employment rates among black men in these regions differed dramatically—63.9 percent in the South Atlantic but only 53.5 percent in the Midwest region, a 10.4–percentage-point gap. In contrast, the white male employment rate was higher in the Midwest than in the South Atlantic region. Virtually the entire regional differential reflected Midwest black men who, if working, would have been employed in low-paid noncollege occupations. Thus, their exclusion artificially enhanced the Midwest occupational distribution for black men.

Over the expansion, many of these missing Midwest black men became employed so that the 1996 regional employment-rate gap was only 8.7 percentage points. As a result of the disproportionate entry of low-paid black workers, however, there was an "unfavorable" shift in the Midwest black occupational distribution. The relative share of black employment in the college-required sector declined, while in the manual sector it increased. In contrast, in the South Atlantic region, the relative share of black employment in the college-required sector increased, while in the manual sector it declined. These shifts

Table 8.2 Decomposition of Changes in the Black-to-White Male Earnings Ratio by Region, 1992–1994 and 1995–1997

	RACIAL EARNINGS RATIO		DECOMPOSITION INTO:			
REGION	1992–1994	1995–1997	Total change	Sector shares	College wage	Noncollege wage
South Atlantic	72.07	73.24	1.17	0.68	-1.01	1.48
Midwest	81.49	80.51	-0.98	-0.25	0.11	-0.84

Source: Author's calculations from the U.S. Bureau of the Census, Current Population Survey Outgoing Rotation Group Files (Washington, D.C.: Government Printing Office, 1992–1997).

reduce regional occupational differences and, indeed, most of the remaining difference is due to the persistence of regional employment-rate disparities.

Wage data are also influenced by the increased employment of low-paid Midwest black workers. At the beginning of the economic expansion, among Midwest black men, the average wage in the combined noncollege labor sector was 61.2 percent as much as the average wage in the college-required sector. The "class" ratio among white men was only 60.6 percent. Over the economic expansion, the class ratio remained the same among Midwest white workers but declined to 58.7 percent among black workers. By contrast, the class ratio among South Atlantic black men actually increased, indicating growing equality among black workers there.

During the economic expansion, the racial earnings ratio among men declined in the Midwest but improved in the South Atlantic region. As with the racial earnings ratio among women in the previous chapter, the overall change can be decomposed into three distinctive components into the sector-shares, college-wage, and noncollege-wage effects (see Table 8.2).

In the South Atlantic region, the racial earnings ratio among men increased by 1.17 percentage points. Black men in this region shifted more rapidly into the college-required sector than white men and, in the noncollege sector, the wages of black men increased by more than the wages of white men. These favorable changes were partially offset by an adverse college-wage effect; the wages of black workers increased by less than the wages of white men in the college-required sector.

As a result of the entry of low-earning, less-skilled black men, the

Midwest racial earnings ratio among men decreased by 0.98 percentage points. Midwestern black men shifted less rapidly into the college-required sector than white men and, in the noncollege sector, the wages of black men increased less than the wages of white men. These adverse effects were marginally offset by a small favorable college-wage effect, as the wages of black workers increased by slightly more than the wages of white workers in the college-required sector.

In the Midwest, the major source of racial earnings ratio decline was the adverse noncollege-wage effect. This was anticipated, given the large entry of low-paid black workers there. However, these entrants did not depress black wages in the manual occupations. Instead, the major source of the adverse effect was the more rapid rise of white than black wages in the skilled occupations. The wages of black workers did not lag because white workers were able to increase their share of employment in the better-paying skilled occupations. Instead, the wages of black men lagged because they were less able to obtain the higher-paid positions within occupations in which they were employed. Thus, black men experienced a glass-ceiling effect where they can enter occupations but not advance at as high a rate as white men.

There are discriminatory barriers to advancement in the skilled labor sector. Indeed, economists Joyce Jacobsen and Laurence Levin estimate that almost one-half of the racial wage differential among noncollege-educated men is the result of differential returns to tenure and experience.[24] There are additional reasons for the growing racial wage gap within skilled occupations. Over the economic expansion black and white Midwest men experienced different sources of labor mobility. For black men, the expansion enabled them to move into full-time employment so that they would be disproportionately at the bottom rung of the ladder in each skilled occupation. At the same time, having secure employment at the beginning of the expansion, white men were able to advance within skilled occupations.

The dynamics in the skilled labor sector were different in the South Atlantic region. Because black men had more secure employment at the beginning of the expansion, they experienced the same rise up the occupational ladder as white workers. In addition, black men were able to shift into the higher-paying skilled occupations. Both of these factors enabled black wages to rise faster than white wages in the skilled occupations.

In the college-required labor sector, at the beginning of the expansion, black men in both regions were somewhat underrepresented in the highest-paying occupations and overrepresented in the lowest-paying ones. The expansion eliminated this racial disparity completely. This improvement contrasted with the experience of black women who lagged behind white women in the ability to gain access to the higher-paying professional and managerial occupations.

In the Midwest, black and white men shifted to the college-required sector in relatively the same proportions, so that black men did not have a disproportionate share of the lowest-rung positions. However, glass-ceiling effects did not lessen, so that there was virtually no change in the relative wages within occupations. In the South Atlantic region, the positive sector-shares effect indicates that black workers increased their share of employment in college-required occupations. Most likely, this reflected a growing number of new black college graduates entering the job market. These new entrants would have disproportionately concentrated at the bottom rung in each occupation. Since this dampened the average growth of black wages within occupations, there was an adverse college-wage effect in the South Atlantic region.

Measuring Labor Market Discrimination

Racial disparities do not necessarily demonstrate labor market discrimination. They could primarily reflect skill and behavioral differences. The data, however, seem to reject this viewpoint, instead indicating that wage gaps among equally educated black and white workers twenty-five to thirty-four years old grew in the 1980s and persisted through the 1990s (see Table 8.3). Using similar findings, Andrew Brimmer estimated that if black men earned the same wages as comparably educated white men, total gross domestic product (GDP) would increase by 2.15 percent.[25]

The pro-market economist June O'Neill—appointed by President Clinton in 1995 to direct the Congressional Budget Office—also found that there were substantial and growing racial earnings gaps among men during the 1980s. Indeed, her reported ratios are lower than those of Mishel, Bernstein, and Schmitt for that time period. However, O'Neill firmly rejected claims that this demonstrated persistent labor market discrimination against black men.[26]

Pro-market economists claim that these estimates are incomplete since they do not fully adjust for skill differences between black and white men. In particular, comparisons must take into account the fol-

Table 8.3 Black-to-White Earnings Ratio (in percent) among Men Twenty-five to Thirty-four Years Old, 1979–1995

| | YEARS OF SCHOOLING | | | |
	8–10	12	13–15	16 and more
	Mishel, Bernstein, and Schmitt*			
1979	81.6	85.8	90.1	92.8
1989	81.1	81.1	81.6	77.6
1995	82.9	80.9	82.4	87.1
	O'Neill**			
1979/80	75.2	80.4	84.6	90.6
1987	81.6	75.5	82.1	74.4

* Hourly wage rate comparisons among all workers who had positive income during that year.

** Usual weekly wage, averaged over a three-year period, including only individuals who worked at least twelve weeks and full-time for at least one-half of the weeks worked.

lowing additional factors: the region of residency, actual work experience, and the measure of basic skills. With these adjustments, O'Neill estimated that young black men in 1987 would have earned 99.1 percent of comparably skilled young white men.

O'Neill's estimate was based on a comparison of the usual weekly wage of men who worked at least twelve weeks during the previous year and were full-time for at least half of the time they worked. Interventionists contend that the choice of income measure and restrictions on which workers are included understates racial earnings disparities. They argue that direct controlled studies of hiring practices are the most effective method of measuring labor market discrimination.

Additional Explanatory Variables

There are substantial differences in the regional residency of black and white men. In 1990, 47 percent of white men but only 31 percent of black men lived in the Midwest, Plains, Mountain, and Pacific regions where the average male weekly wage was $415. In contrast, 55 percent of black men but only 33 percent of white men lived in the three southern regions where the average male weekly wage was $376. We should also take into account that the southern regions have the largest racial wage gaps, while the Pacific, Mountain, Plains, and Pacific regions have the smallest racial wage gaps. If black men had the same residential distribution as white men, more black men would have higher wages and face smaller racial wage disparities. As a result, the racial earnings gap among men would be reduced by almost five percentage points.

Holding age constant, among high school graduates, black men have fewer years of work experience than white men. Racial differentials in work experience, however, may not be a matter of individual choice. For example, let us assume that when black men begin their labor market experience they possess the proper behavioral traits of punctuality and effort. However, suppose that they initially encounter substantial discrimination. As we have seen, this causes black men to have spotty work records, which, given the negative stereotypes they face, makes it more difficult for them to maintain stable employment. As a result, over time the gap in actual work experience between black and white men of the same age grows. The gap grows even more if black workers become discouraged and "adapt" by losing the proper behavioral traits and their focus on legal employment.[27]

At the end of this process, black workers are less experienced, and employers are quite justified to pay them less than comparably educated white men. However, discrimination was responsible for the inability of black men to gain as much work experience as white men. For this reason, many researchers reject the use of actual work experience because it would eliminate an important component of racial earnings disparities—past labor market discrimination. Instead, these researchers use age as a proxy for work experience because if labor markets were nondiscriminatory, black and white men of the same age and educational attainment should have the same work experience.

Using different data sets than Mishel et al. and O'Neill, the labor economist William Rodgers found that in 1989 black college graduates earned 15 to 20 percent less than comparably skilled white college graduates when no quality variable is included. The 1989 racial earnings gap among male college graduates was substantially larger than in 1979 when a much smaller share of black men graduated college. This evidence suggests that as black men gained credentials to enter higher-paying occupations, the cause of racial earnings gaps changed. In the 1970s the racial earnings gap was primarily due to the exclusion of black men from professional employment. However, a decade later it appeared that the gap was primarily due to racial earnings differences within occupations.[28]

Equally educated men, however, do not necessarily have the same skills. For this reason, it would be ideal if a skills measure independent of years of schooling attained could be included. At the college level, class rank where available can provide this measure. Among students who graduated college, black students average two-thirds of a grade lower than whites. As mentioned earlier, former Ivy League college presidents William Bowen and Derek Bok followed a group of male college graduates who matriculated at a group of elite schools in 1976. They found that in 1995 black graduates earned about 17 percent less than white graduates. However, black and white male graduates who had the same class rank had virtually the same 1995 earnings.[29]

The skills measure O'Neill chose to use is the Armed Forces Qualifying Test (AFQT). Racial differences are substantial on this test. Rodgers and Spriggs note that while 56 percent of white men score at least the fiftieth percentile, only 14 percent of black men do so. Since this racial differential is independent of education attainment, they also found that its inclusion reduced substantially the expected earnings gap between comparably educated black and white men.[30]

Rodgers and Spriggs, however, reject the use of AFQT scores because they believe the test presents a racially biased measure of basic skills. Rodgers and Spriggs contend that if AFQT scores were race neutral they should be completely determined by family background, school quality, and psychological variables. After adjusting for these variables, however, they found that black men still score substantially below comparable white men. Rodgers and Spriggs believe that these unexplained racial differences reflect the racial bias of the test.

There is undoubtedly some bias in standardized tests that result in an overstating of the skill differences between black and white men. However, the exclusion of the AFQT variable has little impact on O'Neill's results for men with at least some college education. When the AFQT variable was included, O'Neill estimated that earnings of black workers in this group was 110.4 percent of the earnings of comparably skilled white workers, so that it may be white professionals who face discrimination in labor markets. When the AFQT variable was excluded, blacks were estimated to obtain 98 percent of white earnings, virtual equality. Thus, O'Neill's evidence suggests that eliminating the AFQT variable eliminates only the potential for "reverse" discrimination that her previous estimate suggested.

Standardized test scores play a critical role in the college admissions process. Given their lower scores, black students tend to go to less-prestigious colleges and tend to have lower GPAs, so it should not be surprising if their earnings are lower than comparably educated white college graduates. In contrast, employers rarely make distinctions among the high schools their job applicants graduated when hiring in noncollege occupations. As a result, quality measures should not explain very much of the racial wage gap in this labor sector. For those with no more than a high school education, O'Neill estimated that black earnings were still only 93.8 percent of white earnings when she included the AFQT variable. If excluded, blacks had estimated earnings equal to 88.4 percent of whites. Thus, whether or not AFQT scores were included, O'Neill found that there was significant discrimination against noncollege-educated black men.

Group Profiling and New York City College Graduates

Group profiling based on school attended strongly influences the employment prospects of black college graduates. This is most apparent in New York City. Earlier in this chapter, we noted the high and growing poverty and unemployment rates of New York City college graduates. Studies suggest that this is disproportionately black and Latino graduates from branches of the City University of New York (CUNY). CUNY has eleven separate four-year colleges that differ dramatically in their quality and racial composition. There are five historic senior colleges in which the strongest students and most demanding programs are concentrated. The other six senior colleges were virtually all established after the great expansion of the system in 1970. Few white students attend these less-prestigious colleges.

During the 1990s, the business community and conservative politicians deplored the lack of standards in the CUNY system, by which they meant the six nonhistoric senior colleges. They claimed that CUNY allowed very weakly prepared students to enter these colleges and, through grade inflation, allowed many to graduate with limited skills. This growing criticism of CUNY standards was well covered in the local press, but there was little recognition of its damaging effects on the employability of black and Latino CUNY graduates. With anemic New York City job growth, private-sector demand for college graduates was sluggish. However, New York City produces a disproportionately large share of black and Latino college graduates. Among those twenty-five to sixty-four years old, 18.5 percent of New York City's black residents but only 14 percent of black residents of other large cities are college graduates. Twelve percent of New York City's Latino residents but only 8.1 percent of Latino residents of other large cities are college graduates. As a result, during the 1990s there was an excess supply of black and Latino CUNY graduates seeking New York City employment.

As group profiling theory suggests, having an excess supply of applicants, many New York City employers began rejecting *all* applicants who graduated from these colleges. Group profiling was widespread because these graduates were overwhelmingly black and Latino, reinforcing the racial stereotypes many employers already held. While most black and Latino graduates of the CUNY system found employment, a large group from the weaker colleges suffered.[31]

To change hiring decisions, the CUNY administration floated the idea of having a "rising junior exam." This skill-based, standardized exam would be taken by all CUNY students after they had completed sixty credits. If students did not pass this exam, regardless of their college record, they would be dismissed from the university system. These CUNY administrators argued that this exam was the most effective way to counter the growing stigma attached to black and Latino CUNY graduates, especially those from the weaker colleges. Mayor Rudy Giuliani eventually pushed through, over the protest of the vast majority of CUNY faculty and liberal supporters, a new set of admissions guidelines that restricted somewhat the number of New York City high school graduates who would be able to directly enter the senior colleges. When new more stringent admissions standards were approved, the rising junior exam proposal was delayed.

Choice of Earnings Measure

Critics also note that estimates of the racial earnings gap are sensitive to the measures of earnings used. Whether a worker suffered two or twenty weeks of unemployment, it would not affect the usual weekly or hourly wage measure. Since black men suffer more unemployment than white men, these measures understate the racial earnings gap. The same bias occurs if comparisons are restricted to full-time, year-round workers (or any partial restriction as O'Neill does). All of these measures will show smaller racial gaps than studies that use annual income for all workers with positive income as the earnings measure.

For virtually every year and every educational level, racial earnings disparities are smaller when weekly wage comparisons, rather than annual earnings comparisons, are made. In 1980, black male high school graduates earned 83 percent as much as comparably educated white men when usual weekly wage is used—about the average of the Mishel et al. and O'Neill estimates (Table 8.3). However, the ratio declines to 75.1 percent when annual wages is the measure used, reflecting the lower number of weeks worked by black men compared to white men.[32]

The impact of differential unemployment is particularly noticeable among noncollege graduates. During the 1970s decade, 73 percent of black men, aged twenty-two to fifty-eight years old, were employed full-time, year-round in at least eight years. In contrast, during the 1980s, only 51 percent of adult black men were employed full-time, year-round in at least eight years. For all men, the decline was only from 79 percent to 70 percent. These declines were overwhelmingly experienced by noncollege-educated men. Thus, studies that restrict comparisons to hourly wage rates or usual weekly wage or full-time workers understate the racial earnings gap in noncollege labor markets.[33]

A final criticism builds on another bias of the data used. Virtually all studies eliminate workers with limited work time by requiring some minimum employment requirement. Butler and Heckman found that the apparent improvement during the 1970s was the result of the removal of less-skilled blacks from the labor market while the most productive blacks remained. Building on this, Darity and Myers suggested that if these workers were included, there would have been no improvement. Even pro-market economist James Smith found that one-half of the improvement in the 1970s was the result of black labor force withdrawals. Given the continued high rate of nonemployment among black men, the exclusion of men with little work experience continues to bias results.[34]

Controlled Audit Studies

Interventionists often focus on audit studies to buttress the claims that labor market discrimination persists. These studies are controlled experiments in which two individuals, one black (or Latino) and one white, are matched for all the relevant personal characteristics, such as references, employment backgrounds, and articulation skills, then sent to apply for the same advertised entry-level job openings. Using black and white testers, the Urban Institute conducted audit studies in Washington, D.C., and Chicago during 1990 and 1991. Equal outcomes occurred in 79.9 percent of the audits; in 14.2 percent neither was offered the position and in 65.7 percent both were offered the position. In 14.8 percent of the audits, only the white applicant was offered the position, while in the remaining 5.3 percent, only the black applicant was offered the position.[35]

There was also an audit study done in Denver in 1991. Unlike the Urban Institute studies, however, it found no difference in the treatment or employment outcomes of white and black applicants. The authors suggest that these results stem from two factors. Blacks in Denver made up a smaller fraction of the metropolitan population than did blacks in the Urban Institute audit cities. This lessened racial conflict over jobs, lowering the likelihood that Denver employers would be racially conscious in their hiring decisions. Blacks in Denver also had relatively high educational attainment so that employers there might have fewer negative stereotypes than employers in the Urban Institute audit cities.

The Denver and Urban Institute studies are not completely comparable since they used different methods of matching testers and different schemes of payment to testers. However, Ron Mincy accepts the validity of all three studies so that "each presents reliable evidence of discrimination in the respective labor markets." Unfortunately, participants in the discrimination debate often do not present a balanced assessment of these audit studies. For example, Marc Bendick, Charles Jackson, and Victor Reinoso totally dismissed the Denver study because "its results are contaminated by methodological flaws" but ignored comparable methodological flaws in the Chicago study. President Clinton's chief affirmative action advisor, Christopher Edley, presented only the D.C. study. The Thernstroms emphasize the Denver study and claim that serious methodological flaws in the Washington, D.C., study "severely limit the generalizations that can be drawn from [it]."[36]

A study by James Heckman and Peter Siegelman further illustrates the difficulty in judging the usefulness of audit studies. They analyzed variation in outcomes among the five pairs of testers in the Chicago study. If all five pairs were equally matched, they should have experienced similar outcomes. Heckman and Siegelman found, however, that the racial differences in the aggregate Chicago results were driven by large disparate outcomes experienced by only two of the five test pairs. For this reason, Heckman and Siegelman concluded that the Washington, D.C., study alone had clear evidence of discriminatory hiring practices. However, they criticized the Urban Institute for emphasizing this evidence of discrimination: "By focusing on the disparities between the treatment of majority and minority group members, the Urban Institute studies deemphasize the high proportion of audits in which equal treatment of both partners was found. An appropriate question, therefore, is 'whether the glass is one-quarter empty or three-quarters full?' In all of the audit pair studies it seems quite full to us."[37]

Concluding Remarks

Evidence presented indicates that severe employment problems persist for black men even after the longest uninterrupted economic expansion in U.S. history. This is particularly the case once nonemployment, incarceration, and census undercounting of black men is accounted for. Indeed, only when labor markets tightened after 1997 did racial earnings and employment disparities lessen. Just as with black women, these tight labor markets forced many employers to hire job applicants for whom they held negative stereotypes. This enabled those black men who had some work experience to gain full-time, year-round employment. However, it did not reverse the continued detachment of a significant share of young black men from the labor market.

Black employment problems were most severe in areas that had an excess supply of workers. This was the case in the Midwest at the beginning of the economic expansion and in New York City throughout the expansion. In the Midwest, these employment difficulties were reflected in the particularly high nonemployment rate of black men that artificially made employment and earnings disparities seem smaller. In New York City, these employment difficulties were severe enough to substantially adversely affect college-educated black men.

Racial earnings disparities among college graduates does not appear to be significant, especially if adjustments are made for skills, either through class rank or standardized test scores. Racial earnings disparities in the noncollege labor sector, however, were larger and more persistent. These disparities primarily reflect the inability of black men to advance within skilled occupations. In addition, because of racial profiling, young black men have difficulty gaining employment, limiting their work experience as they age.

Instead of discriminatory practices, liberal economists tend to emphasize structural factors to explain racial disparities within the noncollege labor sector: the increasing use of informal hiring practices and the changing location of manufacturing firms. Since blacks have a weak set of business contacts, they are unlikely to be in the personal network of suburban employers. Since blacks are trapped in central cities, many are unable to commute to suburban jobs. Thus, they argue that the lack of black employment occurs even if employers hold neither racial preferences nor stereotypes.

These economists tend to minimize the extent to which racial preferences and stereotypes influence the decisions of firms about where to locate and what hiring procedures to use. As Wilson and Holzer documented, however, hiring practices were consciously developed so that black workers would have difficulty finding out about job openings. For example, when the Japanese automobile manufacturers expanded production facilities in the United States, their location decisions seemed to be at least partially based on a desire to avoid hiring black workers. They built almost all of their plants in semi-rural locations distant from cities in which black workers were concentrated. One particular example was a decision to locate an auto plant *two* miles outside the census definition of the Columbus, Ohio, metropolitan area. If it had located within the official metropolitan area, the firm would have been subject to equal employment opportunity (EEO) guidelines that require firms to hire in proportion to available labor supplies in the metropolitan area. Since about 20 percent of the Columbus metropolitan area is black, the firm would have been under pressure to hire a work force that was 20 percent black. However, by locating just outside the metropolitan area, the firm could still tap the Columbus labor market but would not be subject to the 20 percent goal since few blacks lived in the particular locality in which it located.

Many conservative policy analysts focus on the personal decisions of noncollege-eduated black men to explain their employment problems. These analysts often claim that much of the problem stems from the unwillingness of black men, especially in the Northeast and Midwest, to take service jobs that they perceive as demeaning. Indeed, this argument surfaced when it was found that black men had a disproportionately low representation among the waiting work force in New York City. Though 26 percent of the city's population in 1996, they represented only 10.5 percent of those employed as waiters. When surveyed, many black waiters "acknowledge that black Americans may be rejecting what they perceive as a servile profession." This reflected not a particular political perspective but the attitudes of white customers. Typical was the experience of one black waiter at an exclusive restaurant who was told, "For a colored boy, you're not too bad."[38]

Black waiters were quick to point out that discriminatory practices are a more important explanation of the low numbers of black
waiters. When he was trying to gain a toehold in the industry, George
Thomas remembered, "I faxed my qualifications to restaurants and they
expressed excitement. Then they saw me in person, and the whole
conversation changed." Given this experience, Harlem political leader
David Paterson suggests that black men don't seek employment as waiters because "they think those jobs are closed off to them." Fortunately,
Mr. Thomas did not give up and worked his way up to becoming waiter
captain at a three-star restaurant.[39]

While racial equality is in reach in the college-required labor sector,
the continuation of EEO policies is still necessary if the remnants of
discriminatory practices are to be rooted out and the advances already
made are to be sustained. In noncollege labor markets, black men continue to be victimized by glass-ceiling effects that limit their ability
to advance. Black men also continue to be last in the hiring queue.
For these reasons, EEO policies must be expanded and strengthened
in the noncollege sector.

In addition, government can be more sympathetic to the employment difficulties faced by black men. Despite poor labor markets, New
York City treats black men as if they were responsible for their joblessness. Rather than hiring them as fully paid workers, they are hired
on workfare programs that pay them minimum wage or lower. The *New
York Times* reporter Steven Greenhouse documented how, between
1994 and 1998, New York City was able to reduce its government work
force by 10 percent through the hiring of 34,000 workfare recipients.
This was most striking in the parks department where government
employees declined from 1,925 to 1,156.[40]

That the government has the ability to absorb young workers with
low education is most apparent in Germany. Economists Francine Blau
and Lawrence Kahn documented that in 1991, among all men aged
eighteen to twenty-nine years old without a high school diploma, 17
percent had government employment in Germany but less than 2 percent had government employment in the United States. Moreover, unlike
workfare programs that pay minimum wages, government employment
in Germany narrowed the wage gap between these workers and private-sector workers. If the government in the United States followed
the German example, the situation of young black men could be improved dramatically.[41]

9 | Employment and Ownership Disparities

What Should the Government Do?

Affirmative action was one of the more contentious issues of the 1990s. While the Bush administration reluctantly supported legislation that strengthened equal employment opportunity policies, by the middle of the decade, another component of affirmative action—set-aside policies that aided the growth of black and female business ownership—was being fundamentally undermined. At least one reason for this divergence is the substantial contrast between the justifications given for EEO policies and those given for set-aside policies.

EEO policies intervene in the hiring process in order to create a "level playing field" on which black and white job applicants can compete fairly. Supporters envision labor markets dominated by meritocratic considerations where EEO policies ensure that the most qualified applicant is hired. In contrast, set-aside programs require that government pursue a fixed percentage of their purchases of goods and services from minority businesses, even if they are as much as 10 percent more costly than nonminority-owned businesses. Unlike EEO policies, set-aside programs give priority to group goals that often override considerations for individual equity.

Affirmative action supporters, including Barbara Bergmann and Andrew Hacker, generally claim that only the force of government has led to modest gains for women and African American men in the last few decades. They predict a return to the patriarchal past for women and Jim Crow–like conditions for blacks if affirmative action policies are terminated. In the words of another supporter, Cornel West, "racial and sexual discrimination would return with a vengeance."[1] As a result, they favor the status quo, defending all affirmative action policies. In contrast, pro-market proponents argue that whether or not affirmative action made sense in the past, it has no positive value for women and African American men in the new millennium. Indeed, pro-market proponents, including the Thernstroms, believe that the ending of all affirmative action policies will have positive effects on women and black men.[2]

Equal Employment Opportunity Programs

Earlier chapters identified two reasons why there might be only a limited number of qualified applicants from underrepresented groups who reach the interview stages of the hiring process: the use of informal hiring procedures and group profiling. In nonprofessional labor markets, firms generally rely on informal networks to attract applicants, sometimes making it more difficult for qualified women and black men to gain employment. In addition, group profiling leads firms to exclude all applicants from groups that are perceived, on average, to have lower qualifications. Firms may use selective advertising of job openings to avoid applicants from these unwanted groups.

EEO policies were enacted to counteract these discriminatory hiring practices. They set hiring guidelines that require firms to advertise in media that will reach underrepresented groups and not to begin interviewing until sixty days after such advertisements appear. These guidelines also stipulate that all institutions and private firms doing business with the government are expected to interview a minimum number of applicants from underrepresented groups or explain why they were unable to do so. Cecilia Conrad estimates that the costs of compliance and enforcement total $1.9 billion or just 0.3 percent of total national production.[3]

The goal of these guidelines is to ensure that, whenever possible, underrepresented groups are able to reach the interview stage of the hiring process. At least at its onset, the goal was not to impose strict hiring requirements. Indeed, the bill's chief sponsor, Hubert H. Humphrey, said at the time of passage: "[If anyone can find] any language which provides that an employer will have to hire on the basis of percentage or quota related to color, race, religion, or national origin, I will start eating the pages one after another because it is not in there."[4] Instead, it was assumed that once firms were forced to interview individuals from underrepresented groups, they would evaluate candidates on individual merit rather than perceived group traits. Thus, it was hoped that EEO requirements would be sufficient to prod firms to overcome discriminatory practices that have plagued their hiring process.

EEO guidelines generally rely on the goodwill of employers: If they follow advertising procedures and interview a sufficient number of applicants from underrepresented groups, firms are still free to hire whomever they believe is the most qualified. Affirmative action supporters fear that this gives too much leeway, enabling personal prejudice to still dominate hiring decisions. They point to evidence that even after a decade or more, black and female representation was often far below the percentages which would have reflected equality, suggesting that even more aggressive intervention is necessary.

However, those who believe the continued lack of equitable representation of various groups demonstrates ongoing discriminatory practices may be wrong. Since white male employees who were hired during periods of discriminatory practices are not fired, equitable employment practices affect only new hires through labor turnover and employment expansions. Suppose that initially a company has two thousand employees, of whom only 20 percent are black. Next, let us assume that 50 percent of the qualified workers in the field are black. Let the black and white share of new hires reflect the distribution of qualified workers available, one hundred white and one hundred black. With two hundred new hires annually, after one year the black employment rises to 23 percent. The next year, if assuming an annual expansion of 5 percent, the percentage of black employment increases still further, to 24.3 percent.[5]

If we simulate the change in the percentage of black employment over a ten-year period, with a 10 percent turnover rate and 5 percent expansion rate, the black share of workers employed grows to 43.6 percent, within striking distance of the anticipated long-run equality rate of 50 percent. However, the growth of black employment shares would be impacted if the turnover rate equaled only 2 percent and employment expansion equaled only 4 percent (see Figure 9.1). In this case, total employment is only 33.5 percent black after ten years. At that point, the share of black employment is growing at less than 1 per-

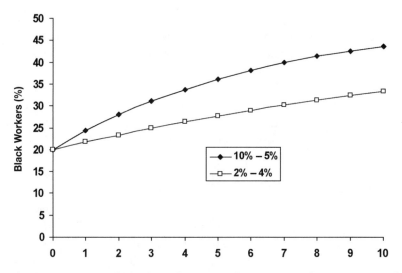

Figure 9.1 Impact of Equal Employment Policies on Racial Composition of Work Force, by Turnover and Expansion Rates.

cent per year so that, even after another decade, the rate would not quite reach 40 percent. Thus, if a firm has relatively few new hires, substantial underrepresentation would persist even after an extended period of time.

During the 1980s there were slow rates of expansion in many industries and occupations. This was particularly true at many universities where enrollment stagnated and government funding fell. Many academic departments continued to be all white and all male despite relatively aggressive efforts by university presidents. In addition, since wage premiums are widely used to reduce turnover, the firms that paid the highest wages tended to have the lowest turnover rates. Thus, in many sectors and among many high-wage firms, affirmative action was not expected to be sufficient to dramatically change the race or gender composition of the work force.

As a result, there was strong pressure on the government to find ways to increase the hirings from underrepresented groups more rapidly. Affirmative action proponents questioned any hiring mechanism that seemed to limit the number of new hires from underrepresented groups. In 1971, they focused on hiring practices at the Duke Power Company in North Carolina. At the time, Duke Power had educational and testing requirements for all positions, including custodial workers—requirements that had been instituted in 1955.

While no one claimed that they had been adopted to exclude black workers, nevertheless this seemed to be an unintended effect. In a unanimous decision, *Griggs v. Duke Power Company,* the Supreme Court ruled that tests that maintained employment divisions of prior discriminatory practices could not be used unless shown to relate directly to job performance. Since it would be inherently difficult to argue that standardized tests or even general educational credentials could be directly related to job performance, hiring practices using these measures could be challenged if they had a disparate impact.

The Thernstroms suggest that this attack on the use of tests and educational credentials turned the 1964 civil rights legislation on its head. To combat discrimination, civil rights groups supported increased use of standardized tests and educational credentials in the hiring process. Ideally, this would have replaced subjective (and discriminatory) hiring practices with merit-based ones. A problem developed because black applicants fared poorly on many standardized tests so that they had a disparate impact on hiring. As a result, the Thernstroms allege that the civil rights leaders attacked the hiring procedures that were expected to combat discriminatory practices because they didn't yield the desired outcomes. Moreover, the Thernstroms contend that the logical implication of *Griggs* was that firms should be hiring black and white workers in proportion to their representation in local labor markets and, hence, supported racial quotas.

The issue of racial quotas did arise in the steel industry. In 1974, the steelworkers union and Kaiser agreed on a set of hiring practices intended to overcome the lack of black representation in skilled craft occupations at a plant in Louisiana. Rather than determine new hires to craft positions by a plantwide seniority list, the agreement created separate black and white seniority lists. One-half of all new hires to craft positions would be from each list, implicitly creating a racial quota system. Brian Weber claimed that this was discriminatory since many more white workers would have qualified for craft positions if plantwide seniority had been used. In *U.S. Steelworkers v. Weber,* the Supreme Court, by a 5 to 4 decision, upheld the agreement between Kaiser and the steelworkers union. Writing for the majority, Justice William Brennan supported the agreement even though he was aware that the use of quotas was explicitly rejected by the Congress that passed the equal rights legislation.

The Thernstroms use this history to build a story that employers, facing the likelihood that they would be forced to pay exorbitant sums for noncompliance, adopted quotas to solve their legal problems. The Thernstroms rely on a few individual cases where companies decided to make substantial out-of-court settlements. In a comprehensive survey of economic studies, however, Lee Badgett and Heidi Hartmann found that during the 1970s, black employment gains from affirmative action were quite modest. For Jonathan Leonard, the reason for this limited impact was fairly obvious. Even during the 1970s, companies had little to fear as long as they provided the necessary paperwork to the government. Leonard noted that the likelihood of a firm being reviewed was small—only 11 percent for nondefense contractors and 24 percent for defense contractors. Moreover, firms that hired more blacks were more likely to be reviewed than those whose black employment lagged. Less than 4 percent of firms reviewed were required to explain their hiring decisions, and more than half of those were for blatant paperwork deficiencies. In 1974, average back-pay awards were only sixty-three dollars per beneficiary in the small number of successful suits. During the entire decade, only twenty-six firms lost the right to compete for government contracts as a result of their noncompliance.[6]

At no time do the Thernstroms mention that, during the 1980s, the federal government under the leadership of the Reagan administration was adamantly opposed to affirmative action. Reagan's appointment to head the civil rights commission, Clarence Thomas, was fundamentally opposed to affirmative action, and few discrimination cases were pursued under his leadership. Describing this period, Jonathan Leonard writes: "Fewer administrative complaints were filed, back-pay awards were phased out, and the already rare penalty of debarment became an endangered species. . . . Affirmative action, such as it was, no longer aided blacks."[7]

While EEO policies had, at best, a modest impact on private-sector hiring, they seemed to have had a substantial effect on government employment. Between 1970 and 1984, 45 percent of all black men in professional or managerial occupations were employed by government agencies. Among black female professionals and managers, 65 percent were employed by government agencies, indicating that EEO policies were dramatically more effective in government than private-sector hirings. Badgett found that this reflected lower levels of discrimination in the government, where affirmative action guidelines were required, than in the private sector where they generally were not.

The disproportionate employment of black professionals and managers by government agencies creates a very tenuous situation. Since the mid-1980s, the growth of nonmilitary government expenditures has declined, reducing the number of new government hires. As a result, prospects for black college graduates have been disproportionately adversely affected. This may help explain why, even with a modest increase in access to private-sector employment, the earnings gap between recent black and white college graduates rose during the 1980s.

The concentration of black college graduates in government employment had another unintended effect. Jewish workers also comprised a disproportionate share of teachers, social workers, and other professionals employed in the nonprofit and government sector. As government employment opportunities diminished in the 1980s, competition over promotions grew so that conflicts between these two groups were inevitable, reinforcing harmful attitudes. Nationwide studies found that the share of the black population with significant anti-Semitic beliefs was almost twice that found among the white non-Jewish population and was stronger among college-educated than noncollege-educated blacks. At the same time, Jews became somewhat more conservative in their voting and more hostile to affirmative action policies.[8]

Though reduced enforcement may have limited the effects of EEO policies, they generally continued to have a beneficial effect on employment practices. For example, Judith Fields and Edward Wolff studied how discrimination affects the size of the wage premiums paid by many companies. They found that among private-sector firms required to file affirmative action reports, there was a smaller gender gap in wage premiums. More generally, Rodgers and Spriggs found that black employment grew more rapidly in these private-sector firms than in those not covered by affirmative action regulations.[9]

In another study, Badgett measured the adverse impact race had on the share of black men and women who gained professional or managerial employment in California. After adjusting for other determinants, including education, she found that being a black woman reduced the probability of being a professional or manager by 11 percentage points in 1970. This adverse impact fell to 3.9 percentage points by 1980 and to 1 percentage point by 1990. The adverse impact for black men fell from 3.5 percentage points in 1970 to 2.3 percentage points in 1980, but rose to 2.7 percentage points by 1990. For white women, Badgett found an even more dramatic change. In 1970, white women were 15 percentage points less likely to be managers or professionals than comparably skilled white men. This adverse impact dropped to 4 percentage points in 1980 and completely disappeared by 1990. Thus, it appears that access to professional and managerial employment for women continued to improve during the 1980s but not necessarily for black men.[10] It also reinforces the belief that the main barrier college-educated women face today is glass ceilings not exclusionary practices.

Studying hiring practices in the 1990s, pro-market economists Harry Holzer and David Neumark found that EEO policies have been beneficial to black and female workers. They found that these policies expand the recruitment efforts of firms and raise their willingness to hire workers from stigmatized groups by relying more on formal evaluation of applicants. This led to an increased number of black and female applicants being hired. Most important, they noted that when affirmative action was used in recruiting, it did not lead to hiring women and black applicants with lower credentials than the white applicants hired. Indeed, they found that even when affirmative action is used in hiring, though "it yields minority employees whose credentials are somewhat weaker, . . . performance generally is not." They concluded, "Overall, the more intensive search, evaluation, and training that accompany Affirmative Action appear to offset any tendencies of the policy to lead to hiring of less-qualified or less-productive women and minorities."[11]

Black Business Ownership

Some participants in the 1970s Black Power movement claimed that an important component of black liberation was the growth of black business ownership. This reflected a perception that black unemployment was partially caused by the racial attitudes of white owners and the lack of employment networks available to black workers. Black workers would be more likely to find out about employment openings in black-owned firms and so would be more likely to be hired. For these reasons, it was believed that having more black owners would improve the employment of black workers and provide them upward mobility.

In order to increase black business ownership, many civil rights advocates proposed government policies to support the creation of black businesses. Known as set-aside programs, they required government agencies to purchase a fixed percentage of their goods and services from minority-owned firms. Begun at the federal level in 1977, set-aside programs were widely adopted by local and state governments during the 1980s. Despite these efforts, black business ownership continues to be below the national rate, and especially lower than the rate among many immigrant groups. What explains the low rates of black entrepreneurship? Why haven't set-aside programs been more successful in correcting this disparity?

Understanding Ethnic/Racial Business Ownership

Throughout the 1950s, Jewish ownership predominated in black neighborhoods, creating tensions between black and Jewish civil rights proponents. In the post–civil rights era, Jewish ownership has waned but it has not been replaced by indigenous black ownership. Instead, a variety of immigrant groups have filled the void, and there is some evidence of the growth of ethnic ownership. The rate of Asian American ownership (5.94 percent) in 1987 was almost four times the rate of black ownership (1.50 percent). Moreover, Asian American firms were twice as large, having annual sales equal to $112,800 per firm compared to $56,400 per black firm. Even Latino entrepreneurship was above black levels (see Table 9.1).

During the next five years, black entrepreneurship lagged still further behind these immigrant groups. The number of Latino-owned firms grew more rapidly in absolute numbers, as well as on a per capita basis, than black-owned firms. Moreover, while there was a healthy growth in Latino-owned firms as measured by sales per firm, black-owned business actually declined in size during this period.

The statistics from the Department of Commerce (Table 9.1) actually *overstate* the rate of black ownership since it includes all firms that have annual sales receipts of at least $500. Suppose we define *meaningful* firms as businesses that have annual receipts of at least $25,000. During the five-year period studied, the share of black-owned businesses that had annual sales of at least this level declined from 25 to 23 percent. As a result, if we restrict our comparisons to meaningful firms, the gap between black and immigrant communities grows even larger. In 1992, the number of meaningful businesses that were black-owned, Latino-owned, and Asian-owned equaled 142,777, 246,453, and 265,500, respectively. Moreover, black-owned businesses are much more fragile, as is apparent when looking at survival rates. In 1996, 72.1 percent of Asian-owned businesses and 66.5 percent of

Table 9.1 Size and Number of Firms by Group, 1987 and 1992

CATEGORY	BLACK		LATINO		ASIAN	
	1987	*1992*	*1987*	*1992*	*1987*	*1992*
Firms (000)	424	621	422	772	355	565
Sales ($mil)*	23.9	32.2	29.9	72.8	40.1	94.9
Population (mil)	28.4	30.3	19.9	24.3	6.0	7.8
Firms/Pop (%)	1.50	2.05	2.12	3.18	5.94	7.24
Sales/Firm ($000)	56.4	51.9	70.9	94.4	112.8	168.0

SOURCE: U.S. Department of Commerce, *Survey of Minority-Owned Businesses* (Washington, D.C.
Bureau of the Census, 1987, 1992).
* 1987 Sales and Sales/Firm are in 1992 dollars.

Latino-owned businesses had survived compared to only 59.1 percent
of black-owned businesses.[12]

The government classification of Asian is quite broad, including
Native Americans, East Asians, and Asian Indians. In addition, Table
9.1 includes both native-born and immigrant owners. If we focus specifically on immigrant groups, the entrepreneurial differences are
clearer. In particular, five immigrant groups have exceptionally high
rates of entrepreneurship: those from the former Soviet Union, Middle
East, India, China/Taiwan, and Korea. In 1997, the average rate of business ownership among men from these groups was 20.4 percent compared to 11.8 percent for all men. Moreover, 58.4 percent of these male
immigrant owners were college graduates, while only 6 percent had
less than a high school degree. By comparison, 29.7 of all male owners were college graduates and 8 were high school dropouts.[13] Black
and Latino immigrants, especially from Mexico, Guatemala, El Salva-
dor, Haiti, and the Dominican Republic, have much lower rates of business ownership. On average, the ownership rate among immigrant men
from these countries averaged 5.5 percent. Among those who became
owners, 50.5 percent were high school dropouts, while only 9.2 percent were college graduates.[14]

Many observers have tried to explain these large ethnic and racial differences in ownership rate. One of the earliest theories was proposed by the sociologist E. Franklin Frazier, who claimed that blacks
had a lower ownership rate because they had no tradition of business
enterprise. In contrast, Jews were perceived to have a high rate of ownership because of their long tradition of business enterprise. The economists Robert Fairlie and Bruce Meyers find no empirical support for

this thesis. They cite the example of Greek immigrants from fishing villages, with no experience in business ownership, coming to the United States and establishing a dominant position in the restaurant industry in many cities. Surveying twenty-nine different immigrant groups, Fairlie and Meyers found that there was no correlation between the rate of business ownership in country of origin and their rate of ownership in the United States.[15]

Fairlie further explored the reasons why black men are one-third as likely to be self-employed as white men. He found that black men were one-half as likely to begin a business and, once starting a business, were twice as likely as white owners to terminate ownership. One important factor is that personal wealth is a much more constraining factor for black men, suggesting that white men have much greater access to credit markets. Having a self-employed father also explains a significant portion of the racial disparity. However, Fairlie believes that discrimination is a significant explanation for racial differences in access to credit. This point will be discussed later in this chapter.[16]

Another set of explanations focuses on the disparity in the educational background of business owners. Entrepreneurs from groups that have high rates of business ownership tend to be highly educated individuals, while the opposite is true for entrepreneurs from groups with low rates of business ownership. This suggests that education may be a necessary condition for successful entrepreneurship. Clearly, education can improve the managerial skills necessary for business ownership. In addition, educated individuals have greater access to capital than less-educated individuals. Indeed, one of the great myths of Jewish entrepreneurship is that poor Jewish immigrants at the beginning of the twentieth century became business owners almost immediately by relying on revolving credit associations (RCA) for start-up capital. Evidence indicates, to the contrary, that Jewish ownership at that time was primarily among second- and third-generation German Jews who had migrated to the United States in the 1850s, not their eastern European brethren who dominated the Great Immigration wave at the turn of the century. Thus, Jewish entrepreneurship was concentrated among those men who had education and access to capital.[17]

A similar myth today claims that Asian immigrants are able to immediately start businesses through their access to RCAs. The economist Timothy Bates rejects this view after studying the sources of financial capital for Korean and Chinese firms. He found that RCAs, which tend to have extremely high interest rates, are much less important than traditional debt sources, such as commercial loans. Indeed, it was only the most marginal firms that relied on RCAs. Bates found, however, that the most important source of start-up capital is personal equity of owners and their partners.[18]

Jewish entrepreneurship at the turn of the century also had striking similarities to the Korean and Chinese entrepreneurship today. In both cases, barriers to professional advancement caused well-educated men to choose self-employment. In the case of Jews, it was direct discrimination that barred them from many fields of employment. Today, due to language barriers and certification requirements, many highly educated East Asian immigrants cannot compete successfully for professional or governmental employment positions. Instead, they shift to entrepreneurial activities shunned by comparably educated and skilled blacks.[19]

Roger Waldinger offers another explanation: Immigrant entrepreneurs often begin with a captive group of consumers and workers who, due to language barriers, must shop in and work for immigrant firms. In addition, Waldinger suggests that immigrant entrepreneurs succeed by developing ethnic niches in a variety of industries. Korean-owned fruit stores and Indian-owned newsstands in New York are but two examples. Waldinger contends that as these niches are consolidated, and as employers increasingly rely on ethnic networks for recruitment, they displace black-owned firms.[20]

Set-Aside Programs

Proponents have justified set-aside programs as a corrective to the employment discrimination black workers experience. Studies consistently find that black-owned firms are much more likely to hire black workers. Typical is a study by the economist Timothy Bates. He found that in nonminority communities, the majority of employees are minorities in 86.7 percent of black-owned but only 20.4 percent of white-owned small businesses. Whereas the majority of employees are minorities in 96.2 percent of black-owned small businesses in minority neighborhoods, this occurs in only 37.6 percent of white-owned small businesses.

Cecilia Conrad found that these hiring disparities are partially explained by the different recruiting strategies used by black and white employers. White employers tend to primarily use newspaper ads, whereas black owners tend to use employee referral services, such as schools or community agencies. As mentioned earlier, advertising in selective newspapers often enables employers to target certain communities. In particular, white employers tend to advertise in local newspapers in white communities so that, not surprisingly, Conrad found that led to the hiring of more white employees. Also, school and agency referral services are disproportionately located in black neighborhoods so that employers using them are more likely to hire black workers.[21]

Even after adjusting for recruiting strategies and location, Conrad still found that black owners tended to hire more black workers than white owners. Bates contends that these disparities reflect the use of informal hiring practices by small business owners, as well as negative stereotypes of black workers held by white owners: "If most of the jobs available in the small-business sector are found in white-owned firms, and most of the white-owned firms prefer to hire relatives, family members, friends and friends of friends—few of whom are black—then it follows that black job seekers will fare poorly in this sector. . . . In such a world, expanded black ownership of small business is an option that is worthy of serious consideration."[22]

In pursuit of the goal of increased black ownership, the government began setting aside a portion of its purchases for minority-owned or female-owned business enterprises (MWBEs). Initially, this was done through the Section 8(a) program of the Small Business Administration (SBA), whereby it serves as the prime contractor for goods and services to various federal agencies. The SBA then provides subcontracts to firms that are owned by individuals from socially and economically disadvantaged groups. Enhanced by President Nixon's promotion of black capitalism as the centerpiece of his agenda for aiding distressed minority communities, preferential procurement policies were formally legislated in the 1977 Public Works Employment Act. Congress mandated that primary contractors had to ensure that 10 percent of the subcontracts went to black and other minority-owned firms. Less than three years later, in *Fullilove v. Klutznick*, a 6 to 3 majority of the Supreme Court ruled that this act was constitutional.

Spurred by *Fullilove*, more than one hundred local municipalities, as well as the majority of states, enacted set-aside legislation during the 1980s. Ordinances were enacted in order to remedy past societal discriminatory practices that had limited the number of black firms capable of competing on equal footing against white-owned firms. Not surprisingly, black self-employment rates rose in cities that had set-aside programs by 20 percent more than they did in cities that did not. Most telling, disproportionate self-employment growth was pri-

marily in the construction sector, the area most identified with exclusionary practices and emphasized in all set-aside programs. In the construction sector, self-employment rates were unchanged in cities that
did not have set-aside programs but doubled in cities that did.[23]

In 1983, Richmond, Virginia, passed an ordinance requiring that
all construction firms engaged in municipal work subcontract at least
30 percent of the dollar amount of the prime contract to MWBEs. Six
years later, in *Richmond v. Croson,* a majority of the Supreme Court
rejected the argument that past societal discrimination alone is sufficient to justify remedial relief for disadvantaged groups. This ruling
adversely affected black self-employment rates.

New Jersey was typical of the way the ebbs and flows of government programs impacted the share of business going to minority-owned
firms. As a result of the institution of set-aside programs, the share of
government money spent going to minority-owned firms increased from
0.5 to 3.2 percent between 1984 and 1988. However, after *Croson,* government awards to minority-owned firms were halved. Tom Larsen reported: "MWBE utilization decreased from 37% to 24% in Atlanta,
from 32% to 11% in Richmond, and from 25% to only 3.5% in Philadelphia. In Tampa, MWBE utilization essentially disappeared decreas-
ing by 99%."[24] The adverse impact of *Croson* helps explain why the
growth in black ownership lagged during the 1987 through 1992 period (Table 9.1) and why over the entire period of 1982 through 1992,
the black self-employment grew as much in cities that did not have
set-aside programs as they did in cities that did.[25]

In the wake of *Croson,* local municipalities undertook studies to
identify the discrimination they were seeking to remedy. These studies were often sufficient to enable some local municipalities to reestablish their targeted procurement policies. However, in the 1995
Adrade v. Pena ruling, by a 5 to 4 vote, the Supreme Court extended
to all federal programs the requirement that race-based actions meet
the demanding test of strict scrutiny—narrow tailoring to serve a compelling state interest. As with *Croson,* affirmative action proponents
felt no need to mend set-aside programs. The Clinton administration
defends every one of the 160 programs that awarded financial benefits to federal contractors who help meet racial or ethnic goals.[26]

Though set-aside programs seem to have had a modest impact on
black self-employment rates during the mid-1980s, there was evidence
that these programs were open to abuse because of poor monitoring
procedures. For example, Bates and Williams used the experience in

New Jersey to demonstrate the problems inherent in applying race-based procurement policies. In 1985, New Jersey set a goal of 7 percent of state procurement spending to go to MWBEs. There were, however, a number of problems. The state had to determine which businesses were truly minority owned. Just as important, the state had no monitoring procedure to determine whether it was meeting its goal since it tracked primary contractors but not subcontractors. Bates and Williams concluded, "Using the state's haphazard procurement records to determine the impacts of New Jersey's preferential procurement program upon the minority business community was quite impossible."[27]

Bates and Williams suggested that "some of these young MWBEs may be front companies," set up by white firms to win a specific set-aside contract and then disbanded.[28] Indeed, in 1998, Jesse Jackson protested the awarding of four television licenses to Edwin Edwards through a federal set-aside program for exactly this reason. At the time, Edwards already owned seven television stations, including stations in Pittsburgh, Baltimore, and Milwaukee. Jackson found that 97 percent of the stock in Edwards's media company, Glencairn, was owned by representatives of the Smith family, who also owned Sinclair Broadcasting. In every city, Edwards had ceded to Sinclair, for a fee, control over programming, personnel, and advertising. Moreover, in every city in which Glencairn owned or was seeking ownership of a television station, Sinclair also owned one. The companies used the same bank and the same loan officer. When Sinclair transferred four television stations to Glencairn, Edwards seemed unaware of the actual price his company paid. His detractors noted that confusion over the cost of a transaction that expanded his television empire by two-thirds "was evidence that he was merely a figurehead for his company and therefore unfamiliar with the transactions that were being carried out in his name."[29] Conveying this sentiment, Hacker stated: "Thus far, fewer minority firms can be said to have graduated from dependence on their 'set aside' cushion. . . . An additional concern is that some companies seeking 'set aside' contracts have not in fact been owned by blacks or other minority entrepreneurs. As successive prosecutions have shown, firms have frequently been underwritten by white businessmen, with some black or other minority executive displayed as figureheads."[30]

As an alternative to preferential procurement policies, the federal government could instead focus on factors that undermine the ability of MWBEs, particularly black-owned businesses, to compete.[31] Black communities have long argued that banks have practiced "redlining"—

that is, not granting loans for properties and to businesses located in certain neighborhoods. When analyzing mortgage loans in 1992, the Federal Reserve Bank of Boston found that whites had a 10 percent reject rate, whereas blacks had a rejection rate of 28 percent. After controlling for the large number of variables collected to establish the credit worthiness of the borrowers, blacks were still 7 percent less likely to be granted the loan. In addition, audit studies that sent "identical" applicants for mortgage loans found that significant discrimination existed. Using data from the Small Business Administration, studies have found substantial discrimination against black loan applicants. Blacks are almost three times as likely as whites to have their loan application denied. Even after controlling for credit-worthiness and other relevant factors that distinguish black- and white-owned business, blacks are still about twice as likely to be denied credit. In addition, blacks who have their loans approved tend to pay higher interest rates than those charged to white borrowers of similar credit-worthiness. These findings probably understate the amount of racial discrimination because many potential black-owned firms are not in operation due to lack of credit and many in business may be too afraid to apply.[32]

Federal programs have attempted to compensate for the borrowing problems faced by black owners. In 1972, congressional legislation initiated the Minority Enterprise Small Business Investment Company (MESBIC) to facilitate capital formation in minority communities. By 1982, 141 MESBICs were chartered, but only 32 were still operating in 1994. Bates finds that the failure rate is particularly high for small MESBICs.[33] For these companies, labor costs and loan losses consume 68 percent of total revenues as compared to only 38 percent for larger companies. Most discouraging, Bates finds that both small and large MESBICs have been unsuccessful in raising the value of equity in the firms in which they invest. Twenty-five years after government support for targeted capital lending began, the investment capital gap between minority and nonminority firms remained large: Average start-up capital reported by black and Latino stores was less than one-half the amount reported by nonminority firms. Bates provides a number of sensible reforms to improve the performance of these subsidized investment companies. This must be a priority of government efforts if black businesses are to grow.

While Bates desires to mend set-aside programs, Harvard Business School economist Michael Porter believes that, as a strategy to improve the economic well-being of black inner-city residents, they should be abandoned. Instead, Porter claims that with a modest amount of government subsidies, established businesses can be convinced to locate in inner-city neighborhoods because of the consumer markets they can attract and because of the locational advantages and underused labor resources available. In a broader sense, Porter focuses on a location-based strategy—encourage inner-city business formation—rather than a people-based strategy—encourage black ownership.[34]

Porter's thesis seems to capture at least some of recent economic dynamics. Beginning in the mid-1990s shopping centers have been built in inner-city neighborhoods, as national chains find that their sales per square foot are higher in these locations than in their suburban stores. Multiplex movie theaters have opened in south-central Los Angeles and the east New York section of Brooklyn—some of the poorest neighborhoods in urban America. Megastores have located in inner-city locations for exactly the reasons Porter noted: cost advantages, consumer markets, and a ready supply of local workers. Interestingly, the modest government subsidies that are given are often opposed by black and Latino leaders. They complain that entering firms do not enhance black ownership but, instead, threaten the profitability of the small black and Latino family businesses that are located in these areas.

Of course, Porter's thesis has been criticized. As already noted, nonminority-owned businesses, even those that locate in inner-city neighborhoods, have not necessarily hired local residents. Second, the discriminatory lending policies of local financial institutions may have been responsible for the limited number of black-owned enterprises in the first place. These critics contend that government could increase black employment more by improving black business access to loans than by subsidizing the location decisions of nonminority-owned firms. Finally, critics wonder how effective location-based strategies can be, given the increased mobility of both workers and firms. For many of these critics, with all its warts, set-aside programs remain an important component of any black economic development strategy.[35]

Concluding Remarks

Given the ascendancy of pro-market values, especially during the Reagan administration, EEO policies have become less effective than they had been. Moreover, EEO policies have generally been directed at discriminatory practices in professional and managerial labor markets. The emphasis on these labor markets has occurred because many interventionists have become convinced that for both economic and noneconomic reasons, capitalists will support the break-down of the remaining employment barriers in the upper tier of the corporate structure. Interventionists suggest that with a growing multi-cultural society it is good business to have racial and gender diversity in corporate leadership. It is profitable because a multicultural leadership will be more sensitive to consumer demands and to orga-nizing and evaluating a multicultural work force. For example, one of the ways that Sears Roebuck has been invigorated has been through the tailoring of each store's merchandise to the ethnic makeup of its clientele. This new strategy began when Latino managers in Los An-geles convinced the corporate hierarchy to allow them to adjust fea-tured appliances and clothing to match the preferences of its Latino clientele.

Barbara Bergmann points out that every time affirmative action has been under attack, the corporate elite has been its strongest de-fender. She does not believe, however, that their motivation was sim-ply greater corporate profitability. Bergmann suggests: "They worry that the antisocial behavior of those who feel left out of mainstream America is detrimental, even dangerous, to the society that constitutes the cor-poration's environment and they know that such behavior has expen-sive consequences."[36]

In support of this viewpoint, advances for black and white women into professional and managerial positions continued even after the Reagan administration reduced affirmative action enforcement. Unfor-tunately, advances for all black and female workers have too often been judged by changes in professional and managerial labor markets alone. Supporters of this strategy seem to believe that there will be a trickle-down effect, whereby the benefits from greater female and black rep-resentation in these occupations will trickle down to their working-class counterparts.

This trickle-down approach is problematic. There is little evidence that improved employment and earnings for female and black non-professional workers will occur simply as a result of changes in the racial and gender composition of corporate managers and profession-als. Indeed, there is a danger that the gains for women and black men in professional labor markets will make it easier to ignore the persis-tent discrimination suffered by others. Thus, interventionist efforts should be redirected so that EEO policies can be invigorated and more focused on nonprofessional labor markets.

Though data demonstrate that black ownership does make a difference with respect to the racial composition of the work force employed, it may not substantially affect the employment of black *inner-city* residents. After all, William Wilson's study found that many black owners tended to have similar stereotypes of inner-city residents as white owners. Moreover, black businesses do not generally locate in inner-city neighborhoods. Even in Atlanta, noted for its vibrant black entrepreneurship, only one-quarter of those firms aided by set-aside programs located in poor neighborhoods.[37] Moreover, if the fear is that nonminority-owned businesses located in the inner city will not hire black workers, the solution may be greater enforcement of EEO policies. For these reasons, government efforts should focus more on correcting discriminatory lending policies and on supporting businesses created by new, less-educated entrepreneurs than on expanding set-aside programs.

10 New Harmony, Not Religious Wars

How to Promote Diversity at Elite Universities

One of the more contentious issues of the 1990s has been whether or not special admissions policies at elite colleges should be maintained. In Michigan, Texas, and California legal challenges to these policies have been mounted, confronting fundamental issues of equity and diversity. Battle lines have been drawn, and combatants are so driven by deeply held ideologies that these conflicts can be characterized as "religious" wars.

Special admissions supporters claim that only the force of government has led to modest gains for women and black men in the last few decades. They predict that selective colleges will become all-white, closing access to elite corporate and professional employment to vast numbers of qualified blacks and Latinos. From this perspective, any admission that there are even modest problems with current policies creates a fault line, which will be seized by opponents who want nothing less than their total dismantling. Thus, even those who favor a more nuanced approach—mend it, don't end it—have been forced to attack all reforms of college admissions practices unless they are clearly cosmetic.

Similarly, opponents of special admissions policies reject compromise. As more blacks and Latinos gain economic success, they increasingly contend that hard work and perseverance have become more decisive in determining outcomes. Opponents point to numerous high-profile blacks who have reached the top of their professions despite not going to the most elite colleges. Thus, they suggest that the modest barriers that might remain if government intervention were terminated should be considered minor impediments.

More nuanced positions are also limited because they lack institutional support. Opponents of special admissions can rely on the Olin Foundation and the Manhattan Institute, while proponents can rely on political institutions, including the NAACP and the National Urban League. Even when some liberals propose alternatives, their support is based upon the presupposition that its effect on black and Latino enrollment will be negligible, the strong inference being that only policies that maintain current enrollment patterns are acceptable.

The most influential individual who has promoted a more nuanced position is Glenn Loury. Loury has deeply rooted antipathies for preferential programs. He points to the hollow victories achieved by racial preferences, where a modest number of additional blacks and Latinos may benefit, but at the price of sustaining a negative stigma: "The outside reputations of most blacks will be lowered."[1] In the past, these antipathies led Loury to join forces with opponents of special admissions programs. However, in the mid-1990s Loury began to distance himself from them, partially because he believes opponents should be more gracious victors: "The Civil Rights movement as a force capable of shaping the moral and political sensibilities of the American public on questions of race was all but finished a quarter century ago, . . . Who cannot see racial preferences, minority-business set-asides, race-norming of employment tests, and the like are on the way out?"[2] However, Loury primarily rejects the color-blind absolutism of opponents of special admissions for other reasons. He notes that part of the race stigma blacks face is the persistence of white attitudes that "all blacks think alike" when there are too few blacks on campus to undermine this stereotype. Most important, Loury distinguishes between preferential policies that lower the bar from those which increase the pool of qualified underrepresented minorities applicants. At the university, this reflects developmental affirmative action programs that target underrepresented minorities for special pre-college, skill-enhancing activities.[3]

Loury is right to believe that special admissions programs are tottering. However, proponents may have more staying power than Loury anticipated and have begun to present a body of work that has reenergized the defense of the remaining special admissions programs. William Bowen and Derek Bok's evidence on the benefits to blacks from special admissions policies at selective universities, Claude Steele's empirical work on black test-taking problems, and Patricia Gurin's studies on the beneficial effect of diversity on white students have all coalesced in a spirited defense of the special admissions programs at the University of Michigan.[4]

This chapter will look more closely at the University of Michigan case and the dynamics in post–Proposition 209 California. Rather than eliminating race-based special admissions completely, I argue that its more constrained use must be combined with class-based affirmative action. Preferential policies must be undergirded by programs that increase the pool of underrepresented minorities who have the minimum skills necessary to succeed in highly competitive universities. By seeing these three distinct sets of policies as complementary, a "new harmony" can be created to replace the current religious wars.

Special Admissions Policies

Unlike equal employment opportunity policies, special admissions policies make no claims that the same standards are applied to all applicants. The use of differential standards is most apparent when combined Scholastic Aptitude Test (SAT) scores of special admissions students are compared to the combined SAT scores of others admitted to the same colleges. At the University of Michigan, the SAT gap between students accepted in 1994 that had underrepresented minorities status (UMS) and those that did not was about two hundred points.[5]

Special admissions proponents claim that SAT scores are poor predictors of college performance. Claude Steele indicates that after high school performance is accounted for, SAT scores add little to the ability to predict college grades. Moreover, he offers a troubling explanation for poor black test scores. Steele contends that black students carry a heavy psychological burden into the testing environment—the negative stereotype that they are unable to perform well on standardized tests. Steele found that black students who excel in college math courses did poorly on stressful math tests because of this psychological burden. However, they did just as well as comparable white students when freed from that stigma.[6]

While SAT scores might have little predictive power at most colleges, they are reasonably correlated with graduation rates at the most selective schools. For example, among freshmen who entered UCal Berkeley in September 1988, the proportion that graduated by 1994 was positively correlated with SAT scores, rising from a 60 percent graduation rate for students with combined SAT scores below 900 to 88 percent for students with combined SAT scores above 1,300. Given their mean combined SAT score of a bit over 900, not surprisingly, the black graduation rate was only 59 percent compared to the white graduation rate of 84 percent.[7]

Most of this disparity, however, reflected the substantial difficulty black students with *very low* SAT scores had graduating. At Berkeley, once combined SAT scores were over 1,000, the difference in graduation rates was much narrower, and other factors, such as income constraints, may explain the remaining differences. Indeed, the most vocal critics of special admissions programs, Stephan and Abigail Thernstrom, make this very point in their discussion of graduation rates at the main state university campuses in Mississippi, Georgia, and South Carolina. They point out that in all of these universities, there are minimum SAT requirements which bar students who are likely to experience severe academic difficulties. These policies substantially limit the percentage of black students accepted. For example, at the University of Mississippi only 9 percent of entering freshmen are black even though blacks comprise 35 percent of the state's population. However, these policies do eliminate racial disparities in graduation rates.[8]

The University of Michigan has tailored its admissions policies to meet ambitious diversity goals: having blacks, Latinos, and native Americans comprise 15 percent of its study body. First, it reduced substantially the value of high SAT scores. In its selection index, applicants receive 10 points if their combined SAT score is between 1,010 and 1,190 out of a maximum of 12 points. In contrast, applicants receive an additional 2 points for each one-tenth of a point rise in their high school GPA. Though its admissions procedure places relatively little value on high SAT scores, the University of Michigan realized that it still would not be able to reach its diversity goals without racial preferences. As a result, Michigan adds 20 points to an applicant's selectivity index when the applicant is a member of an underrepresented minority group.[9]

Despite these preferential policies, the University of Michigan claims that the overwhelming focus of its admissions process is on merit, noting that more than two-thirds of the selection index is based on high school performance and test scores. The distribution of total points, however, is not important. What is crucial is how much of the *variation* in total scores is explained by each component. A UMS ap-

Table 10.1 Racial Percentage Point Differences in Acceptance Rates by SAT Scores and High School GPA, University of Michigan, 1994

| | SCHOLASTIC APTITUDE TEST (SAT) SCORES | | | | | |
HS GPA	800– 899	900– 999	1,000– 1,099	1,100– 1,199	1,200– 1,299	1,300– 1,399
4.00	0	21	21	0	0	0
3.80–3.99	50	46	46	0	0	0
3.60–3.79	50	71	71	21	0	0
3.40–3.59	50	71	71	46	46	0
3.20–3.39	67	71	71	71	46	21
3.00–3.19	67	71	71	71	71	71
2.80–2.99	42	71	71	71	71	71

SOURCE: Adapted from *Washington Post*, 5 December 1997, A35

plicant with a 2.8 high school GPA and a 950 SAT score would have a higher point total than a non-UMS applicant with a 3.5 high school GPA and a 1,300 SAT score; a UMS applicant with a 3.0 high school GPA and a 1,050 SAT score would have a higher point total than a non-UMS applicant with a 3.8 high school GPA and a 1,450 SAT score.

As might be expected, both black and white applicants, with high SAT scores and high GPAs, are virtually assured admittance so that there was little racial differences in acceptance rates for black and white applicants with those qualifications. There is the same racial equality for students with low SAT scores and low GPAs. However, there are substantial racial differences in acceptance rates among applicants who have qualifications in the mid-range. Here, the enhanced point total for UMS applicants gives them a decisive advantage.

The *Washington Post* documents this disparity (see Table 10.1). Each cell identifies a specific set of qualifications—same SAT score and same high school GPA. The value for each cell was derived by taking the difference between the percentage of black applicants with those qualifications that were accepted and the percentage of white students that were accepted. For example, let us look at the cell reflecting applicants with combined SAT scores between 1,100 and 1,199 and GPAs between 3.0 and 3.19. Approximately 93 percent of black students with these qualifications were accepted, while the acceptance rate for white applicants was only about 22 percent. As a result, for this cell, the racial difference was 71 percentage points.

Given its crucial role, eliminating underrepresented minority status from the admissions process would have a devastating effect on diversity. Stephen Raudenbush simulated the impact if UMS applicants had the same probabilities of admittance as non-UMS applicants in each of the GPA-SAT cells in Table 10.1. For the 1995 freshman class, he estimated that the percentage of UMS students admitted would have declined from 14.3 percent to 5 percent.[10]

Under the 1995 admissions policies, 97.55 percent of non-UMS applicants who were admitted had at least a 3.20 high school GPA and combined SAT scores of at least 1,000. By contrast, only 43.88 percent of UMS applicants admitted met both these standards. Using admissions data for Michigan residents, I simulated the effect on UMS admissions if minimum standards would have been enforced for all admits. In this case, UMS applicants could still benefit from preferential policies but only if they met minimum high school grade point and/or SAT standards.

Among Michigan residents, UMS applicants comprised 14.01 percent of those accepted for the fall 1995 entering class. If a minimum high school GPA of 3.20 had been instituted but no minimum SAT score required, UMS share of admittances would have been reduced modestly to 12.29 percent. Instead, if there were no minimum GPA requirement but a minimum combined SAT score of 900 or 1,000 was instituted, UMS admissions would have dropped to 10.21 and 7.21 percent, respectively. If the minimum combined SAT score was set at 1,000 *and* minimum GPA at 3.20, UMS admissions would have dropped to 6.91 percent. Thus, it is the inability of UMS applicants to meet minimum standards, especially SAT scores, which would be primarily responsible for the dramatic decline in diversity which Raudenbush projects.

A final point often ignored is that the black beneficiaries of special admissions programs are primarily applicants from middle-class backgrounds. As the National Task Force on Minority High Achievement found, there are substantial achievement gaps between blacks and whites from middle-class backgrounds. Brent Staples offers a series of explanations. He claims that compulsory ignorance "created a legacy of alienation from books and reading," leading blacks to embrace the notion that defines "brain work as an exclusively white activity." He also points to "teachers and counselors who cannot conceive of [black students] as academically inclined and discourage them from taking advanced courses." Staples concludes, "[W]hat is already clear is that the leap from averageness to excellence for children of the black middle class will require discarding attitudes and preconceptions that were hundreds of years in the making." William Julius Wilson contends that the performance gap persists because black middle-class households are "weighed down by the accumulation of disadvantages that stem from racial restrictions."[11]

Diversity Goals

Increasingly, supporters of special admissions policies have shifted their defense. Elite universities have always adjusted admissions standards in order to have a diverse geographic pool of students. Special admissions supporters contend that there is even more legitimacy to have racial diversity as one of its goals. Barbara Bergmann states: "The major justification for affirmative action in the workplace is its use as a systematic method of breaking down the current discrimination against blacks and women. The desirability of diversity provides the strongest justification for affirmative action in college admissions."[12]

Racial diversity was the basis given by Justice Lewis Powell for his deciding vote when special admissions policies at UCal Davis's medical school were challenged in the federal courts in 1978. Casting the fifth vote in favor of the medical school's policies, Justice Powell said it was legal to incorporate preferential procedures in order to meet diversity goals so that the university could select "those students who will contribute the most to the robust exchange of ideas."

Powell left unsettled, however, how much race could be taken into account and how many individuals from a particular group are necessary to fulfill diversity. Though the number of black students sufficient for diversity may be much lower than their share in the population, diversity advocates generally support the goal of proportional representation. Moreover, in their rationale for diversity they often make the dubious assumption that there is an "authentic" black viewpoint. For example, Barbara Bergmann states:

> Diversity prevents power from being concentrated in any one group and promises sympathetic and fair treatment to all sections of the public. . . . Another benefit of diversity is the differing points of view, insights, values, and knowledge of the world that members of various groups bring to their roles. . . . We cannot have white leaders who spend their college years in segregated institutions and never interact with African Americans or hear their point of view.[13]

This widely accepted notion that one can project values and viewpoints onto individuals based on their racial background leads to dangerous stereotypes. As David Wasserman notes:

> An urban police force wants to hire more black and Hispanic officers because it thinks that they are likely to have a far better rapport with the disaffected and wary youth of those neighborhoods than their white counterparts. . . . An urban school system wants more black and Hispanic teachers because it thinks they will generally be better than their white counterparts at spotting talent in, and motivating, alienated black and Hispanic students, as well as relating to parents and the broader community.[14]

Moreover, there is no guarantee that the blacks and Latinos accepted will be "authentic," providing the expected set of values and viewpoints. I doubt proponents would argue that Clarence Thomas, by bringing racial diversity to the Supreme Court, has prevented power from being concentrated among conservatives and promises sympathetic treatment to blacks and the poor. I doubt that the new crop of black executives singled out by *Fortune* have values and viewpoints which make them significantly different from their white counterparts.[15] This certainly has been the pattern of behavior of female executives that the feminist Suzanne Gordon has observed: "Women now strive to be treated as equals to men in a man's world rather than to change the masculine marketplace men have made. In addition, . . . many women have even begun to adopt traditional male attitudes of disdain for the caregiving activities of women that have nurtured, empowered, and sustained the human community for centuries."[16]

There is an alternative reason to promote diversity. As Loury points out, diversity is valuable precisely because it will break down stereotypical views. It is valuable for white students to meet black students with a *variety* of political and social views in an atmosphere in which they think of one another as equals not simply socially, but academically as well. It is important for white students to see that though, not surprisingly, black students have strong views on racial discrimination, they do not have a single set of policies to promote equality. As the University of Michigan psychologist Patricia Gurin writes: "Social diversity is especially likely to increase effortful, active thinking when institutions of higher education capitalize on these conditions in the classroom and provide a climate in which students from diverse backgrounds frequently interact with each other."[17]

Gurin marshaled substantial empirical evidence from local and national data to support her claims concerning the linkage between diversity and learning:

> Students who experienced the most racial and ethnic diversity in classroom settings and in informal interactions with peers showed the greatest engagement in active thinking processes, growth in intellectual engagement and motivation, and growth in intellectual and academic skills. . . . Students educated in diverse settings are more motivated and better able to participate in an increasingly heterogeneous and complex democracy.[18]

While Gurin's work shows the positive benefits of diversity, her findings also suggest that there are some problems created by the enrollment of *weak-skilled* African American students. She finds that white students are much less likely to be involved in study groups with blacks than they are with Asians or Latinos, even though the black student body is five times larger than these two other groups. Her findings also suggest that weaker black students disproportionately seek refuge in ethnic studies courses, reducing their role in promoting multicultural campus interactions. Thus, the elimination of the weakest-skilled black students might further diversity goals even more.

There is also the possibility that students admitted as a result of special admissions programs may not benefit. In particular, the Thernstroms point to the high black failure rate at the selective colleges included in the Bowen and Bok study. They also highlight Linda Wightman's study, which found that "more than a fifth of the black law students who owed their admission to racial preferences failed to graduate; even worse, 27 percent of those who got through law school were unable to pass a bar exam within three years, a failure rate nearly triple that of blacks who were admitted under regular standards, and almost seven times the white failure rate."[19]

The Thernstroms suggest that even though special admissions supporters are aware of its harmful long-term effects, they continue to support these policies because of liberal guilt. "Racially well-meaning whites, terrified of the label racist, remake themselves as angels of mercy, embracing policies built on deference to black victimization through which they can display their racial virtue."[20] Interestingly,

Andrew Hacker seems to agree: "Since [special admissions programs] will almost inevitably bring in students who will have difficulty keeping up with their classmates, it seems appropriate to ask why [elite] schools persist in this kind of effort. The candid answer is that many professors and quite a few students regard the paucity of black faces on their campuses as a cause for shame. To raise the minority presence eases a lot of academic guilt."[21]

The Thernstroms overstate their case. First, the vast majority of black students in elite colleges graduate and, thus, are likely to benefit from special admissions policies which enabled them to enroll there. Second, there is some evidence that black students are *more* likely to graduate from the most selective colleges than if they had attended less selective ones. In particular, William Bowen and Derek Bok claim that black students with equal SAT scores had higher earnings if they attended the most selective colleges (SEL-1) rather than somewhat less selective (SEL-2) ones. They conclude: "Black students admitted to the most selective [schools] did not pay a penalty in life after college for having attended such competitive institutions. On the contrary, the black matriculants with academic credentials that were modest by the standards of these schools appear to have been well advised to go to the most selective schools to which they were admitted."[22]

At closer inspection, the data used by Bowen and Bok do not completely support their claims. Among black male and black female students, with combined SAT scores below 1,000, those that had attended SEL-1 colleges had higher 1995 incomes than those who had attended SEL-2 colleges. This should not be surprising since they would have been weak students in either group of colleges. Since the most selective schools have the most status and also the highest retention rates, weak black students benefit from attending them.

When we look at the record of black students with combined SAT scores between 1,000 and 1,199, however, the evidence is less compelling. For black men, with combined SAT scores between 1,100 and 1,199, and black women, with combined SAT scores between 1,000 and 1,099, it was beneficial to attend an SEL-1 rather than an SEL-2 school. Among black men with combined SAT scores between 1,000 and 1,099, however, their 1995 earnings were $83,600 and $91,800 if they had attended an SEL-1 and an SEL-2 school, respectively. Similarly, black women with combined SAT scores between 1,100 and 1,199 had lower earnings if they attended an SEL-1 rather than an SEL-2 school—$73,500 versus $83,600. Thus, Bowen and Bok's data suggest that black students with *competent* skills do not consistently benefit when special admissions programs enable them to attend the most selective schools.[23]

If the only black students who consistently benefit from special admissions programs are the weakest-skilled students, there is an unintended adverse side affect: the reinforcement of negative attitudes among whites and Asians about the capability of blacks. As the most selective schools have become more desirable, the competition at them has become more intense. In this environment, while the weakest-skilled African American students might very well graduate and use those credentials to gain high salaries, the racial performance gap will grow. Indeed, Bowen and Bok found that at their selective schools, among the class of 1991, more than one-half of all black matriculants ranked in the lower quarter of their graduation classes.[24] These disparities only reinforce perceptions of black inferiority and the racial stigma that Claude Steele found so damaging to even high-achieving black students.

The impact of special admissions programs on racial differentials in performance is not limited to selective colleges. Black students who have records consistent with attendance at the less-competitive schools are attending selective colleges due to special admissions policies. Since less-competitive schools are unable to recruit these black students, they must dip lower into the academic pool to meet their diversity goals. Thus, less-competitive schools will also have a racial disparity in course performance, again reinforcing racial stereotypes.

Besides poorer school performance, special admissions policies may reinforce a siege/tribal mentality among black students at elite colleges. Black students fear criticizing openly other blacks because it will give "ammunition" to white racists, and a culture develops which strongly encourages blacks to maintain segregated patterns of socialization. As Gurin's data suggest, ethnic studies programs often serve as segregated safe havens for weakly prepared students rather than places of demanding intellectual pursuits. For these reason, an overuse of race-based special admissions programs may hinder racial interaction and help sustain racial stigmas.

Class-Based and Developmental Policies

For most people, race- and ethnic-based special admissions policies conflict with notions of equity. Not surprisingly, in 1996, 54 percent of California voters approved Proposition 209, which outlawed state agencies using race in any way to determine hirings, procurement contracts, or college admissions. This majority included one-quarter of Latino and black voters.[25] The passage of Proposition 209 increased the visibility of an alternative *class-based* set of special admissions policies, as well as support for policies to provide resources to prepare disadvantaged students to meet the same admissions standards as other applicants.

Class-based special admissions allows for preferences based on socioeconomic characteristics. Applicants from poor households, those raised by a single parent, or those providing evidence of overcoming other obstacles, would gain some preference. The movement to class-based admissions policies has gained momentum for two reasons. First, many liberals *and* conservatives support class-based policies, undermining opposition.[26] Second, and probably more important, given the impending elimination of race-based special admissions policies, this shift is seen by many as a tactical retreat. As Ethan Bonner reported: "In anticipation of a sharp drop in minority admissions, Berkeley officials said, they overhauled their admission procedure, relying less on grade point averages and scores on standardized tests like the SAT and more on essays and a mix of criteria like whether the applicant had overcome difficult barriers."[27]

Prior to the adjustment, Berkeley's admissions policy was based on total points, generated by counting high school performance and standardized test scores equally: a possible 4,000 points based upon high school performance and a possible 4,000 points based on five SAT scores. While total points were distributed equally, each component did not have an equal impact on admissions. To see how this is possible, suppose that everyone who applied had an A average so that they each received 4,000 points for their high school performance. In this case, each applicant's *relative* ranking would be determined *solely* by SAT performance.

This is close to the way variation in total points occurs since there is some but not very much variation in high school performance of applicants to Berkeley. Virtually all students who apply to Berkeley have strong high school records. With upward adjustments, probably 90 percent of the applicants received at least 3,700 out of a possible 4,000 points. With such a slight difference in high school performance, almost all of the variation in total points was due to variations on the SAT component. For example, a student who averaged 670 on the five

SAT tests would total 3,350, while a student who averaged 500 would obtain only 2,500 points.

This retreat seemed acceptable to many since it should make little difference to inner-city black youths if they receive compensation for their racial or low socioeconomic background. However, among students from low-income households (less than $20,000 annual income), blacks do substantially worse than whites, Asians, and Latinos. As a result, special admissions proponents feared that "low-income whites and Asians would end up with almost all of the 'race-blind' awards, since most of them have better records from a strictly scholastic standpoint. This is why affirmative action that aims at helping blacks must take race into account."[28]

These expectations for class-based special admissions policies were fairly accurate. The 1998 freshmen classes at Berkeley and UCLA declined substantially when race-based special admissions were replaced by class-based procedures. The number of black and Latino freshmen at Berkeley each declined by about one-half, while at UCLA, each declined by about 30 percent. As Bonner reported: "Some officials said they had postulated that by taking into account other factors like individuality, as well as socioeconomic status, the number of black and Hispanic students would remain high. But Bob Laird, director of undergraduate admissions at Berkeley, said that many low-income whites and Asians also overcame such barriers so it did not especially benefit minorities."[29]

These results duplicate changes that had already occurred in acceptance rates at state medical schools. In 1995, these medical schools began eliminating underrepresented minority status as an admissions factor and began substituting socioeconomic status. Just as with the undergraduate enrollment, this shift to a class-based preference system adversely affected both black and Latino applicants. As a result, black admittances fell by two-thirds, while Latino admittances were halved.[30]

To provide further insights into the initial effect of the ending of race-based special admissions, let us look at enrollment for Berkeley and UCLA—the two flagship universities in the UCal system (see Figure 10.1). Each campus is allowed to supplement those admitted through the regular process—in which special admissions played a significant role—through the discretion of its president. For this reason, enrolled students are separated into those who were admitted through the regular

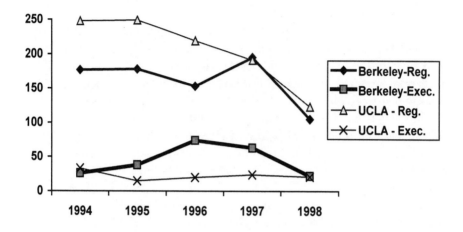

Figure 10.1 Entering Freshman Class, 1994–1998. *Source: University of California Office of the President, Application Flow Report for New Students (various years).*

admissions process and those who entered through executive exceptions.

During the mid-1990s, the number of black freshmen enrolled through the regular admissions process stagnated or declined at the two flagship campuses, Berkeley and UCLA. However, their response differed. To compensate, Berkeley increased substantially in 1996 and 1997 the number of blacks entering through executive exceptions and increased black enrollment through the regular process in 1997. In contrast, UCLA chose not to increase its use of executive exceptions so that total black admission declined continuously. As a result, in 1997, 27.48 percent of all black freshmen enrolled in the UCal system were at Berkeley, while only 16.72, 15.10, and 9.62 percent of Asian, Latino, and white UCal freshmen, respectively, were enrolled there. These distinctive efforts at Berkeley explain why its black freshman enrollment declined disproportionately once race and ethnic preferences were purged from both the regular admissions and executive exceptions procedures.

The enrollment patterns at the other six UCal campuses prove most interesting. Starting in 1997, black enrollment through the regular admissions process began to increase at these campuses so that they reduced the numbers admitted through executive exceptions. Between

1997 and 1998, the number of black freshmen enrolled through the regular admissions process increased from 375 to 450. Even after taking into account the drop in those admitted through executive exceptions, the total number of black freshmen at these schools increased from 476 to 490; total Latino freshmen enrollment increased from 2,087 to 2,246. Thus, to some extent, the ending of race-based special admissions in the UCal system led to a shifting of black and Latino students within the system. Indeed, in 1998, 16.51 percent of all black freshmen enrolled in the UCal system were at Berkeley, more in line with that of other groups.

The initial reports on black and Latino fall 1998 freshman enrollment at Berkeley caused a number of critics of race-based admissions programs like Nathan Glazer to rethink their position. However, given Proposition 209, supporters of race-based policies realized that they would have to rely on class-based policies and looked to the experience in Texas. There, too, the court-ordered *Hopkins* decision eliminated race-based preferences. In response, a coalition developed between black, Latino, and white state legislators from low-income areas. They successfully passed legislation which required that the two state flagship universities—Texas A&M and the University of Texas at Austin—must admit anyone who ranked in the top 10 percent of their high school graduation class.

The California legislature adopted a similar policy. All students who rank in the top 4 percent of their graduating class are now guaranteed enrollment at a school in the UCal system. In addition, Berkeley modified its admissions procedure still further so that socioeconomic disadvantage was given more weight. These changes were expected to increase modestly the number of black and Latino students eligible for the UCal system.

Despite the doomsday forecast, black and Latino enrollment rebounded dramatically. By 2000, Chicano admissions were 13 percent higher, and freshman enrollment 10 percent higher than in 1997. Black admittance matched 1997 admittance. However, black freshman enrollment was still 14 percent below its 1997 peak though it grew by 13 percent between 1999 and 2000. This reduced black enrollment seems to be primarily due to an unwillingness of many of those admitted to attend the less-prestigious campuses. In particular, total 2000 black freshman enrollment at the eight UCal campuses other than Berkeley matched 1977 enrollment.[31]

Even if class-based special admissions policies lowered black and

Latino admissions, many reject a return to unrestricted race-based policies. Opponents of race-based policies claim that "the worst aspect of racial preferences is that they encourage dependency on entitlements, rather than our own initiative."[32] They believe that once race-based preferences are eliminated, blacks and Latinos will be forced to increase their own efforts, raising their skill levels and gaining more satisfaction when they succeed. Just as free market advocates contend that "tough love" policies are good for the poor because they break the cycle of welfare dependencies, many suggest that the same is needed to break special admissions dependencies.

Unlike these opponents, however, Loury rejects a complete abandonment of taking race into account. He advocates government funding for preparatory efforts which enable disadvantaged black youth to become better prepared to meet desired standards because it takes "black underdevelopment in late twentieth-century America seriously."[33] Loury characterizes this approach as *developmental* affirmative action in contrast to *preferential* affirmative action.

With little systemwide support, the Riverside campus of the UCal system undertook developmental affirmative action programs in the early 1990s. It initiated skill-enhancement programs to increase the supply of UCal-eligible high school students from the surrounding black and Chicano communities. This program has been a resounding success. Whereas throughout the state the fraction of UCal-eligible students had declined, in Riverside and adjoining San Bernardino counties, it rose from 6 percent to 8.1 percent.

With the ending of race-based admissions policies, California is finally taking seriously similar programs to increase the number of UCal-eligible students. As James Traub writes:

> UC[al] campuses are now reaching down into the high schools, the junior highs and even the elementary schools to help minority students achieve the kind of academic record that will make them eligible for admissions, thus raising the possibility that diversity without preferences will someday prove to be more than a fond hope. Academics and administrators throughout the system admit that the university would never have shouldered this burden had it not been for the elimination of affirmative action; and many say that the price is worth paying.[34]

Thanks to the 10 percent program, the share of black and Latino students at the University of Texas at Austin returned to the levels achieved under race-based special admissions policies. This enrollment was aided by Longhorn scholarships to students from historically underrepresented schools so that they can afford to attend. As a result, a large number of low-income students admitted lacked the skill background provided by high schools in wealthier areas. The university has aided these less-prepared students by providing smaller classes in key technical courses like calculus rather than have them attend lecture sections with five hundred students.[35]

The presence of skill deficiencies in these high-achieving students has been a catalyst to educational improvements in schools that serve the poorest students. A long-time participant in outreach programs, Phillip Uri Treisman contends that there has been an increased desire of university officials to go into the public schools to correct skill deficiencies as soon as possible. "When I first came here it was clearly a controversial issue . . . [but] has that turned around. Now, there's, 'How can we do this, how fast, what do you need?'"[36] As a result, Treisman is hopeful that students in underfunded schools are beginning to have access to the same skill-development programs as students in wealthier school districts.

Skill-development programs have been particularly effective in the U.S. Army. Just as universities, the army found that poor performance on standardized tests limited the number of blacks who met minimum academic requirements. However, the army chose not to create differential academic standards but, instead, initiated developmental policies.

The army increased the number of black college graduates entering commissioned officers training schools by its special focus on the historically black colleges and universities (HBCU). Charles Moskos and John Butler report, "A black applicant to an ROTC program is twice as likely as a white applicant to be awarded an ROTC scholarship because a special scholarship allotment . . . exists for the HBCUs."[37] While this increases the black pool, the army found that because of low skills among ROTC cadets at the HBCUs, it was necessary to have developmental programs to ensure that they would pass entrance examinations to officers training programs. Since 1985, all ROTC cadets at the HBCU are evaluated for basic written, oral, and math skills. Average or below-average scorers are required to enroll in the Enhanced Skill Training (EST) program funded by the army. The EST has raised skill levels so that 99 percent of its enrollees pass the Officer Basic Training Course, the screening program that all new second lieutenants take after commissioning. As a result, nearly one-half of all African American officers recruited from ROTC programs attended HBCUs.

The army also used a preparatory program to increase the number of black applicants entering West Point. The U.S. Military Academy Preparatory School (USMAPS) enrolls students who have been recommended for the academy but who have SAT scores too low to meet entrance requirements. About 60 percent of those enrolled enter West Point after successfully completing its full-year skill-enhancing program. While USMAPS alumni make up one-sixth of the entire West Point student body, USMAPS alumni comprise 40 percent of the black student population.

Among black USMAPS alumni who enter West Point, 94 percent graduate four years later, compared to 79 percent for the entire West Point entering class. Loury believes that selective state universities should pattern their admissions policies after the army's policies, provisionally accepting promising applicants who "first go to a less exclusive school to improve their math and verbal aptitudes."[38]

A similar approach has been taken in New York City to increase the number of black and Latino students enrolled in the three elite public high schools. In 1996, black students comprised only 4.8 percent of those enrolled at Stuyvesant and 9.8 percent of those enrolled at Bronx High School of Science, the two most competitive of the elite public high schools, even though they comprised 34 percent of all New York City high school students. Latino students are also underrepresented in these high schools. In addition, over 90 percent of the students accepted at Stuyvesant come from thirteen of the thirty-three school districts. In response, the New York City Board of Education began an enrichment program, the Math/Science Institute (MSI), available to students from the twenty underrepresented school districts.

Students accepted to the Math/Science Institute participate in a program beginning the summer following the sixth grade. The students attend the program daily from the beginning of July to the second week in August and continue twice each week during their seventh-grade school year. The students spend a second summer in the Math/Science Institute, and in the autumn of the eighth grade, the students attend a test preparation course. Participants in the program take the Specialized Science High School Admissions Test in December with the other applicants throughout New York City. Students must attain the required score in order to be admitted to the desired specialized high school for the following autumn.

In its first year, 419 students were enrolled and 310 completed the eighteen-month program. Almost three-quarters of the students completing the program were either black or Latino, and they had a 50 percent passing rate on the entrance exam, compared to a passing rate among all applicants of only 22 percent. These acceptances help increase black enrollment at Stuyvesant by 20 percent and Latino enrollment by 60 percent. The second Math/Science Institute graduating class increased black and Latino enrollment still further. More broadly, in 1998, MSI students comprised only 6 percent of all students admitted to Stuyvesant but 28 percent of all those students admitted from the twenty underrepresented school districts. As a result of these position achievements the program has been expanded to four sites with a total of 1,100 students.[39]

Concluding Remarks

Since race-based special admissions policies require preferential treatment, there should be clear justification and persuasive evidence demonstrating their effectiveness. It is insufficient to point to the dearth of black and Latino students at elite programs if special admissions policies required substantial inequities in admissions standards. Most telling, these preferential policies have not expanded the small pool of qualified black and Latino students. Indeed, they have hindered the shift to programs that are the most likely vehicles to expand the pool of blacks and Latinos with the skills to succeed. In addition, these preferential programs make it more difficult to defend and *expand* EEO hiring policies.

Campus diversity can only be beneficial when black and Latino students are on reasonably equal footing with other students. If weakly prepared students are admitted, negative attitudes held by white and Asian students are reinforced. Moreover, the evidence that these weakly prepared students benefit simply from the credentialization they receive may only hold for the weakest students admitted to the most elite schools. Today, with much more competition among well-qualified students, it is less likely that simply gaining a degree will be sufficient to ensure success. Thus, requiring minimum high school GPAs and SAT scores must be a part of any continued race-based special admissions programs.

While modified race-based policies can be useful in some situations, class-based policies should be emphasized because they maximize efforts to aid working-class households that have yet to be given equal access to professional careers. The class-based 10 percent program in Texas exposed the glaring inequities between high schools in poor and wealthy areas. Similarly, Proposition 209 focused attention on the inadequate educational resources provided to working-class communities. Developmental programs have been used successfully elsewhere and will likely be just as successful in California and Texas if state funding for these efforts is made available.

By narrowing the scope of special admissions to only those who meet minimum academic standards, and emphasizing class-based and developmental policies, more underrepresented minorities can be aided without undermining notions of equity. There is always the danger that by offering developmental programs for a small number of students who excel, movements to improve public schools that serve all black and Latino students can be undermined. However, such fears cannot justify rejecting specialized programs that promote the upward mobility of working-class black and Latino students. Indeed, only by supporting developmental policies can we expect to overcome the racial stigma that has historically burdened them.

11 | Setting Policy Priorities
What Works Best Politically?

Many books conclude with a laundry list of recommendations, and in a sense this one will be no different. Indeed, the last two chapters detailed ways in which affirmative action policies can be improved, and earlier, pay-equity proposals were presented as a means of overcoming the lower pay in female-dominated occupations. Black and female workers can also gain from policies aimed at raising wages of all low-paid workers in the noncollege labor sector.

Other writers have focused on class-specific recommendations. This was the main approach taken by the sociologist William Julius Wilson in his book, *The Truly Disadvantaged.* It is also found in *Why Americans Hate Welfare* where the political scientist Martin Gilens documents how race has shaped the way Americans judge government welfare policies. He finds that the U.S. public, as a result of biased and sensationalistic media coverage, associate welfare with undeserving blacks who would rather take handouts than strive to better themselves. Gilens is compelling in his presentation of how these falsehoods have mobilized racial prejudice without seeming to be racist. Despite the centrality of race, however, Gilens emphasizes that race-neutral policies are better than race-conscious policies. Thus, he focuses on job training and other skill-enhancing programs that he believes are capable of attracting wider political support.[1]

My support of class-specific policies is also based in part on political judgments. Surveys continue to find wide differences in black and white attitudes concerning race. On the one hand, whites often admit that they have a better chance of getting ahead in today's society, while few believe that affirmative action has enabled blacks to be advantaged. On the other hand, one-third of white Americans believe that too much is being made of problems facing black Americans, and only one-quarter of whites believe race relations to be one of the most important issues in U.S. society.[2] Moreover, class-specific policies are much less vulnerable to attack because they serve a broader constituency. These factors may explain why whites have broadly supported the replacement of race-specific affirmative action by class-specific preferential policies in the college admissions process in both Texas and California. However, I also focus here on class-specific policies for other reasons.

Without trivializing the disparities among professional workers, this book has argued that racial and gender gaps are much larger and more resistant to change in the noncollege labor sector. Informal hiring practices have made it more difficult to break down exclusionary barriers, and glass ceilings persist even when female and black workers are able to enter higher-paying occupations in this sector. Certainly more aggressive enforcement of equal employment opportunity policies can help. However, reliance on enhanced EEO policies would still leave significant disparities as long as employers use informal hiring practices, especially when labor supplies are relatively abundant. Moreover, occupational wage differences in this sector are not dominantly based on skill differences, so skill-enhancing policies may have limited success. For these reasons, policies that raise the earnings of workers at the bottom of the labor market, independent of skill, are necessary to substantially eliminate race and gender disparities in the noncollege labor sector. Besides pay equity, these policies include increased unionization, minimum wage and living wage legislation, enhancement of the earned income tax credit, and macroeconomic policies that maintain tight labor markets.

Trade Unions

Initiated by white men, craft unions served only skilled workers. However, the industrial unions that rose in the 1930s served a broader constituency. Seeking to unite both skilled and unskilled workers within each industry, they were forced to overcome racial divisions, particularly in industries like meatpacking and steel, in which there were a significant number of black workers. Indeed, thanks to these unionization efforts, gains in the late 1930s and early 1940s "represented more industrial and occupational diversification for Negroes than had occurred in the seventy-five preceding years."[3]

Unfortunately, after World War II progress within the union movement stalled. Indeed, few of the industrial unions that organized black and white workers had more than token black representation among its leadership. The struggle against discriminatory practices at the workplace was compromised even more when the industrial unions merged with the craft unions in 1955 to form the AFL-CIO. Union retreat often resulted from the anticommunist purges of left-wing activists—the group most committed within unions to racial equality—as well as an accommodation to the racial attitudes of white workers. Economic studies, however, continued to find that in the 1960s, unions still raised the overall racial earnings ratio by about 3 percent.[4]

This retreat was most apparent within the Union of Automobile Workers. Though an industrial union, at its inception in the 1930s, the UAW gave the all-white skilled craft section veto power over any contract negotiated. Over the next thirty years, the skilled occupations within the unionized industry remained virtually all white, and black workers continued to be relegated to the more difficult, lowest-paid positions. In Detroit, a UAW bastion, white workers elected conservative Republican Albert Cobo mayor three times during the 1950s because he ran on a platform of protecting white neighborhoods from integration. White auto workers formed the core of Alabama governor George Wallace's victory in the 1968 Democratic presidential primary and provided the foundation of the subsequent Republican strategy of winning over a conservative Democrat.[5]

Union bureaucratic indifference to concerns of black (and female) workers continued to grow, and by the 1980s few progressives considered AFL-CIO leadership an ally in the fight against gender and racial inequities. Together with other problems within the union movement, and shifts in the location of production, the share of private-sector workers who were union members declined to 10 percent from a peak of 35 percent at the time of the AFL-CIO merger. This deunionization has been linked to rising wage inequality and to the lowering of real wages. The labor economist Richard Freeman estimates that approximately 20 percent of this increased earnings inequality is attributable to declining union density.[6]

Since the 1995 election of John Sweeney to leadership of the AFL-CIO, however, there has been a renewed hope that the union movement will again become an ally of black and female workers. For the first time in decades, aggressive union organizing campaigns have increased labor ranks, and some of the major organizing campaigns have focused on low-wage black and female workers. The most exemplary of the recent organizing efforts has been the Janitors for Justice (J for J) campaign. Throughout the 1980s, in cities across the country, unionized janitors were replaced with nonunionized contractors who employed immigrant workers. Nowhere was this more evident than in Los Angeles where union membership shrank from 5,000 in 1978 to 1,800 in 1985, and unionized employment at $7.00 per hour was replaced by nonunionized minimum wage workers. In response, Sweeney, who then headed the Service Employees International Union (SEIU), set up the J for J campaign to reunionize the janitors who worked in the nation's class-A office properties.

The campaign has been national since a large proportion of the properties is owned by national companies, Real Estate Investment Trusts (REITs), or pension funds. Moreover, the janitorial services owners used were national companies, including American Building Maintenance and OneSource. As a result, the SEIU coordinated efforts in major cities and began negotiating directly with the national companies. In addition, the SEIU built alliances with community organizations and supported nonunion issues that were of importance to immigrant communities, including support for amnesty legislation that would allow illegals to gain permanent residency status. In California, the SEIU became a potent political force, resulting in widespread support among elected officials for the J for J campaign.[7]

When the SEIU struck in Los Angeles in 2000, it was able to rely on support from other local unions who had historically shown little interest in the plight of immigrant workers. In particular, the elevator operators, members of one of the best-paid and most conservative unions, refused to cross picket lines. In addition, the SEIU began setting up picket lines at sites in other cities owned by the same corporations. As a result, property owners—for whom janitorial services are a small expense—put pressure on the contracting companies to settle quickly. As a result, unionized janitorial workers in Los Angeles received a 26 percent pay increase spread over three years, and the spillover effect on the wages of nonunionized janitors in noncovered buildings was also substantial.

A second major area in which union organizing has aided the lowest-paid workers has been in the hotel industry. In 1999, 53 percent of housekeeping workers were black and Latino, while 83 percent were women. Their average weekly wage was just under three hundred dollars. The Hotel Employees and Restaurant Employees (HERE) union has spearheaded organizing drives that have gained wage and working-condition benefits for many of these workers across the nation. The most visible success has been in Las Vegas. Due to successful organizing drives, 29 percent of hotel-casino workers there are unionized compared to only 1.5 percent in Reno.

The sharp contrast between these two casino resort areas in Nevada is also reflected in salary differences. The average wage of workers in occupations in Las Vegas with substantial union coverage is 24 percent higher than the average wage in identical occupations in Reno. These wage benefits are received by nonunionized Las Vegas workers in those occupations. The union sets the standard, and it's a powerful enough force in the labor market that if the nonunion properties want to get the same quantity and quality labor, they pretty much have to meet the union standard. These benefits prevent Las Vegas hotel and casino workers from falling into financial despair. Whereas fourteen of the twenty-one hotel-casino service job classifications in Reno had average wages below the poverty level, this is true of only four classifications in Las Vegas. Once more, unions aid black and female workers by lifting the wage floor in the lowest-paid occupations.

Minimum Wage and Living Wage Policies

The minimum wage sets a floor below which wages cannot be paid. As of July 2000, it stood at $5.15 per hour. The minimum wage has historically been supported as an effective means of aiding less-skilled workers. However, beginning in the late 1970s, critics began suggesting that the higher wages make it unprofitable for firms to hire many low-skilled workers. Indeed, in the 1980 presidential debate, candidate Ronald Reagan claimed that the minimum wage was the principal reason for high black youth unemployment, and later in the decade, the liberal *New York Times* editorialized for its elimination. Given this rhetoric, it is not surprising that between 1979 and 1989 there was no increase in the minimum wage. While there have been a number of increases since then, in 2000, after adjusting for inflation, the minimum wage is still more than 30 percent below its value in the late 1960s.

The ability to mount campaigns to increase the minimum wage has been aided by recent studies that demonstrate that there are at most very small adverse employment effects. Indeed, after the minimum wage was increased in 1991, the economists Laurence Katz and Allan Krueger found no adverse effect on employment in Texas fast-foods restaurants. If fast-foods restaurants in a low-wage state did not change their employment decisions, these researchers considered it unlikely that other firms whose labor costs were less sensitive to changes in the minimum wage would do so. Then economists Jared Bernstein and John Schmitt analyzed the two-stage 1996–1997 minimum wage increase. They focused on teenagers and adults with less than a high school degree, the two groups thought to be most likely to suffer lost employment. Using a variety of tests, they could not find any statistically significant adverse employment effects. These findings made it highly unlikely that many workers would suffer earnings losses from minimum wage increases.[8]

These studies led pro-market economists to shift to another reason to oppose the minimum wage. They pointed to evidence that, at the time of the 1991 increase, only 17 percent of minimum wage workers lived in poor households and only another 14 percent lived in near-poor households—those with incomes between 100 and 150 percent of the poverty income threshold. Thus, pro-market economists claimed that the minimum wage is an inefficient anti-poverty program, primarily increasing earnings of workers who live in middle-class households.[9]

Bernstein and Schmitt reject this viewpoint. When the minimum wage was raised in two stages in 1996 and 1997, nearly 10 million workers had their wage raised as a direct result. An additional 10 million workers, who had an hourly wage between $5.15 and $6.15, probably also benefited. Female workers comprised 58.2 percent of those 20 million workers. It also benefited disproportionately nonwhite women since in 1996, 13.7, 19.4, and 27.5 percent of white, black, and Latino female workers, respectively, earned $5.78 per hour or less.[10]

Households in the bottom 20 percent of the income distribution receive only 5 percent of total family income but received 35.4 percent of the benefits of the minimum wage increase. In addition, 18 percent of minimum wage workers were single heads of households, while among other households, the minimum wage workers contributed on average 44 percent of the household's income. Thus, raising the minimum wage disproportionately aids poor and near-poor households and is an important policy to raise the wages of working women.[11]

Working full-time, year-round at the minimum wage still yields earnings insufficient for a family to escape poverty unless supplemented by other sources of income, such as government transfers or other wage earners in the household. Moreover, a large proportion of low-wage workers and their families are among the 40 million Americans without health insurance. Living wage campaigns attempt to overcome these problems by setting the wage rate high enough for full-time workers to escape poverty solely on the basis of their earnings. If an annual income of $15,000 is set as the goal and we assume two thousand hours of employment, this yields a living wage rate of $7.50 per hour. In addition, fringe benefits, including medical coverage, are often included as proposed requirements. In a sense the living wage movement reflects the goals of the earlier family wage movement without its patriarchal component.

The contemporary living wage movement began in Baltimore in 1994. At the time, government jobs there were being shifted to the private sector through privatization. These private companies paid much lower wages and provided fewer benefits than government employees had received. In order to stem this cheapening of labor, community organizations and unions spearheaded a successful campaign for a living wage that required all firms providing government services to pay their workers at least $6.10 per hour in 1996, rising to $7.70 per hour by 1999.

Living wage legislation was enacted in Minnesota in 1997. Welfare reform advocates understood that this legislation would aid former recipients in attaining an acceptable living standard when welfare benefits were eliminated. In Boston and Los Angeles the focus was on firms that were receiving government subsidies. In return, it was argued that these corporations had a responsibility to pay living wages to their employees. In Chicago, the living wage legislation covered home health-care workers working for private agencies that receive reimbursements from the city government. For these workers there was an immediate raise of $2.15 per hour to the mandated wage of $7.60 per hour.[12] The most ambitious legislation to date has been the 1997 Los Angeles living wage ordinance that not only mandated wages of $7.25 per hour, but also required firms to provide up to $1.25 per hour in health benefits, and at least twelve paid days off per year to the portion of their workers who either work on city contracts or in activities for which the company received a city subsidy. By 2000, at least forty local governments had some form of living wage legislation.

Living wage ordinances have often been successful because they generally cover only a small number of workers. In most cities, as little as a few hundred but no more than a few thousand workers have been directly affected. For example, the Los Angeles legislation directly covered only 6,500 full-time–equivalent workers; equally divided between firms that provide services to the city and firms that received city subsidies. However, there is likely to be a ripple effect whereby other workers employed by covered firms would also receive some wage increase. In addition, the health benefits and paid days off included in the Los Angeles legislation would lead these firms to provide these benefits to some of their workers who are not covered. Ripple effects were estimated to cover an additional eight thousand workers.[13]

For the typical covered firm in Los Angeles, the direct and indirect costs averaged about 1.5 percent of the firm's total cost, clearly not very significant. In 86 percent of the affected firms the share of workers covered was less than 10 percent. In these firms, living wage legislation raised costs by 0.8 percent. In only 7 percent of firms did the legislation cover more than 20 percent of workers. In these firms, the legislation did have substantial impact—generally raising total costs by more than 10 percent. According to the efficiency wage theory, however, these additional costs would be somewhat compensated for by a reduction in labor turnover, reduced training costs, and increased productivity as a result of a more highly motivated and experienced work force.

The initial legislation has sometimes acted as a catalyst for expanding coverage. For example, the legislation in Oakland, California, covered only three hundred workers. However, it became a catalyst for pressuring other private-sector employers to comply. Soon afterward, a local hotel agreed to voluntarily comply, and now a coalition is setting their sights on three thousand low-wage workers under the jurisdiction of the Port of Oakland. Similarly, union and local activists are attempting to expand the living wage ordinance in Santa Monica to include all hotels located in this resort area.[14] Moreover, it is hoped that once a reasonable number of low-wage workers are covered, there will be increased pressure on many other employers to offer similar wages and benefits. This can help raise citywide wage floors, disproportionately aiding black and female workers.

Expanding the Earned Income Tax Credit

The EITC is a credit against federal personal income tax liability. Unlike all other tax credits, the EITC is refundable: If the credit exceeds tax liability, the taxpayer receives the difference in cash from the U.S. Internal Revenue Service. While available to a limited number of childless workers, this section focuses on the component that is available to families with children. Benefits vary with number of children and wage income. Credits rise with earnings according to a fixed percentage for an initial range of income called the phase-in range. The effect is the same as a wage subsidy. Once the taxpayer's wages push benefits up to the legal maximum, the benefits stay constant for an additional range of income, called the "plateau." Finally, at a certain point, with additional income, credits decrease at a fixed rate until eligibility ends. The phase-out rate also varies depending on children. The program presently costs over $30 billion annually, making it the largest entitlement program in the federal budget, aside from health programs and social security.

For a family with two children, the phase-in rate is 40 percent. In other words, for each $100 of wages in the phase-in range, the taxpayer is entitled to a credit of $40. For 1999, the phase-in range extended to $9,500, at which point the maximum credit was $3,816. Between income of $9,500 and $12,500, the credit remained constant. Between income of $12,500 and $30,850, the credit phased out at a 21 percent rate. At incomes above $30,850 households were ineligible for credits. The amounts are indexed for inflation so that they automatically rise each year.

The EITC is more effective in moving families over the poverty line than any other government program. Participation in the EITC is high, compared to income support programs; over 85 percent of those who are eligible for the credit apply for it. A major motive for preferring a tax credit such as the EITC to traditional public assistance is the hoped-for boost to work incentives. From 1984 to 1996, employment rates for single mothers with children increased significantly, and researchers attribute the bulk of this increase to repeated expansions of the EITC. In this sense, in the pre–welfare reform environment, the EITC acted as an effective "carrot" to prod some recipients to choose work rather than welfare.[15]

While the EITC has very positive anti-poverty effects, it has two major weaknesses. Households in the phase-out range can face a high

implicit tax rate, and many single heads face a severe marriage penalty. In addition, if we look at the combined effects of the major child-
related benefit programs, they appear inequitable since benefits per
child are less for lower-middle-class families than either poorer or
richer families.

Households benefit from higher earnings to the extent that their
disposable income rises. The implicit tax rate is the proportion of any
earnings increase that goes to the government as either additional taxes
or a reduction in benefits from government programs. At the beginning of the phase-out range, virtually all families with children are
not subject to federal or state taxation. However, many of these households currently receive benefits from means-tested programs. In each
of these programs, benefits are also reduced as income rises. For each
additional $100 of income, food-stamp benefits decline by $24 and
rents in government low-income housing projects rise by $30. House-
holds also have to pay social security and medicare taxes that are a
combined 7.65 percent of income. EITCs are also phased out. For a
family with two children for each additional $100 of earnings over
$12,500, credits fall by $21. As a result, even though this household
does not pay income tax on the additional income, the implicit tax
rate would be as high as 83 percent if the household is collecting food
stamps and housing subsidies. In this case, for each additional earnings of $100, disposable income increases by only $17. To the extent
the household would have to incur additional child-care expenses, the
net benefits from additional work are even less. In 1998, the House
Ways and Means Committee estimated that for a female head of household with two dependent children, if her gross income rose from
$15,000 to $20,000, after taking into account the additional taxes, lost
benefits, and additional child-care and commuting expenses, the family
would gain only an additional $861 of discretionary income.[16]

For households with a bit more income, the implicit tax rate is
also high. Their incomes are too high for food stamps or housing subsidies so that they no longer have these losses if they earn additional
income. However, now when they earn an additional $100, they must
pay federal and state income taxes. Together with the social security
and medicare taxes, and the lost earned income tax credits, the increase in disposable income would still only be $50 to $55.

The high implicit tax rate makes it difficult for these families to
rise above near poverty because extra work adds so little to discretionary income. Indeed, from a social standpoint, it may be best for

these households to *reduce* market labor time, especially if children are young. Studies have shown, however, that few EITC recipients understand its relationship to their implicit tax rate. Almost all families receive the EITC as a lump sum at the end of the tax year and are unaware how the credits change depending upon income. As a result, the EITC probably has only a modest effect on labor supply decisions on households in the phase-out range.[17] However, our main concern should not be that the EITC distorts employment decisions. Instead, we should be concerned because of the inappropriateness of having low-income families facing higher tax rates than millionaires and how this can trap them in near poverty.

A second problem is the marriage penalty. For married couples, their separate incomes must be combined to determine eligibility and benefits. In general, if the householder with dependent children has labor income of at least $8,000 and marries a partner earning at least that amount, the couple will have a lower combined disposable income than if they remained single. The marriage penalty rises as the income of the childless partner increases. For example, if a householder, with two dependent children and $10,000 in labor income, marries a childless partner, with wage income of $20,000, virtually all of the $3,816 of credits received would be lost. While there are some compensating tax benefits, their combined disposable income is reduced by over $3,000 if they marry. The penalty is even more severe if both partners have dependent children. Once more, the phasing out of credits causes economic losses.

Finally, the combination of the EITC and other child-related tax benefits families receive creates additional inequities. In order to judge equity of treatment of families with children, we should aggregate benefits from the following three child-related provisions of the tax code: EITC, child credit, and dependent allowance. The federal tax code exempts $2,750 from taxation for each dependent child. Since the personal income tax has increasing marginal rates, the higher one's tax bracket, the more an exemption is worth. The tax exemption is worth (0.28) ($2,750) or $770 in tax savings for those in the 28 percent tax bracket. For the wealthiest taxpayers in the top 39.6 percent bracket— well under 1 percent of all taxpayers—the exemption saves (0.396) ($2,750) or $1,089 per child in taxes. For a majority of taxpayers who are in the 15 percent bracket, the savings are (0.15) ($2,750) or $413 per child. In 1998, the federal government enacted a child credit of $500 per child. Like the benefits of the dependent exemption, the child

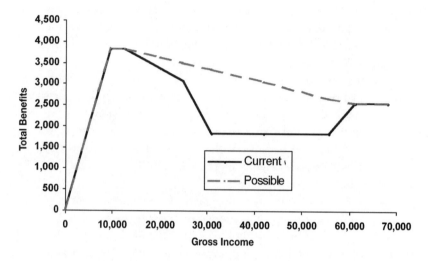

Figure 11.1 Child-Related Tax Benefits to Married Couples with Two Children.

credit received cannot exceed tax liability so that most poor families do not fully benefit from these two provisions of the tax code.

Consider the tax benefits currently from these three tax provisions for married couples with two children (see Figure 11.1). The calculations assume only wage income with all households taking the standard deduction and having no other tax credits or adjustments to income. At incomes of $12,500 or less these households receive no benefits from either child credits or dependent allowances because their incomes would be too low to be subject to taxation. As a result, in this income range, the only child-related benefits they receive are from the EITC.

These combined benefits rise in the phase-in range, reaching the maximum of $3,816 at income of $9,500. As income rises above $12,500 credits begin to decline. The loss of credits is partially offset by the benefits households start receiving from the dependent allowance and the child credit—because of these provisions families avoid paying federal income tax, at a 15 percent rate, on additional income. At income of $24,866 the benefits of the child credit and dependent allowances for households in the 15 percent tax bracket are completely phased in. At that point, the tax benefits equal $3,067—$1,000 from child credits, $825 from dependent allowances, and $1,242 from EITC. After this point, the EITC continues to be phased out and the combined benefits decline sharply. At $30,850, households no longer qualify for the EITC, and tax benefits are reduced to $1,825—the value of the child credits and dependent allowances.

Benefits of $1,825 continue as income rises. At some point—income of $55,750—in the absence of children, the next dollar would be taxed at a higher 28 percent rate. Now the dependent allowances are worth more so that once the household gains the full effect, at income of $61,250, the combined benefits equal $2,540. This combined benefit schedule indicates that poor and near-poor households gain substantially, due to the EITC, and those over $60,000 gain substantially because the dependent allowance is worth more to them than to households in the 15 percent bracket. As a result, the children of middle-class households receive fewer combined benefits than either their wealthier or poorer counterparts.

Together with an economist at the Economic Policy Institute, Max Sawicky, I have developed a tax proposal to correct these inadequacies of the current tax system. At the time this book was written, it had been proposed in legislation sponsored by Dennis Kucinich (Democrat, Ohio) and Thomas Petri (Republican, Wisconsin).[18] Called the Universal Unified Child Credit (UUCC), it combines the three child-related benefit programs. Its basic structure and its ability to solve the three inadequacies mentioned can be shown if we refer back to Figure 11.1. The UUCC benefits for households up through $12,500 could be equivalent to those currently being received from the EITC, maximizing at $3,816. They could then be reduced continuously (the dotted line in Figure 11.1) until benefits are phased down to $2,540 at $61,250, which is the amount that these households are currently receiving from their child credits and dependent allowances. Since $1,276 ($3,816–$2,540) of benefits is phased out over $48,750 ($61,250–$12,500), the necessary phase-out rate would be 2.6 percent, much smaller than the current 21 percent phase-out rate. A similar expansion of the EITC can be done for households with one child where the maximum benefits of $2,312 can be phased down to $1,270, also requiring a much smaller phase-out rate than the current 16 percent.

While some important adjustments are made in the actual proposal, the UUCC enables the phase-out rates to be dramatically lowered, and this substantially eliminates all three of the inadequacies of the current system. With such a small phase-out rate, households do not lose significant credits if they earn additional income nor if they marry. With a 2.6 phase-out rate, for each additional $100 of income, credits decline by only $2.60. This lowers the implicit tax rate, most dramatically when households are currently subject to both the phase-out rate and federal taxation. For married couples with two children, this is above income of $24,866. For single heads with one child it is above $15,167. In these situations, the UUCC would lower implicit tax rates by eleven percentage points.

In our previous example when a householder with two children and income of $10,000 married a childless partner with income of $20,000, over $3,400 of credits are lost. With the new phase-out rate, only $458 of credits are lost. The actual UUCC proposal reduces the marriage penalty by more than $1,000 for a wide variety of potential marriage partners. Finally, the UUCC benefits will be at least $1,270 per child for all families and decline slightly—by the new phase-out rate—as household income rises. This is much more equitable than the present system.

Full Employment Policies

While legislating pay scales and providing wage subsidies can be effective, the most important policy initiative for aiding lower-paid workers may be the maintenance of tight labor markets. The 1990s witnessed unemployment rates falling to historic peacetime levels with dramatic benefits to less-educated, young workers. In addition, welfare recipients were absorbed into the paid labor force as employers overcame their resistance to hiring them. Together with minimum wage increases in 1996 and 1997, those at the bottom of the job market disproportionately benefited. Between 1994 and 1998 the hourly wage rate for the worker at the lowest decile rose by 7.5 percent compared to 4.1 percent for the average worker.[19] Moreover, these workers were disproportionately able to move from part-time to full-time employment so that their usual weekly earnings increased by even more.

These gains, however, were put at risk by the Federal Reserve Board's decision to stem the perceived harmful inflationary effects of these wage increases. In 1999, the Fed began raising interest rates in order to reduce the demand for goods and services. With less spending by consumers and businesses, the demand for labor would be reduced and so too would be the pressure to raise wages and benefits. Currently, the economy must grow at 3 percent annually just to absorb new entrants and replace the jobs lost to labor productivity increases. The Fed desired to reduce growth to 2.5 percent so that the national unemployment rate would rise from 4 percent to at least 4.5 percent, still low by post–Vietnam war standards.

Traditionally, anti-inflationary policies were based upon a perception that substantial unemployment persists even when the economy is producing enough jobs to match the total number of job seekers. Some of the unemployed would not have the right skills or live in the right places and would be what economists call "structurally" unemployed. Others would be searching for even better job prospects than the offers that they could immediately obtain. These workers comprise the frictionally unemployed. According to conventional economists, the high unemployment during most of the 1980s was not caused by a lack of job creation but by a rising share of the work force that was either structurally or frictionally unemployed. Indeed, this provided the basis for the widespread belief that the target unemployment rate for federal policies—labeled by economists the nonaccelerating inflation rate of unemployment (NAIRU)—should be between 5.5 and 6.0 percent. According to conventional economists, if unemployment fell below NAIRU, labor shortages would become widespread, causing wage and price increases to accelerate.

Embracing this viewpoint, Federal Reserve chair Alan Greenspan began raising interest rates in 1994 when the national unemployment rate declined below 6 percent. The Clinton administration rejected this conventional wisdom. The head of his Council of Economic Advisors, Laura D'Andrea Tyson, claimed that there were a number of myths concerning inflation that underpinned the Fed's approach. In particular, she argued that there was still plenty of underemployed labor so that wage increases would not be substantial if the expansion continued.

Over the next two years, President Clinton and his supporters counter Alan Greenspan's desire to clamp down on economic growth. First, Clinton's appointment to the Federal Reserve, Alan Blinder, openly argued that if contractionary policies were undertaken, the Fed had an obligation to inform the public that this meant rising unemployment. Second, Clinton floated the name of New York City investment backer Felix Rohatyn as a nominee to the Federal Reserve Board. Rohatyn was widely known as a strong advocate of economic expansion even if it risked increasing inflation rates somewhat. Entering the presidential campaign of 1996, Clinton then seemed to reach an "understanding" with Greenspan. For the two openings on the nine-member Federal Reserve Board, Clinton would nominate individuals with views similar to Greenspan, and in return Greenspan would allow the economic expansion to continue. Indeed, Greenspan began to increase credit availability, and the expansion grew more robust, no doubt helping Clinton win reelection.[20]

When Greenspan was poised to begin slowing down the economy in 1997, an Asian economic crisis forced a reappraisal. Rising unemployment and a slowdown in wage growth would cause U.S. households to reduce their purchases of goods and services. Since a significant portion of purchases would be on goods that were directly or indirectly produced in these Asian countries, Fed anti-inflationary policies would further weaken economies already devastated by banking and currency problems. As a result, Greenspan decided to aid the U.S. expansion, allowing national unemployment rates to decline to below 5 percent.

Most conventional economists were surprised that the expansion did not cause inflation to increase. Their dire forecast had underestimated the number of qualified workers available. Whereas in the early 1990s there were six million part-time employed workers who sought full-time employment, by the late 1990s that number had dropped to less than three million. Many of the less-educated workers who moved from part-time to full-time employment, as well as former welfare recipients thrust into the labor market, were quite capable. The doubling of H-1B visas also expanded available labor supplies and limited wage increases among computer, engineering, and other scientific workers. Finally, firms chose to offer their workers more extensive overtime, easing the need to hire additional workers.

This lack of rising inflation rates did not surprise some economists. Using standard economic models, in 1995 Robert Eisner simulated the effect of a reduction of the national unemployment rate from 5.8 to 3.8 percent on inflation. After a few periods, the inflation rate did accelerate from 3 percent to almost 8 percent. However, in conflict with conventional expectations, inflation rates did not continue to rise but remained at 8 percent for a number of subsequent periods. What most surprised Eisner, the predicted inflation rate began to drop, reaching 5 percent and remaining at that value thereafter.[21]

In addition, Tyson's successor at the Council of Economic Advisors, Joseph Stiglitz, likened the conventional view to a precipice: Take one step over it, and you fall into a spiral of rapidly accelerating inflation. In contrast, Stiglitz found that maintaining low unemployment rates would have a limited effect on the inflation rate and, as Eisner, he did not believe that these increases would accelerate if low unemployment rates were sustained. Stiglitz thought, "Small mistakes have only small consequences." Hence, policy makers should not fear that declining unemployment rates could create costly problems. These findings made it more difficult to justify anti-inflationary policies even after the Asian crisis became more manageable.[22]

While the theoretical support for preemptive anti-inflationary actions by the Fed waned, there were still groups with vested interests in avoiding inflationary surprises. Historically, they included those on fixed incomes. However, social security is now indexed to the inflation rate so that this group no longer faces adverse consequences from inflation. Today, it is households that have substantial long-term bonds and stock holdings who are harmed. If inflation rates move upward by two or three percentage points, so too will interest rates. The price of stocks will be adversely affected since rising interest rates would cause at least some investors to shift to these new higher-yielding bonds. In addition, the market price of already owned bonds would decline so that they could pay a competitive interest rate. It is primarily this influential group that favors anti-inflationary policies no matter how damaging they may be to those at the bottom of the economic ladder.

In 1965, buoyed by the civil rights movement, Nobel Prize economist James Tobin proposed that the government should promote low unemployment rates—3.0 to 3.5 percent—in order to close the racial employment gap. He feared, however, that economic policies would be governed by the desires of the "vast comfortable white middle class, who are never touched by unemployment, and prefer to safeguard the purchasing power of their [financial assets] rather than to expand opportunities for the disadvantaged and unemployed." We should continue to heed Tobin's advice: support tight labor markets that will benefit the most vulnerable workers and reject anti-inflationary policies that primarily benefit stock and bondholders.[23]

Concluding Remarks

In this book, I have tried to be as pragmatic as possible when considering ways to combat race and gender earnings disparities. In particular, besides recommending expanded government-funded child-care services to aid working women, there has been no call for significant expansions of government funding. Clearly, given the very large budget surpluses projected for the next decade, there is room for needed expansions of health-care and educational expenditures in poor and working-class communities. Every child should be provided decent health-care and educational resources. These are entitlements in virtually all other major industrialized countries and should be legislated here. A Canadian-style universal health-care system and new, well-equipped schools in poor neighborhoods with financial incentives to attract qualified teachers should be a part of any progressive agenda. However, until a political movement strong enough to demand these changes arises, the more incremental policies described here can be effective. Indeed, they may provide the building blocks for the progressive movement capable of gaining larger structural changes.

This book has also ignored social and cultural factors that may influence labor market behavior of employers and employees. Why do employers gravitate so easily to racial and gender stereotypes? What can be done about the dysfunctional behavior that limits the upward mobility of some poor black youths? In a sense, this book suggests that if society creates a more favorable employment environment for disadvantaged workers, stereotypes will be broken down and dysfunctional behavior will be overcome. Moreover, recent experience has indicated that tight labor markets can become a catalyst for the development of social programs that aid the transition of welfare recipients and idle youth into the labor market. While this approach might seem facile, it does avoid the quagmire of issues that must be confronted if one becomes engaged in social engineering and cultural policy making.

Finally, this book has avoided looking at the larger issue in capitalist societies. While I strongly believe that capitalism does not need race and gender labor market divisions, it suffers from other ills: maintenance of class inequities, promotion of endless consumerism, sacrifice of the environment, and indifference to the suffering of the most vulnerable members of society. Some of these ills reflect the downside of rampant individualism which capitalism encourages. A generation or two ago, to combat individualism people sought social solutions through reliance on an invasive government. Today, people seek personal solutions, often through religion. However, the appropriate role of individualism in a more humane communal society is beyond the scope of this book.

These limitations should not detract from the value of this book. I have tried to present both the strengths and the weaknesses of market mechanisms in the struggle against race and gender inequities and both the strengths and weaknesses of current affirmative action programs. I have presented policies to lift the wage floor for the lowest-paid workers. It is my hope that you have gained understandings and insights into the workings of labor markets and the public policies that are required to combat inequities and that this book has helped in a small way to build a movement for the more humane society we all seek.

Notes

CHAPTER 1. DECIDING WHO GETS THE GOOD JOBS

1. Diane Lewis, "Stop Bias, Greenspan Urges," *Boston Globe*, 23 March 2000, A1; Constance Hays, "Coke's Black Employees Step Up the Pressure," *New York Times*, 23 March 2000, D1.
2. Stephan Thernstrom and Abigail Thernstrom, *America in Black and White* (New York: Simon and Schuster, 1997); Roy Johnson, "The New Black Power," *Fortune*, 4 August 1997, 46–83.
3. Laurence Mishel et al., *The State of Working America, 1996–1997* (Armonk, N.Y.: M. E. Sharpe, 1997).
4. Randy Albelda et al., *Unlevel Playing Fields* (New York: McGraw-Hill, 1997).
5. Natalie Angier, "Among Doctors: Pay for Women Still Lags," *New York Times*, 12 January 1999, F7.
6. William Darity and Samuel Myers, *The Underclass* (New York: Garland, 1994); William Darity and Samuel Myers, "The Impact of Labor Market Prospects on Incarceration Rates," in *Prosperity for All? The Economic Boom and African Americans,* ed. Robert Cherry and William Rodgers (New York: Russell Sage, 2000), 279–306.
7. Finis Welch, "Economic Well-Being in the United States," *American Economic Review* 89 (May 1999): 1–16.
8. Ellen Meiksins Wood, "An Interview," *Monthly Review* 51 (May 1999): 81–82.
9. Frederick Engels, "The Origins of the Family, Private Property, and the State," in *Selected Works,* ed. Karl Marx and Frederick Engels (London: Lawrence and Wishart, 1972), 455–593.
10. Karl Marx, *Early Writings,* ed. T. Bottomore (London: Watts, 1963).
11. Ellen Meiksins Wood, "An Interview."
12. Oliver Cox, *Caste, Class, and Race* (New York: Monthly Review Press, 1970).
13. Harold Baron, "Racial Dominance in Advanced Capitalism: A Theory of Nationalism and Divisions in the Labor Market," in *Labor Market Segmen-*

tation, ed. Richard Edwards et al. (Lexington, Mass.: D. C. Heath, 1975), 173–216; Allan Johnson, *The Gender Knot: Unraveling Our Patriarchal Legacy* (Philadelphia: Temple University Press, 1997).

14. William Bowen and Derek Bok, *The Shape of the River: Long-Term Consequences of Considering Race in College and University Admissions* (Princeton, N.J.: Princeton University Press, 1998).

15. Paul Baran and Paul Sweezy, *Monopoly Capital* (New York: Monthly Review Press, 1965); Ray Franklin and Solomon Resnik, *The Political Economy of Racism* (New York: Random House, 1973).

16. Robert Cherry, "Impact of Tight Labor Markets on Black Employment," *Review of Black Political Economy* 27 (summer 2000): 27–41.

17. Robert Cherry, "Black Jobs: Missing in Action," *Dollars and Sense* (November/December 1998): 24; Heather Boushey and Robert Cherry, "Exclusionary Practices and Glass Ceiling Effects across Regions," in *Prosperity for All?*, ed. Cherry and Rodgers, 160–187.

18. Allan Wolfe, "Welfare Policy," *New York Times,* 25 September 1999, A27.

19. Heidi Hartmann, ed., *Comparable Worth: New Directions for Research* (Washington, D.C.: National Academy Press, 1985).

20. Judith Stein, "History of an Idea," *Nation*, 14 December 1998, 12–17.

21. Robin Kelley, "Integration: What's Left?" *Nation*, 14 December 1998, 17–19.

22. Ibid.

23. Data presented in the Expert Witness Report of Stephen Raudenbush, in *Gratz et al. v. Ballinger et al.,* No. 97–75–7531 (E.D. Mich., 22 January 1999).

CHAPTER 2. THE PROFIT MOTIVE

1. Steve Sailer, "How Jackie Robinson Desegregated America," *National Review* 97 (8 April 1996): 38.

2. George Fitzhugh, "Sociology for the South," in *Slavery Defended: The Views of the Old South*, ed. Eric McKitrick (Englewood Cliffs, N.J.: Prentice Hall, 1963), 34–50, esp. p. 36.

3. For a detailed discussion of Adam Smith's views on poverty, see Geoffrey Gilbert, "Adam Smith on the Nature and Causes of Poverty," *Review of Social Economy* 55 (fall 1997): 273–291.

4. For a detailed discussion of Adam Smith's views on market wage determination, see Donald Stabile, "Adam Smith and the Natural Wage," *Review of Social Economy* 55 (fall 1997): 292–311.

5. Booker T. Washington, *Up from Slavery* (Garden City, N.Y.: Doubleday, 1963), 160.

6. Ibid., 158, 161.

7. Ibid., 160.

8. George Soros, "The Capitalist Threat," *Atlantic Monthly* 279 (February 1997): 45–58.

9. Paul Krugman, "In Praise of Cheap Labor," *Slate* (20 March 1997).

10. Lin Lean Lim, *The Sex Sector* (Geneva: International Labour Office, 1998).

11. Skip Barry, "Taking Aim at Child Slavery," *Dollars and Sense* 220 (March/April 1997): 10.

12. Steven Greenhouse, "Activism Surges at Campuses Nationwide," *New York Times*, 29 March 1999, A17; Internet site: www.sweatshopwatch.org.

13. Dorothy Smith, "Women's Inequality and the Family," in *Families and Work*, ed. Naomi Gerstel and Harriet Gross (Philadelphia: Temple University Press, 1987), 23–54.

14. John Kenneth Galbraith, *Economics and the Public Purpose* (Boston: Houghton Mifflin, 1973), 74.
15. Karl Marx, *Capital*, vol. 1 (New York: International Publishers, 1967), 462.
16. Ibid., 470.
17. Robert Cherry, "Racial Thought and the Early Economics Profession," *Review of Social Economy* 33 (1976): 147–162.
18. Hugh Murray, "The NAACP Versus the Communist Party," in *The Negro in Depression and War*, ed. Bernard Sternsher (New York: Schocken, 1969), 267–280.
19. Gunnar Myrdal, *An American Dilemma: The Negro Problem and Modern Democracy* (New York: Harper and Row, 1944).
20. Robert Cherry, "The Culture of Poverty Thesis and African Americans: The Views of Gunnar Myrdal and Other Institutionalists," *Journal of Economic Issues* 29 (December 1995): 1–14.
21. Gordon Allport, *The Nature of Prejudice* (Reading, Mass.: Addison Wesley, 1954).
22. St. Clair Drake and Horace Cayton, *The Black Metropolis* (New York: Harcourt and Brace, 1945).
23. Gary Becker, *The Economics of Discrimination*, 2d ed. (Chicago: University of Chicago Press, 1971).
24. Robert Cherry, "Should We Rely on the Marketplace to End Discrimination? What the Integration of Baseball Tells Us," in *Jackie Robinson: Race, Sports and the American Dream*, ed. Joseph Dorinson and Joram Warmund (Armonk, N.Y.: M. E. Sharpe, 1998), 214–233.
25. Sailer, "How Jackie Robinson Desegregated America," 39.
26. Thomas Sowell, *Markets and Minorities* (New York: Basic Books, 1981).
27. Peter Bohmer, "The Impact of Public Sector Employment on Racial Inequality: 1950 to 1984" (Ph.D. Diss., University of Massachusetts, 1985).
28. Sowell, *Markets and Minorities*, 49–50.
29. Milton Friedman, *Capitalism and Freedom* (Chicago: University of Chicago Press, 1962), 112.

CHAPTER 3. IT'S NOT PERSONAL

1. Gerald Scully, *The Business of Major League Baseball* (Chicago: University of Chicago Press, 1989), 171.
2. Ibid., 172.
3. Claudia Golden and Cecilia Rouse, "Orchestration Impartiality: The Impact of 'Blind' Auditions on Female Musicians," National Bureau of Economic Research Working Paper 5903, 1997.
4. Marc Bendick et al., "Measuring Employment Discrimination through Controlled Experiments," *Review of Black Political Economy* 23 (summer 1994): 25–48. See also Jerome Culp and Bruce Dunson, "Brothers of a Different Color: A Preliminary Treatment of Black and White Youth," in *The Black Youth Problem*, ed. Richard Freeman and Harry Holzer (Chicago: University of Chicago Press, 1986), 233–259.
5. Charles Bagli, "The Ciprianis Are Accused of Sex Bias in Hiring," *New York Times*, 25 August 1999, B1. For a discussion of similar hiring by the steakhouse Smith and Wollensky, see Barbara Bergmann, *In Defense of Affirmative Action* (New York: Basic Books, 1996).
6. Barbara Bergmann, *The Economic Emergence of Women* (New York: Basic Books, 1986).

7. Ronald Ferguson and Randall Filer, "Do Better Jobs Make Better Workers? Absenteeism from Work among Inner-City Black Youth," in *The Black Youth Employment Crisis*, ed. Richard Freeman and Harry Holzer (Chicago: University of Chicago Press, 1986), 261–298.
8. Warren Whatley and Stan Sedo, "Quit Behavior as a Measure of Worker Opportunity," *American Economics Review* 88 (May 1998): 363–367.
9. Philip Shenon, "Black FBI Agent's Ordeal," *New York Times*, 15 January 1988, A1.
10. Philip Shenon, "FBI to Promote 11 Hispanic Agents in Bias Case," *New York Times*, 20 September 1990, B4.
11. Bob Herbert, "Bias Intensified by Inertia," *New York Times*, 14 January 1997, A24.
12. Ken Sack, "Racism Found aboard Government Dredge," *New York Times*, 2 May 1997, A22.
13. Peter Frisch and Allamma Sullivan, *Wall Street Journal* series on Texaco; 5 November 1996, B10; 11 November 1996, A3; 12 November 1996, A3.
14. Ira Gissen, "A Study of Jewish Employment Problems in the Big Six Oil Company Headquarters," *Rights* 9 (1978): 3–10. See also American Jewish Committee, *Summary of Report on First Fifteen Banks* (New York: Author, 1973).
15. Quoted in Richard Zweigenhalf, "Recent Patterns of Jewish Representation in the Corporate and Social Elites," *Contemporary Jewry* 6 (1982): 36–46.
16. Stephen Slavin and Mary Pradt, *The Einstein Syndrome: Corporate Anti-Semitism in America Today* (Washington, D.C.: University Press of America, 1982).
17. Michael Reich, *Racial Inequality* (Princeton, N.J.: Princeton University Press, 1981).
18. Mishel et al., *The State of Working America*.
19. David Chalmers, *Hooded Americanism* (Garden City, N.Y.: Doubleday, 1965).
20. This example is taken from Ronald Ehrenberg and Robert Smith, *Modern Labor Economics*, 5th ed. (New York: HarperCollins, 1994), 385; the primary source is Daniel Raff and Lawrence Summers, "Did Henry Ford Pay Efficiency Wages?" *Journal of Labor Economics* 5 (October 1987): S57–S86. For a summary of the efficiency wage literature, see Lawrence Katz, "Efficiency Wage Theories: A Partial Evaluation," in *Macroeconomics Annual, 1986*, ed. Stanley Fischer (Cambridge, Mass.: MIT Press, 1986).
21. David Gordon et al., *Segmented Work, Divided Workers: The Historical Transformation of Labor in the United States* (Cambridge: Cambridge University Press, 1982).
22. David Gordon, *Fat and Mean* (New York: Free Press, 1996), 77.
23. Albelda et al., *Unlevel Playing Fields*, 186.
24. Ibid.

CHAPTER 4. RACE BEFORE CLASS

1. Jacqueline Jones, *The Dispossessed: America's Underclasses from the Civil War to the Present* (New York: Basic Books, 1992).
2. Teresa Amott and Julie Matthaei, *Race, Gender, and Work* (Boston: South End Press, 1991).
3. Much of the general backdrop of this section is taken from Gavin Wright, *Old South, New South* (New York: Basic Books, 1986).
4. C. Vann Woodward, *The Strange Career of Jim Crow* (New York: Oxford University Press, 1966).

5. Robert Margo, *Race and Schooling in the South, 1890–1950* (Chicago: University of Chicago Press, 1990).

6. Wright, *Old South, New South;* Robert Higgs, *Competition and Coercion* (Cambridge: Cambridge University Press, 1977). In contrast, Jones (*The Dispossessed*, 87) claims that "the assertion that 'equal wage payments [for blacks and whites] was the prevailing rule' ignores the social and racial structure of the South's agricultural work force."

7. Wright, *Old South, New South,* 190.

8. Roger Ransom and Richard Sutch, *One Kind of Freedom* (Cambridge: Cambridge University Press, 1977).

9. Ibid., 219.

10. Higgs, *Competition and Coercion.*

11. Woodward, *The Strange Career of Jim Crow,* 90.

12. George Strauss and Sidney Ingerman, "Apprenticeship," in *Negroes and Jobs,* ed. Louis Ferman et al. (Ann Arbor: University of Michigan Press, 1968), 298–322.

13. Wright, *Old South, New South,* 196.

14. Allan Chase, *The Legacy of Malthus* (New York: Alfred A. Knopf, 1977).

15. Jones, *The Dispossessed;* Jay Mandle, *Not Slave, Not Free* (Philadelphia: Temple University Press, 1992).

16. Stanley Lieberson, *A Piece of the Pie* (Berkeley: University of California Press, 1980).

17. Warren Whatley and Gavin Wright, "Race, Human Capital, and Labor Markets in American History," in *Labour Market Revolution,* ed. George Graham and Mary MacKinnon (London: Routledge, 1994), 282.

18. Warren Whatley, "African American Strikebreaking from the Civil War to the New Deal," *Social Science History* 17 (winter 1993): 525–558; Richard Vedder and Lowell Gallaway, "Racial Differences in Unemployment in the United States, 1890–1990," *Journal of Economic History* 52 (fall 1992): 696–702.

19. W.E.B. Du Bois, "The Philadelphia Negro," in *The Black Worker,* vol. 4, *The Black Worker during the Era of the American Federation of Labor and the Railroad Brotherhoods,* ed. Phillip Foner and Ronald Lewis (Philadelphia: Temple University Press, 1979), 356.

20. Herbert Hill, "The Problem of Race in American Labor," *Reviews in American History* 24 (June 1996): 197.

21. Lieberson, *A Piece of the Pie,* 351.

22. Jones, *The Dispossessed,* 114.

23. Mark Aldrich, "Progressive Economists and Scientific Racism: Walter Willcox and Black Americans, 1895–1910," *Phylon* 40 (March 1979): 1–14; Allan Morrison, "The Secret Papers of FDR," in *The Negro in Depression and War,* ed. Sternsher, 66–77; Robert Zangrando, "The NAACP and a Federal Anti-Lynching Bill," in *The Negro in Depression and War,* ed. Sternsher, 181–192.

24. Phillip Foner and Ronald Lewis, eds., *The Black Worker,* vol. 5, *The Black Worker from 1900 to 1919* (Philadelphia: Temple University Press, 1980), 241.

25. Ibid.

26. Charles Johnson, "How Much Is Migration a Flight from Persecution?" in *The Making of Black America,* vol. 2, ed. August Meier and Elliot Rudwick (New York: Atheneum, 1971), 180–183.

27. Jones, *The Dispossessed,* 75.
28. Eva Mueller and William Ladd, "Negro-White Differences in Geographic Mobility," in *Negroes and Jobs,* ed. Ferman et al., 382–399.
29. Foner and Lewis, *The Black Worker,* 4:256, 286, 311, 331.
30. Kelley Miller, "The City Negro," in *The Black Worker,* 5:11; W.E.B. Du Bois, "The Negro Artisan," in *The Black Worker,* 5:88; Lieberson, *A Piece of the Pie,* 322; Foner and Lewis, *The Black Worker,* 5:250.
31. Will Winn, "The Negro: His Relationship to Southern Industry," in *The Black Worker,* 4:256.
32. St. Clair Drake and Horace Cayton, *Black Metropolis,* vol. 1 (New York: Harper and Row, 1945), 45–46.
33. Ibid., 73.
34. Foner and Lewis, *The Black Worker,* 5:26.
35. Ibid., 28, 32, 39.
36. Ibid., 42–43.
37. Du Bois, "The Negro Artisan," 57.
38. Du Bois, "The Philadelphia Negro," 352.
39. Foner and Lewis, *The Black Worker,* 5:41.
40. Wright, *Old South, New South,* 224.
41. Michael Honey, *Southern Labor and Black Civil Rights* (Urbana: University of Illinois Press, 1993); Ernest Obele-Stark, *Black Unionism in the Industrial South* (College Station: Texas A&M Press, 2000).
42. Wright, *Old South, New South,* 224.
43. Ibid., 230.
44. Ibid., 235.
45. Honey, *Southern Labor and Black Civil Rights,* 59.
46. Wright, *Old South, New South,* 236.
47. Ibid., 259.
48. Elizabeth Jacoway and David Colbrun, *Southern Businessmen and Desegregation* (Baton Rouge: Louisiana State University Press, 1982), 5, 7, 8, 11.
49. Wright, *Old South, New South,* 286, 268.
50. Robert Cherry, "Race and Gender Aspects of Marxian Macromodels," *Science and Society* 55 (spring 1991): 60–78.
51. David Gordon et al., *Divided Work, Segmented Workers* (New York: Cambridge University Press, 1982); Thomas Kochan et al., *The Transformation of American Industrial Relations* (New York: Basic Books, 1986).
52. William Quay, *The Negro in the Chemical Industry* (Philadelphia: University of Pennsylvania Press, 1970), Table 15; Stanley Greenberg, *Race and State and Capitalist Development* (New Haven, Conn.: Yale University Press, 1980), 228.
53. Herbert Northrup, *The Negro in the Automobile Industry* (Philadelphia: University of Pennsylvania Press, 1969); Theodore Purcell and Daniel Mulvey, *The Negro in the Electrical Manufacturing Industry* (Philadelphia: University of Pennsylvania Press, 1971).
54. James Heckman and Brook Payner, "Determining the Impact of Federal Antidiscrimination Policy on the Economic Status of Blacks," *American Economics Review* 79 (1989): 138–178.
55. Taylor Branch, *Parting the Waters* (New York: Simon and Shuster, 1988).

CHAPTER 5. GENDER BEFORE CLASS

1. Peggy O'Crowley, "Another Gender Gap: A Study Finds That Men Have More Free Time than Women," *New Jersey Star Ledger,* 21 March 2000, A1.

2. Heidi Hartmann, "The Unhappy Marriage of Marxism and Feminism," in *Women and Revolution,* ed. Lydia Sargent (Boston: South End Press, 1981), 1–42; Jane Humphries, "Class Struggle and the Persistence of the Working-Class Family," *Cambridge Journal of Economics* 1 (1977): 241–258.

3. Sonya Rose, "Gender Antagonism and Class Conflict: Exclusionary Strategies of Male Trade Unionists in Nineteenth-Century Britain," *Social History* 13 (May 1988): 191–207.

4. Ibid.

5. Quoted in Jane Humphries, "The Working-Class Family, Women's Liberation and Class Struggle," *Review of Radical Political Economics* 9 (fall 1977): 34–35.

6. Jane Mark-Lawson and Anne Witz, "From 'Family Labour' to 'Family Wage'? The Case of Women's Labor in Nineteenth-Century Coalmining," *Social History* 13 (May 1988): 151–174.

7. Rose, "Gender Antagonism and Class Conflict," 206.

8. Jane Lewis, quoted in Colin Creighton, "The 'Family Wage' as a Class-Rationale Strategy," *Sociological Review* 44 (May 1996): 208.

9. Susan Pedersen, *Family, Dependence, and the Origins of the Welfare State: Britain and France, 1914–1945* (Cambridge: Cambridge University Press, 1993), 38.

10. Ibid., 60, 69.

11. Quoted in Hugh Vibrant, *Family Allowances in Practice* (London: P. S. King and Son, 1926), 10–11.

12. Ibid., 46.

13. Pedersen, *Family, Dependence, and the Origins of the Welfare State,* 130.

14. Vibrant, *Family Allowances in Practice,* 151.

15. Ibid., ch. 10.

16. Michele Barrett, *Women's Oppression Today* (London: Verso, 1980).

17. Martha May, "Bread before Roses: American Workingmen, Labor Unions and the Family Wage," in *Women, Work, and Protest,* ed. Ruth Milkman (Boston: Routledge and Kegan Paul, 1985), 1–21.

18. Teresta Amott and Julie Matthaei, *Race, Gender, and Work* (Boston: South End Press, 1991), 103.

19. Ibid., 114.

20. George Stigler, "Domestic Servants in the United States, 1900–1940." Occasional Paper #24, National Bureau for Economic Research, 1946.

21. Amott and Matthaei, *Race, Gender, and Work,* 104.

22. May, "Bread before Roses," 8.

23. Ron Rothbart, "'Homes Are What Any Strike Is About': Immigrant Labor and the Family Wage," *Journal of Social History* 23 (winter 1989): 274.

24. Martha May, "The Historical Problem of the Family Wage: The Ford Motor Company and the Five-Dollar Day," *Feminist Studies* 8 (summer 1982): 414.

25. Ibid., 413–414.

26. May, "Bread before Roses," 10.

27. Maurine Weiner Greenwald, "Working-Class Feminism and the Family Wage Ideal: The Seattle Debate on Married Women's Right to Work, 1914–1920," *Journal of American History* 76 (June 1989): 128.

28. Ibid., 149.

29. Claudia Goldin, *Understanding the Gender Gap: An Economic History of American Women* (New York: Oxford University Press, 1990), 163.

30. Ibid., 176.
31. See Gary Becker, *Treatise on the Family* (Chicago: University of Chicago Press, 1981); Talcott Parsons, "The Social Structure of the Family," in *The Family: Its Function and Destiny*, ed. Ruth Anshen (New York: Free Press, 1949), 173–201.
32. See Hartmann, "The Unhappy Marriage of Marxism and Feminism."
33. For a more complete presentation of this marriage model, see Robert Cherry, "Rational Choice and the Price of Marriage," *Feminist Economics* 4 (spring 1998): 27–49.
34. Elaine McCrate, "Trade, Merger, and Employment: Economic Theory on Marriage," *Review of Radical Political Economics* 19 (spring 1987): 79.
35. Hartmann, "The Unhappy Marriage of Marxism and Feminism," 10.
36. See Amott and Matthaei, *Race, Gender, and Work.*
37. Dorothy Smith, "Women's Inequality and the Family," in *Families and Work*, ed. Gerstel and Gross, 29.
38. McCrate, "Trade, Merger, and Employment," 83.
39. For a summary of time allocation studies, see Cherry, "Rational Choice."
40. See Jan Stets, "Modeling Control of Relationships," *Journal of Marriage and the Family* 57 (May 1995): 489–501; Ann Ferguson and Nancy Folbre, "The Unhappy Marriage of Patriarchy and Capitalism," in *Women and Revolution,* ed. Sargent, 313–338.
41. Ruth Milkman, "Women's Work and Economic Crisis: Lessons from the Great Depression," *Review of Radical Political Economics* 8 (spring 1976): 69–97; Veronica Beechey, "Women and Production," in *Feminism and Materialism,* ed. Annette Kuhn and AnnMarie Wolpe (London: Routledge, 1978), 157–175.
42. Edward McCaffery, *Taxing Women* (Chicago: University of Chicago Press, 1997), 77.
43. Barrett, *Women's Oppression Today*; Julie Matthaei, *An Economic History of Women in America* (New York: Schocken Books, 1980), 325.
44. McCaffery, *Taxing Women,* 210.
45. Quoted in Cherry, "Rational Choice," 42.
46. Kathryn Edin, "Few Good Men," *American Prospect* 11 (January 2000): 42–43; the genesis of this traditionalist attack is Charles Murray, *Losing Ground* (New York: Basic Books, 1984). For a general critique of Murray, see Robert Cherry, *Discrimination: Its Economic Impact on Blacks, Women and Jews* (Lexington, Mass.: Lexington Books, 1989), ch. 7; and Sara McLanahan et al., *Losing Ground: A Critique* (Madison, Wis.: Institute for Research on Poverty, 1987).
47. Elaine McCrate, "Labor Market Segmentation and Relative Black-White Teenage Birth Rates," *Review of Black Political Economy* 18 (spring 1990): 37–53.
48. Barbara Ehrenreich, *The Hearts of Men: Flight from Commitment* (Garden City, N.Y.: Anchor Press, 1983).
49. William J. Wilson, *The Truly Disadvantaged* (Chicago: University of Chicago Press, 1987).
50. Mishel et al., *The State of Working America,* Fig. 6G.
51. Edin, "Few Good Men," 29.
52. Ibid.
53. Ibid., 31.
54. Ibid., 29.

55. Center for Impact Study, *Domestic Violence and Birth Control Sabotage* (Chicago: Center for Impact Studies, 2000); website: www.impactresearch. org; see also Jody Raphael, *Saving Bernice* (Boston: Northeastern University Press, 2000).

56. Jody Raphael and Richard Tolman, *Trapped in Poverty, Trapped in Abuse* (Chicago: Taylor Institute, 1997), 14. For a broader discussion of domestic abuse and sexual coercion, see Robert Cherry, "Sexual Coercion and Limited Choices," in *Sex without Consent,* ed. Merril Smith (New York: New York University Press, forthcoming).

57. Martha Roldan, "Renegotiating the Marital Contract," in *A Home Divided: Women and Income in the Third World,* ed. Daisy Dwyer and Judith Bruce (Stanford, Calif.: Stanford University Press, 1988), 228–247.

58. The numerical exercise and material in this section is adapted from McCaffery, *Taxing Women.*

59. Jennifer Kingson, "Women in Law Say Path Is Limited by 'Mommy Track,'" *New York Times,* 8 August 1988, A1.

60. Nancy Fraser, "After the Family Wage," *Political Theory* 22 (November 1994): 591–618.

61. Compilation of quotes from the *New Yorker* and *Time Magazine* found in Michael Males, *The Scapegoat Generation: America's War on Adolescents* (Monroe, Maine: Common Courage Press, 1996), 1.

62. For an excellent discussion on child-rearing costs, see Nancy Folbre, *Who Pays for the Kids?* (New York: Routledge, 1994).

CHAPTER 6. THE IMMIGRATION CONTROVERSY

1. John Tierney, "A 1911 Fire as Good TV, Bad History," *New York Times,* 18 November 1999, B1.

2. George Borjas, "The Economics of Immigration," *Journal of Economic Literature* 23 (December 1994): Table 1; Immigration and Naturalizaton Service, *Statistical Yearbook* (various years).

3. Jeffrey Passell and Barry Edmonstron, *Immigration and Race in the United States* (Washington, D.C.: Urban Institute, 1992).

4. Immigration and Naturalization Service, *Statistical Yearbook* (various years).

5. Paul Donnelly, "Indefinitely Temporary: Senate Boost to High-Tech Guest Workers Will Block Green Cards" (Washington, D.C.: Center for Immigration Studies, Backgrounder, 2000).

6. Gregory DeFreitas, "Immigration, Inequality, and Policy Alternatives," Working Paper #82 (Russell Sage Foundation, 1995); Keith Bradsher, "Skilled Workers Watch Jobs Go Overseas," *New York Times,* 28 August 1995, A1.

7. Donald Bartlett and James Steele, *America: Who Stole the Dream?* (Kansas City, Mo.: Andrews and McMeel, 1996), 80–82.

8. Gregory DeFreitas, "Unionization among Racial and Ethnic Minorities," *Industrial and Labor Relations Review* 46 (January 1993): 284–301.

9. Ze'ev Chafets, *Devil's Night and Other True Tales of Detroit* (New York: Random House, 1990).

10. Booker T. Washington, *The Negro in the South* (New York: Carol Publishing Group, 1970), 59–60.

11. Booker T. Washington, *Up from Slavery* (Garden City, N.Y.: Doubleday, 1963), 16; Washington, *The Negro in the South,* 58–61.

12. Irving Fisher, "Address," *American Labor Legislation Review* 7 (March 1917): 9–23. For a background of Irving Fisher and his contemporary economists, see Robert Cherry, "Racial Thought and the Early Economics Profession," *Review of Social Economy* 34 (April 1976): 147–162.
13. Peter Brimelow, *Alien Nation* (New York: Random House, 1995), 43.
14. Ibid., 46.
15. Ibid., 216.
16. Thomas Sowell, *The Economics and Politics of Race* (New York: Quill, 1983), 71.
17. Thomas Sowell, *Ethnic America: A History* (New York: Basic Books, 1981), 296.
18. Pat Buchanan, "Immigration Should Be Suspended to Preserve the Nation," in *Immigration Policy*, ed. Scott Barbour (San Diego, Calif.: Greenhaven Press, 1995), 31–33.
19. Ibid., 32.
20. Ibid.
21. Joel Perlmann, "'Multiracials,' Racial Classification and Mexican Intermarriage—The Public Interest," Jerome Levy Economics Institute Working Paper 195, Bard College, 1997; Joshua Goldstein, "Kinship Networks That Cross Racial Lines: The Exception or the Rule?" *Demography* 36 (August 1999): 399–407; Douglas Besharov and Timothy Sullivan, "The Interracial Generation," *Washington Post*, 21 July 1996, C1.
22. Cherry, *Discrimination*.
23. George Borjas, "The Economic Benefits from Immigration," *Journal of Economic Perspectives* 9 (spring 1995): 3–22.
24. Steven Camarota and Leon Bouvier, *The Impact of New Immigrants: A Review of the New Americans* (Washington, D.C.: Center for Immigration Studies, 1999).
25. Bartlett and Steele, *America*, 103.
26. Norman Matloff, "High-Tech Trojan Horse: H-1B Visas and the Computer Industry" (Washington, D.C.: Center for Immigration Studies, Backgrounder, 1999).
27. Marc Cooper, "The Heartland's Raw Deal," *Nation*, 3 February 1997, 16.
28. Michael Piore, *Birds of Passage* (New York: Cambridge University Press, 1979).
29. Thomas Muller, *Immigration and the American City* (Cambridge: New York University Press, 1993), 137.
30. Ibid., 121.
31. David Card, "The Impact of the Mariel Boatlift on the Miami Labor Market," *Industrial Labor Relations Review* 43 (January 1990): 245–257; Robert LaLonde and Robert Topel, "Labor Market Adjustment to Increased Immigration," in *Immigration, Trade, and the Labor Market*, ed. John Abowd and Richard Freeman (Chicago: University of Chicago Press, 1991), 167–200.
32. David Card, "In Migration Mobility and Immigration Flows," Working paper, Princeton, 1996; Randall Filer, "The Impact of Immigrant Arrivals on Migratory Patterns of Native Workers," in *Immigration and the Work Force*, ed. George Borjas and Richard Freeman (Chicago: University of Chicago Press, 1992), 245–269; William Frey, "Immigration and the Changing Geography of Poverty," *Focus* 18 (fall 1996): 26.
33. Roger Waldinger, *Still the Promised City? New Immigrants and African-

Americans in Post-Industrial New York (Cambridge, Mass.: Harvard University Press, 1996).

34. Thomas Espenshade et al., "Immigration and Social Policy," *Focus* 18 (fall 1996): 5.

35. George Vernez et al., "Surveying Immigrant Communities," *Focus* 18 (fall 1996): 19–23.

36. Joseph Altonji and David Card, "The Effects of Immigration on the Labor Market Outcomes of Less-Skilled Natives," in *Immigration, Trade, and the Labor Market*, ed. Abowd and Freeman, 201–234; Steven Camarota, *Importing Poverty* (Washington, D.C.: Center for Immigration Studies, 1999); James Smith and Barry Edmonstron, eds., *The New Americans* (Washington, D.C.: National Academy Press, 1997); George Borjas et al., "On the Labor Market Impacts of Immigration and Trade," in *Immigration and the Work Force*, ed. Borjas and Freeman, 213–244.

37. Cordelia Reimers, "Unskilled Immigration and Changes in the Wage Distributions of Black, Mexican American, and Non-Hispanic White Male Dropouts," in *Help or Hindrance? The Economic Implications of Immigration for African Americans*, ed. Daniel Hamermesh and Frank Bean (New York: Russell Sage, 1998), 107–148.

38. Roger Waldinger, "Who Makes the Beds? Who Washes the Dishes?" Manuscript, Department of Sociology, UCLA (February 1992); David Howell and Elizabeth Mueller, "The Effect of Immigration on African-American Earnings." Working Paper, New School for Social Research, New York, 1997; Editorial, "Hasty Call for Amnesty," *New York Times,* 22 February 2000, A22.

39. Vernon Briggs, *Class, Immigration and Nation* (Armonk, N.Y.: M. E. Sharpe, 1992), 56.

40. See Robert Higgs, "Race, Skill and Earnings: American Immigrants in 1909," *Journal of Economic History* 31 (June 1971): 420–428; See also Tierney and Sowell, *Ethnic America.*

41. George Borjas, "Illegal Immigrants Are Not Exploited," in *Illegal Immigration*, ed. Barbour, 122–127.

42. Paul McGouldrick and Michael Tannen, "Did American Manufacturers Discriminate against Immigrants before 1914?" *Journal of Economic History* 37 (September 1977): 723–747; Lawrence Mishel et al., *The State of Working America, 1996–1997* (Armonk, N.Y.: M. E. Sharpe, 1997), Table 3.7.

43. Wendel Primus, "Immigration Provisions of the New Law," *Focus* 18 (fall 1996): 14–18; Frank Bean et al., "Public Assistance Use by Immigrants," *Focus* 18 (fall 1996): 41–46; Camarota, *Importing Poverty.*

44. Richard Vedder et al., "The Immigration Problem: Then and Now," *Independent Review* 4 (fall 2000): 347–364.

45. Smith and Edmonstron, *The New Americans.*

46. Barry Chiswick, "The Effect of Americanization on the Earnings of Foreign-Born Men," *Journal of Political Economy* 86 (October 1978): 897–921; Harriet Orcutt Duleep, "Measuring Immigrant Wage Growth," *Demography* (May 1997): 239–249; for a less positive view, see Vilma Ortiz, "The Mexican-American Population," in *Ethnic Los Angeles*, ed. Roger Waldinger and Mehdi Bozorgmehr (New York: Russell Sage, 1996), 247–278.

47. Vedder et al., "The Immigration Problem."

48. Carry Kirby, "No Shortage of Experience," *San Francisco Chronicle*, 19 May 2000, A1; Coalition for Fair Employment in Silicon Valley, "Testimony."

Presented to Hearing Subcommittee on Immigration and Claims, House Judiciary Committee, 25 May 2000. Website: www.house.gov/judiciary/hink0525.htm.

CHAPTER 7. THE RISE OF WORKING WOMEN

1. Francine Blau et al., *The Economics of Women, Men, and Work*, 3d ed. (Upper Saddle River, N.J.: Prentice Hall, 1998), Table 5.10.
2. Robert Cherry, "Race and Gender Aspects of Marxian Macromodels," *Science and Society* 55 (spring 1991): 60–78.
3. Ibid.
4. Blau et al., *The Economics of Women, Men, and Work*, Table 4.5.
5. Heather Boushey and Robert Cherry, "The Economic Boom and Women: Issues of Race, Class, and Regionalism." Paper presented at the International Association for Feminist Economics conference, Ottawa, Canada (16 June 1999).
6. This claim is sensitive to measurement procedures. Instead of comparison of averages between the two sectors, we could compare the highest-paid to the lowest-paid workers. This alternative measure also finds a growing inequality among women. However, because of the extremely high pay of the best-paid men, inequality is still larger among men than among women by this measure. See John Heintz and Nancy Folbre, *Field Guide to the U.S. Economy* (New York: New Press, 2000).
7. Gary Becker, *Human Capital* (New York: Columbia University Press, 1964), 51–52.
8. Joyce Jacobsen, "Trends in Worker Sex Segregation, 1960–1990," *Social Science Quarterly* 75 (March 1974): 204–211; Robert Cherry and Pamela Mobilia, "Trends in Various Dissimilarity Indexes," *Review of Radical Political Economics* 25 (September 1993): 93–103.
9. Blau et al., *The Economics of Women, Men, and Work*, Table 6.4.
10. Ibid., Table 6.5.
11. Author's calculation from U.S. Bureau of Labor Statistics, *Employment and Earnings* (Washington, D.C.: Government Printing Office, 2000), Table 11 and Table 36.
12. Bowen and Bok, *The Shape of the River*. Note that the 65 percent figure compares men and women who ranked in the middle third of the graduating class.
13. Robert Wood et al., "Pay Differences among the High Paid," *Journal of Labor Economics* 11 (July 1993): 417–441.
14. Anne Royalty, "Job-to-Job and Job-to-Nonemployment Turnover by Gender and Educational Level," *Journal of Labor Economics* 16 (summer 1998): 392–443.
15. Joyce Jacobsen and Laurence Levin, "Looking at the Glass Ceiling," in *Prosperity for All? The Economic Boom and Blacks*, ed. Cherry and Rodgers, 217–244.
16. Joyce Jacobsen, *The Economics of Gender*, 1st ed. (Cambridge, Mass.: Blackwell, 1994), Table 6.2.
17. Catalyst, *Census of Women Corporate Officers and Top Earners* (New York: Author, 2000). Website: www.catalystwomen.org.
18. Ibid.
19. Heather Boushey and Robert Cherry, "Exclusionary Practices and Glass Ceiling Effects across Regions," in *Prosperity for All? The Economic Boom and Blacks*, ed. Cherry and Rodgers, 160–187.

20. Jane Osburn, "Interindustry Wage Differentials: Patterns and Sources," *Monthly Labor Review* 123 (February 2000): 34–46.
21. Joyce Jacobsen, *The Economics of Gender*, 2d ed. (Cambridge, Mass.: Blackwell, 1998); Jerry Jacobs and Suet Lim, "Trends in Occupational and Industrial Sex Segregation in 56 Countries, 1960–1980," *Work and Occupations* 19 (November 1992): 450–486; Maria Charles, "Cross-National Variations in Occupational Sex Segregation," *American Sociological Review* 57 (August 1992): 483–502.
22. Ingrid Robeyns, "Hush Money or Emancipation Fee? A Gender Analysis of Basic Income," *Basic Income on the Agenda: Policy Objectives and Political Chances*, ed. Loek Groot and Robert Jan van der Veen (Amsterdam: Amsterdam University Press, forthcoming).
23. Steven Greenhouse, "Companies Pay $1 Million in Harassment Suit," *New York Times*, 1 June 2000, A12.
24. John Bound and Laura Dresser, "Losing Ground: The Erosion of the Relative Earnings of African American Women during the 1980s," in *Latinas and African American Women at Work*, ed. Irene Browne (New York: Russell Sage, 1999), 61–104.
25. Ibid.
26. Blau et al., *The Economics of Women, Men, and Work*, Table 4.5; *Employment and Earnings* (January 2000).
27. Jason DeParle, "Shrinking Welfare Rolls Leave Record Share of Minorities," *New York Times*, 27 July 1998, A1.
28. Sandra Danziger et al., "Barriers to the Employment of Welfare Recipients," in *Prosperity for All? The Economic Boom and Blacks*, ed. Cherry and Rodgers, 245–278.
29. Irene Browne and Ivy Kennelly, "Stereotypes and Realities: Images of Black Women in the Labor Market," in *Latinas and African American Women at Work*, ed. Browne, 302–326.
30. Mark Levitan, *New York City's Labor Market, 1994–1997* (New York: Community Service Society of New York, 1999).
31. Sandra Danziger et al., "Barriers to the Employment of Welfare Recipients."
32. Robert Pear, "Welfare Workers Rate High in Job Retention at Companies," *New York Times*, 27 May 1998, B1; Danziger et al., "Barriers to the Employment of Welfare Recipients."
33. Michael Reich, *Racial Inequality* (Princeton, N.J.: Princeton University Press, 1981).
34. Catalyst, *Women of Color in Corporate Management: Opportunity and Barriers* (New York: Author, 1999). Website: www.catalystwomen.org.
35. Robert Pear, "Changes in Welfare Bring Improvements for Families," *New York Times*, 1 June 2000, A1.

CHAPTER 8. JOBS FOR BLACK MEN

1. Robert Cherry, "Impact of Tight Labor Markets on Black Employment," *Review of Black Political Economy* 27 (summer 2000): 27–41; Chinhui Juhn, "Decline of Male Labor Market Participation," *Quarterly Journal of Economics* 107 (February 1992): 79–121.
2. Barry Bluestone and Mary Stevenson, "Racial and Ethnic Gaps in Male Earnings in a Booming Urban Economy," *Eastern Economic Journal* 25 (spring 1999): 209–238.
3. Kim Clark and Lawrence Summers, "The Dynamics of Youth Unemployment," in *The Youth Labor Market Problem,* ed. Richard Freeman and David

Wise (Chicago: University of Chicago Press, 1982), 199–230; Richard Freeman and James Medoff, "Why Does the Rate of Youth Labor Force Activity Differ across Surveys?" in *The Youth Labor Market Problem*, ed. Freeman and Wise, 75–114.

4. Elijah Anderson, "Some Observations on Black Youth Unemployment," in *Youth Employment and Public Policy*, ed. Bernard Anderson and Isabel Sawhill (Englewood Cliffs, N.J.: Prentice-Hall, 1980), 37–46; Harry Holzer, "Black Youth Nonemployment: Duration and Job Search," in *Black Youth Employment Crisis*, ed. Freeman and Holzer, 23–74; Christopher Jencks, "Genes and Crime," *New York Review of Books* 12 (February 1987): 33–41; Kip Viscusi, "Market Incentives for Criminal Behavior," in *Black Youth Employment Crisis*, ed. Freeman and Holzer, 301–346; Andrew Hacker, *Two Nations: Black and White, Separate, Hostile, Unequal* (New York: Random House, 1995).

5. Wilson, *The Truly Disadvantaged;* Darity and Myers, *The Underclass*, 150.

6. Clark and Summers, "The Dynamics of Youth Unemployment."

7. John Bound and Richard Freeman, "What Went Wrong? The Erosion of the Relative Earnings of Young Black Men during the 1980s," *Quarterly Journal of Economics* (February 1992): 215n; Marc Breslow, "The Racial Divide Widens," *Dollars and Sense* 197 (January/February 1995): 10–11.

8. Harry Holzer, *What Employers Want: Job Prospects for Less-Educated Workers* (New York: Russell Sage, 1996).

9. William J. Wilson, *When Work Disappears* (New York: Vintage, 1996), 134.

10. Ibid., 136–137.

11. Holzer, *What Employers Want;* Joleen Kirshenman and Kathryn Nickerman, "'We'd Love to Hire Them But . . . ': The Meaning of Race for Employers," in *The Urban Underclass*, ed. Christopher Jencks and Paul Peterson (Washington, D.C.: Brookings Institutions, 1991), 203–234.

12. Wilson, *When Work Disappears*, 139.

13. Ibid., xix.

14. Ibid., 58–59.

15. Chinhui Juhn, "Black-White Employment Differential in a Tight Labor Market," in *Prosperity for All? The Economic Boom and African Americans*, ed. Cherry and Rodgers, 88–109.

16. Richard Freeman and William Rodgers, "Area Economic Conditions and the Labor Market Outcomes of Young Men in the 1990s Expansion," in *Prosperity for All? The Economic Boom and African Americans*, ed. Cherry and Rodgers, 50–87.

17. Ibid.

18. Sylvia Nasar and Kirsten Mitchell, "Booming Job Market Draws Young Black Men into Fold," *New York Times*, 23 May 1999, A1.

19. Ibid.

20. Greg DeFreitas, "Urban Racial Employment Differentials: The New York Case," in *Prosperity for All? The Economic Boom and African Americans*, ed. Cherry and Rodgers, 110–126.

21. John Ballen and Richard Freeman, "Transitions between Employment and Unemployment," in *Black Youth Employment Crisis*, ed. Freeman and Holzer, 223–274; Bruce Elmslie and Stanley Sedo, "Persistent Consequences of Initial Discrimination: Young Black Workers in the 1960s," *Review of Black Political Economy* 24 (spring 1996): 97–110.

22. Greg DeFreitas, "More Work, More School, More Poverty?" (New York: Community Service Society of New York, 2000).

23. Boushey and Cherry, "Exclusionary Practices and Glass-Ceiling Effects across Regions," 160–187.

24. Joyce Jacobsen and Laurence Levin, "Looking at the Glass Ceiling: Do White Men Receive Higher Returns to Tenure and Experience?" in *Prosperity for All? The Economic Boom and African Americans,* ed. Cherry and Rodgers, 211–238.

25. Andrew Brimmer, "The Economic Cost of Discrimination Against Black Americans," in *Economic Perspectives on Affirmative Action,* ed. Margaret Simms (Washington, D.C.: Joint Center for Political and Economic Studies, 1995), 11–29.

26. June O'Neill, "The Role of Human Capital in Earnings Differences Between Black and White Men," *Journal of Economic Perspectives* 4 (fall 1990): 25–46; Mishel et al., *The State of Working America,* Table 3.56.

27. Gerald Ottinger, "Statistical Discrimination and the Early Career Evolution of the Black-White Gap," *Journal of Labor Economics* 14:1 (1996): 52–78.

28. William Rodgers, "Male Sub-Metropolitan Black-White Wage Gaps," *Urban Studies* 34:8 (1997): 1201–1213; Robert Cherry and Pamela Mobilia, "Changing in Measures of Race and Gender Dissimilarity Indexes," *Review of Radical Political Economy* 25:1 (1993): 72–77; Boushey and Cherry, "Exclusionary Practices and Glass-Ceiling Effects across Regions," 160–187.

29. Bowen and Bok, *The Shape of the River;* Brent Staples, "Preaching the Gospel of Academic Excellence," *New York Times,* 5 June 2000, A28.

30. William Rodgers and William Spriggs, "The Effect of Federal Contract Status on Racial Differences in Establishment-Level Employment Shares: 1979–1992," *American Economics Review* 86 (May 1996): 290–293; see also Jeff Grogger, "Does School Quality Explain the Recent Black/White Wage Trend?" *Journal of Labor Economics* 14:2 (1996): 231–253.

31. For statistics on black and Latino CUNY graduates, not broken down by college groupings, see David Lavin and David Hyllegard, *Changing the Odds* (New Haven, Conn.: Yale University Press, 1996).

32. Cherry, *Discrimination,* Table 5–1.

33. Sylvia Nasar, "More Men in Prime of Life Spend Less Time Working," *New York Times,* 1 December 1994, D1.

34. James Smith, "Comment," *Review of Black Political Economy* 4 (1981): 383–390; William Butler and James Heckman, "The Impact of the Government on the Labor Market Status of Black Americans," in *Equal Rights and Industrial Relations,* ed. Leonard Hausman et al. (Madison, Wis.: Industrial Relations Research Association, 1978), 150–176; William Darity, "Illusions of Black Progress," *Review of Black Political Economy* 10 (1980): 355–379.

35. James Heckman and Peter Siegelman, "The Urban Institute Audit Studies: Their Methods and Findings," in *Clear and Convincing Evidence,* ed. Michael Fix and Raymond Struyk (Washington, D.C.: Urban Institute, 1992), Table 5.1.

36. Marc Bendick et al., "Measuring Employment Discrimination through Controlled Experiments," *Review of Black Political Economy* (summer 1994), 25–48; Franklin James and Steve DelCastillo, *We May Be Making Progress toward Equal Access to Jobs* (Denver: University of Colorado, 1991); Christopher Edley, *Not Black and White: Affirmative Action and American Values* (New York: Hill and Wang, 1996); Thernstrom and Thernstrom, *America in Black and White,* 448.

37. Heckman and Siegelman, 197; Ronald Mincy, "The Urban Institute Audit

Studies: Their Research and Policy Context," in *Clear and Convincing Evidence,* ed. Fix and Struyk, 173.

38. Glenn Collins, "Few Blacks Where Tips Are High," *New York Times,* 30 May 2000, B1.

39. Ibid.

40. Steven Greenhouse, "Many Participants in Workfare Take the Place of City Workers," *New York Times,* 13 April 1998, A1, B6.

41. Francine Blau and Lawrence Kahn, "Gender and Youth Employment Outcomes: The U.S. and West Germany." Cambridge: National Bureau of Economic Research, 1997. Working Paper #6078.

CHAPTER 9. EMPLOYMENT AND OWNERSHIP DISPARITIES

1. Cornell West, *Race Matters* (Boston: Beacon Press, 1993), 68.

2. Bergmann, *In Defense of Affirmative Action*; Hacker, *Two Nations;* Thernstrom and Thernstrom, *America in Black and White.*

3. Cecilia Conrad, "Economic Costs of Affirmative Action," in *Economic Perspectives on Affirmative Action,* ed. Simms, 31–54.

4. Thernstrom and Thernstrom, *America in Black and White,* 425.

5. Finis Welch, "Affirmative Action and Discrimination." in *The Question of Discrimination,* ed. Steven Shulman and William Darity (Middletown, Conn.: Wesleyan University Press, 1989), 153–189.

6. Lee Badgett and Heidi Hartmann, "The Effectiveness of Equal Employment Opportunity Policies," in *Economic Perspectives on Affirmative Action,* ed. Simms, 55–97; Jonathan Leonard, "What Are Promises Worth: The Impact of Affirmative Action Goals," *Journal of Human Resources* 20 (1984): 3–20.

7. Jonathan Leonard, "The Impact of Affirmative Action and Equal Employment Law on Black Employment," *Journal of Economic Perspectives* 4 (fall 1990): 58.

8. Robert Cherry, "Middleman Minority Theories: Their Implications for Black-Jewish Relations," *Journal of Ethnic Studies* 17:1 (1990): 117–138; Gregory Martine and Ruth Clark, *Anti-Semitism in the United States* (New York: Praeger, 1982).

9. Jonathan Leonard, "Wage Disparities and Affirmative Action in the 1980s," *American Economics Review* 86 (May 1996): 285–289; William Rodgers and William Spriggs, "The Effect of Federal Contractor Status on Racial Differences in Establishment-Level Employment Shares: 1979–1992," *American Economics Review* 86 (May 1996): 290–293; Judith Fields and Edward Wolff, "Gender Wage Differentials, Affirmative Action, and Employment Growth on the Industry Level" (Annandale-on-Hudson, N.Y.: Jerome Levy Institute, 1997). Working Paper 186.

10. Lee Badgett, "The Impact of Affirmative Action on Public-Sector Employment in California, 1970–1990," in *The Impact of Affirmative Action on Public-Sector Employment and Contracting in California,* ed. Paul Ong (Berkeley: California Policy Seminar, 1997), 71–94.

11. Harry Holzer and David Neumark, "What Does Affirmative Action Do?" *Industrial and Labor Relations Review* 55 (January 2000): 240–271.

12. Department of Commerce, *Minority-Owned Businesses* (Washington, D.C.: Bureau of the Census, 1992).

13. Steven Camarota, "Reconsidering Immigrant Entrepreneurship" (Washington, D.C.: Center for Immigration Studies, 2000), Table 9.

14. Ibid.
15. Robert Fairlie and Bruce Meyer, "Ethnic and Racial Self-Employment Differences and Possible Explanations," *Journal of Human Resources* 31:4 (1996): 757–793; E. Franklin Frazier, *The Negro in America* (New York: Macmillan, 1957).
16. Ronald Fairlie, "The Absence of African American Ownership," *Journal of Labor Economics* 17:1 (1999): 80–108.
17. Robert Cherry, "American Jewry and Bonacich's Middleman Minority Theory," *Review of Radical Political Economy* 22:2 (1990):139–151.
18. Timothy Bates, *Race, Self-Employment, and Upward Mobility* (Baltimore: Johns Hopkins University Press, 1997).
19. Ibid.
20. Rodger Waldinger, *Still the Promised City? African-Americans and New Immigrants in Postindustrial New York* (Cambridge, Mass.: Harvard University Press, 1996).
21. Cecilia Conrad, "Hiring One's Own Kind: Recruitment Practices of Minority Owned Businesses." Presented at the Allied Social Science Association meetings in Boston, 6 January 2000.
22. Timothy Bates, "Utilization of Minority Employees in Small Businesses," *Review of Black Political Economy* (summer 1994): 113–121.
23. Kenneth Chay and Robert Fairlie, "Minority Business Set-Asides and Self-Employment." Paper presented at Allied Social Science Association meetings in New York, 1999.
24. Tom Larson, "The Impact of Local-Government Affirmative Action Programs for Women and Minority-Owned Businesses in California," in *The Impact of Affirmative Action on Public-Sector Employment and Contracting in California,* ed. Ong, 136.
25. Samuel Myers and Tsze Chan, "Who Benefits from Minority Business Set-Asides?" *Journal of Policy Analysis and Management* 15:2 (1996): 202–226; Thomas Boston, "Trends in Minority-Owned Businesses." Paper presented at the National Research Council Research Conference on Racial Trends in the United States, 1998.
26. Mitchell Rice, "Justifying State and Local Government Set-Aside Programs through Disparity Studies," *Public Administration Quarterly* 52 (summer 1992): 482–490.
27. Timothy Bates and Darrell Williams, "Do Preferential Programs Benefit Minority Business?" *American Economics Review* 86 (May 1996): 294.
28. Ibid., 297.
29. Steven Holmes, "TV Station Deal Draws Opposition," *New York Times,* 11 April 1999, A15.
30. Hacker, *Two Nations,* 128.
31. Bates and Williams, "Do Preferential Programs Benefit Minority Business?"; David Swinton and John Hardy, *The Determinants of the Growth of Black-Owned Businesses: A Preliminary Analysis* (Washington, D.C.: Department of Commerce, 1983); Allan Vidal, "Reintegrating Disadvantaged Communities into the Fabric of Urban Life," *Housing Policy Debate* 6:1 (1995): 169–230.
32. Allan Munnell et al., "Mortgage Lending in Boston: Interpreting HMDA Data," *American Economics Review* 86:1 (1996): 25–53; Cathy Cloud and George Galster, "What Do We Know about Racial Discrimination in Mortgage Markets," *Review of Black Political Economy* 22:1 (1993): 101–120;

David Blanchflower et al., "Discrimination in the Small Business Credit Market." NBER Working Paper, Boston 1998.

33. Timothy Bates, "The Minority Enterprise Small Business Investment Company Program," *Urban Affairs Review* 32 (May 1997): 683–703.

34. Michael Porter, "The Competitive Advantage of the Inner City," *Harvard Business Review* (May-June 1995): 55–71.

35. See various articles in Thomas Boston and Catherine Ross, eds., *The Inner City* (New Brunswick, N.J.: Transaction Books, 1998).

36. Bergmann, "In Defense of Affirmative Action," 164.

37. Wilson, *When Work Disappears;* Thomas Boston and Catherine Ross, "Locational Preferences of Successful Owned Businesses in Atlanta," in *The Inner City,* ed. Thomas Boston and Catherine Ross (New Brunswick, N.J.: Transaction Books, 1998).

CHAPTER 10. NEW HARMONY, NOT RELIGIOUS WARS

1. Glenn Loury, "How to Mend Affirmative Action," *Public Interest* 127 (spring 1997): 39.

2. Glenn Loury, "The Conservative Line on Race," *Atlantic Monthly* (November 1997): 67.

3. Loury, "How to Mend Affirmative Action."

4. See testimony of Bowen, Bok, Gurin, and Steele on "Expert Testimony." Website: www.umich.edu/~newsinfo/Admissions/Expert/summ.html.

5. Stephen Raudenbush, Supplemental Special Report. *Gratz v. Bollinger,* No. 97–75231 University of Michigan (3 March 1999): Table 1.

6. Claude Steele, "A Threat in the Air: How Stereotypes Shape Intellectual Identity and Performance," *American Psychologist* 52 (June 1997): 613–629; Claude Steele and Joshua Aronson, "Stereotype Threat and the Intellectual Test Performance of African Americans," *Journal of Personality and Social Psychology* 69 (November 1995): 797–811.

7. Thernstrom and Thernstrom, *America in Black and White.*

8. Ibid.

9. Selection Index Worksheet, University of Michigan, 1999.

10. Raudenbush, Supplemental Special Report. *Gratz v. Bollinger.*

11. Brent Staples, "How the Racial Literacy Gap First Opened," *New York Times,* 23 July 1999, A26; William J. Wilson, "Affirming Opportunity," *American Prospect* 46 (September-October 1999): 61. See also Stephen Steinberg, "Affirmative Action and Liberal Capitulation," *American Behavioral Scientist* 42 (October 1997): 256–261.

12. Bergmann, *In Defense of Affirmative Action,* 118.

13. Ibid.

14. David Wasserman, "Diversity and Stereotyping," *Philosophy and Public Policy* 17 (winter/spring 1997): 32.

15. Johnson, "The New Black Power," 46–83.

16. Suzanne Gordon, *Prisoners of Men's Dreams* (Boston: Little, Brown, 1991), bookjacket.

17. Patricia Gurin, "Expert Testimony of Patricia Gurin: Summary and Conclusions," 1999. Website: www.umich.edu/~newsinfo/Admissions/Expert/summ.html.

18. Ibid.

19. Abigail Thernstrom and Stephan Thernstrom, "Racial Preferences: What We Now Know," *Commentary* (February 1999): 48.

20. Thernstrom and Thernstrom, *America in Black and White*, 348.

21. Hacker, *Two Nations*, 145.

22. Bowen and Bok, *The Shape of the River*, 144.

23. Ibid., Table 5.1, 143.

24. Ibid., 72.

25. Los Angeles Times, "Exit Polls on Prop 209," *Los Angeles Times*, 10 November 1996.

26. Richard Kahlenberg, "Class-Based Affirmative Action: A Natural for Labor," *New Labor Forum* 2 (spring 1998): 37–43.

27. Ethan Bonner, "Black and Hispanic Admissions Off Sharply at University of California," *New York Times*, 1 April 1998, A1, B11.

28. Hacker, *Two Nations*, 46.

29. Bonner, "Black and Hispanic Admissions Off Sharply at University of California," B12.

30. Cecilia Conrad and Rhonda Sharpe, "The Impact of the California Civil Rights Initiative on University and Professional School Admissions and the Implications for the California Economy," *Review of Black Political Economy* (summer 1996): 13–55.

31. University of California Office of the President, Table 1, Student Academic Services, Management Reports, various years. Note that Latinos include Chicanos. Figures for 2000 enrollment projected from Statement of Intent to Register figures, which were the latest available when this book went to press.

32. Shelby Steele, *The Content of Our Character* (New York: Harper Perennial, 1990), 89–90.

33. Glenn Loury, "Absolute California," *New Republic*, 11 November 1996, 17.

34. James Traub, "The Class of Proposition 209," *New York Times Magazine*, 2 May 1999, 46.

35. Jodi Wilgoren, "New Law in Texas Preserves Racial Mix in State's Colleges," *New York Times*, 24 November 1999, A1.

36. Ibid.

37. Charles Moskos and John Butler, *All That We Can Be* (New York: Basic Books, 1996), 48.

38. Loury, "Absolute California," 20.

39. Pam Belluck, "More Minority Students Enter Elite Schools," *New York Times*, 18 May 1997, B4; Division of Assessment and Accountability, *Final Evaluation Report: The Math Science Institute, 1997–1998* (New York: Board of Education, 1998).

CHAPTER 11. SETTING POLICY PRIORITIES

1. Martin Gilens, *Why Americans Hate Welfare* (Chicago: University of Chicago Press, 1999); Wilson, *The Truly Disadvantaged;* for a review of Gilens, see Robert Lieberman, "All about Race," *American Prospect* 11:15 (2000): 94–95.

2. Kevin Sack and Janet Elder, "Poll Finds Optimistic Outlook but Enduring Racial Divisions," *New York Times*, 11 July 2000, A1.

3. Sterling Spero and Abram Harris, *The Black Worker* (New York: Antheneum, 1931); Horace Cayton and George Mitchell, *Black Workers and the New Unions* (Chapel Hill: University of North Carolina Press, 1939); Robert Weaver, *Negro Labor: A National Problem* (New York: Harcourt and Brace, 1946), 82.

4. Orley Ashenfelter, "Racial Discrimination and Trade Unions," *Journal of Political Economy* (May 1972): 435–464.

5. Thomas Sugrue, "Labor, Liberalism and Race Politics in 1950s Detroit," *New Labor Forum* 1 (fall 1997): 19–25.

6. Richard Freeman, "How Much Has Deunionization Contributed to Male Earnings Inequality," in *Uneven Tides: Rising Inequality in America,* ed. Sheldon Danziger and Peter Gottschalk (New York: Russell Sage, 1993), 147–159.

7. Harold Meyerson, "A Clean Sweep," *American Prospect* 11:15 (2000): 24–29.

8. Lawrence Katz and Allan Krueger, "The Effects of the Minimum Wage on the Fast-Food Industry," *Industrial and Labor Relations Review* 46 (October 1992): 6–21; other studies are summarized in David Card and Allan Krueger, *Myth and Measurement: The New Economics of the Minimum Wage* (Princeton, N.J.: Princeton University Press, 1995).

9. Richard Burkhauser and Allan Glen, "Public Policies for the Working Poor." Working Paper. (Washington, D.C.: Employment Policies Institute, 1993); Daniel Shaviro, "The Minimum Wage, the Earned Income Tax Credit, and Optimal Subsidy Policy," *University of Chicago Law Review* 64 (spring 1997): 405–481.

10. Jared Bernstein and John Schmitt, *Making Work Pay* (Washington, D.C.: Economic Policy Institute, 1998).

11. Ibid.

12. David Moberg, "Martha Jernegons's New Shoes," *American Prospect* 11:15 (2000): 50–53.

13. Stephanie Luce and Robert Pollin, "Can U.S. Cities Afford Living Wage Programs?" *Review of Radical Political Economy* 31 (March 1999): 16–53.

14. Moberg, "Martha Jernegons's New Shoes"; Luce and Pollin, "Can U.S. Cities Afford Living Wage Programs?"

15. Robert Greenstein and Isaac Shapiro, "New Research Findings on the Effects of the Earned Income Tax Credit," #98–022 (Washington, D.C.: Center on Budget and Policy Priorities, 1998); John Karl Scholz, "The Earned Income Tax Credit: Participation, Compliance, and Antipoverty Effectiveness," *National Tax Journal* 47:1 (1994): 59–81; for studies that measured the positive employment effect, see Jeffrey Liebman and Nadia Eissa, "Labor Supply Response to the Earned Income Tax Credit," *Quarterly Journal of Economics* 112 (May 1996): 605–637; Bruce Meyer and Daniel Rosenbaum, "Welfare, the Earned Income Tax Credit, and the Supply of Single Mothers." Northwestern University, manuscript, 1999.

16. U.S. House Ways and Means Committee, *Green Book* (Washington, D.C.: Author, 1998).

17. Liebman and Eissa, "Labor Supply Response to the Earned Income Tax Credit."

18. Robert Cherry and Max Sawicky, *Giving Tax Credit Where Credit Is Due: The Universal Unified Child Credit* (Washington, D.C.: Economic Policy Institute, 2000).

19. David Howell, "Skills and the Wage Collapse," *American Prospect* 11: 15 (2000): 74–77.

20. Laura D'Andrea Tyson, "Five Myths about Inflation," *New York Times,* 13 November 1994, A24; Editorial, "A Valuable Voice for the Fed," *New York Times,* 29 January 1996, A23; Alison Mitchel, "Two New Faces Join Greenspan as Fed Choices," *New York Times,* 23 February 1996, A1.

21. Robert Eisner, "A New View of the NAIRU," in *Improving the Global Economy,* ed. Paul Davidson and Jan Kregel (Brookfield: Edward Algar, 1997), 196–230.

22. Joseph Stiglitz, "Reflections on the Natural Rate Hypothesis," *Journal of Economic Perspectives* 11 (winter 1997): 3–10.

23. James Tobin, "On Improving the Economic Status of the Negro," in *The Negro American,* ed. Talcott Parsons and Kenneth Clark (Boston: Houghton Mifflin, 1965), 462–463.

Index

About the Author

Robert Cherry teaches economics at Brooklyn College. He has published widely on discrimination, including articles in *Review of Black Political Economy, Feminist Economics, Journal of Labor History,* and *Journal of Ethnic Studies.* He coedited *Prosperity for All? The Economic Boom and African Americans* (Russell Sage, 2000). His current work focuses on expanding the Earned Income Tax Credit to benefit more working families.